PENGUIN BOOKS

SOUNDING OFF

Resul Pookutty is a master sound designer, sound editor and mixer. The first Asian to win an Academy Award in a technical category for *Slumdog Millionaire*, Resul has carved a niche for himself in a little over a decade. Beginning his career with the 1997 film *Private Detective: Two Plus Two Plus One*, directed by Rajat Kapoor, he went on to do outstanding work in Bollywood films like *Black*, *Musafir*, *Zinda*, *Traffic Signal*, *Gandhi, My Father*, *Saawariya*, *Dus Kahaniyaan*, *Ghajini*, *Blue*, *Ra.One* and other language films like *Endhiran* (*Robot*), *Nanban 3* and *Pahazssi Raja*, etc.

His recent work in Hollywood includes John Madden's *The Best Exotic Marigold Hotel*. He is currently immersed in several projects in India and abroad, namely *English Vinglish*, *Chittagong*, *Gandhi of the Month* and European films like *Voyage Sans Retour* (France) and *Liv & Ingmar* (Sweden).

Resul was awarded the Padma Shri for his outstanding contribution to Indian cinema in 2009. In the same year, he also received an honorary DLitt from Kalady Sree Sankaracharya University of Sanskrit.

Baiju Natarajan (N. Baiju) studied Malayalam language and literature at the Oriental Research Institute, University of Madras. He has published a volume of poetry in Malayalam, *Akam: 49 Kavitakal* (2001), and edited *Cities of Kerala, Actually Small Towns* (2008), a book on present-day life in nine major urban centres of Kerala. He also works as a consultant and researcher for generating autobiographical narratives for print. He lives in Bangalore and Kochi.

RESUL POOKUTTY

WITH BAIJU NATARAJAN

SOUNDING OFF

THE MEMOIRS OF AN OSCAR-WINNING SOUND DESIGNER

TRANSLATED BY K.K. MURALIDHARAN

PENGUIN BOOKS

An imprint of Penguin Random House

PENGUIN BOOKS

USA | Canada | UK | Ireland | Australia
New Zealand | India | South Africa | China | Singapore

Penguin Books is part of the Penguin Random House group of companies
whose addresses can be found at global.penguinrandomhouse.com

Published by Penguin Random House India Pvt. Ltd
4th Floor, Capital Tower 1, MG Road,
Gurugram 122 002, Haryana, India

First published by Penguin Books India 2012

ISBN 9780143067702

Typeset in Adobe Garamond by Inosoft Systems, Noida

Printed at Repro India Limited

www.penguin.co.in

MIX
Paper from
responsible sources
FSC® C047271

This is a legitimate digitally printed version of the book and therefore might not
have certain extra finishing on the cover.

To Umma and Bappa

CONTENTS

PROLOGUE: LIGHTS! CAMERA! SOUND!

I will kill him!
    It was my moment of glory, but this was the constant refrain playing in a loop in my mind.

Let me explain. As a humble cinema worker, I had reached the pinnacle of success, having just received an Oscar in the Technicolor American twilight of 22 February 2009. Moreover, this had come in the wake of other laurels: the famed BAFTA (British Academy of Film and Television Arts) award and the prestigious CAS (Cinema Audio Society) award which would be the dream of any sound engineer. But that evening I felt a different thrill, holding up the golden-coloured metallic Oscar statuette—weighing all of eight and a half pounds and measuring thirteen and a half inches in length, beautifully designed eighty years ago by an Irish American, Austin Cedric Gibbons. *Slumdog Millionaire* had put me on the map, as it were, and my acceptance speech was selected as one of the most unforgettable speeches of that evening.

From that day forth, cameras always swarmed around me; great men and women squeezed my hands; excited youngsters scratched and pinched my person. The media relentlessly sought my opinion on everything—from what it was like working with director Danny Boyle to what I felt about prevalent issues—in the midst of huge crowds. But no one bothered to take me aside and ask me what exactly was going on in my mind at that very moment.

So I will tell you now. While I was brimming with indescribable joy, pride and love, I could not get this one thought out of my mind: *I will kill him!*

If you ever want to know anything about slavery, my life is there in front of you. Anybody would obviously want to put an end to such misery. So don't be shocked if one of these days you happen to read somewhere that Resul has beaten someone to death.

The man I secretly plan to finish off is none other than my manager, whose sole mission was to put me through an endless series of gruelling and inhuman drills. Somehow I seem to have become his slave. I can only do what he says; I must follow his instructions: go meet this guy, go to this place. He is Kallu alias Baiju Kalluvila. I have known him almost my entire life. We were buddies in our village, Vilakkupara— and now he rules my life (this is perhaps his revenge for our endless squabbling in childhood). He'd gotten me into scrapes almost as often as he'd rescue me from them. And I couldn't help thinking that now, if he did anything to ruin this special moment, that would indeed be the end of him.

My Umma had an endearing description for him: the buck-toothed son of a fraud.

Baiju claims Umma never addressed him in such colourful terms. He would banter rather innocently and loudly: 'Maybe she described me like that to you all in my absence. But why should she refer to me like that anyway? Remember what she used to say to Bappa? Bappa had a dim view of my political alliance with her; when I would hang around her as her general supporter, by ironing her clothes or helping her in some house chore, he would say, "Oh, look at this guy, hanging on her tail all day . . . Why are you wasting your time?" And this only made her angry. "Why don't you keep your advice for your own sons?" she would tell him. So basically, I was her true supporter in most matters.'

Yes, Baiju has a point. Anyway, Umma is not alive any more. So I can't contest my manager's claims.

*

As luck would have it, I spared his life. Of course, that hasn't stopped me from feeling murderous again, my rage exploding in front of Baiju's calm countenance. But I depend on him as much as I deplore him—something he knows too well.

I often get calls like these all the time:

'Saar, we're calling from Kanhangad—what time will you reach here tomorrow?'

And I would have no idea what this was all about.

But the caller would not be discouraged: 'We are calling from AIR. What time will you reach our studio?'

'Oh! Am I coming to your studio?'

'Of course! It's all been agreed. You are not coming?'

The thing is, I have no clue about my comings or goings. The one who knows all is the manager!

Baiju's new technique is to hide the ticket from me. I beg, 'What time are we going, please?'

'Oh. Nine.'

'Where? Air India or the other one?'

'Other one.'

I am the kind who dreads even the thought of missing a flight. So, I would be there at the airport by eight thirty or eight forty-five for a ten o'clock flight. I would tele-check-in and wait. He, on the other hand, would arrive ten minutes before departure. I would be terribly tense. But what to do? He is my manager, I can't leave him behind; and of course, I can't do anything without him.

Once, when I landed at the Mumbai airport after receiving the BAFTA award, Baiju instructed me not to exit the airport until he signalled that I could! He had this tremendous advantage of not knowing anything about the Mumbai airport. If you ask him to wait for you at terminal one, he would promptly wait for you at terminal two. So while I was getting impatient inside the airport, awaiting for the go-ahead from him, he was busy waiting at the wrong terminal with the press and all that jazz!

He had done a similar thing when I was returning after the Oscars. Apparently, he had organized a surprise; but if he had told me about it, I would have done a better job of surprising myself!

I had called him from Frankfurt. He said, 'Come, all is

organized.' I repeatedly demanded to know the nature of the arrangements he claimed to have made. I begged, 'Please don't make a mess like you did last time with the BAFTA thing.'

'No, no, no. You'll see when you land here.'

And when I did arrive, it was quite a scene. What he had organized was a full-blown stampede! The police had to rescue me. They took me away as if I were a petty thief. The manager had an explanation: 'Do you think it's a small affair to create a stampede at the Mumbai airport, that too at three in the morning? We have shattered some concepts.'

'What concepts? If you had told me, I would have landed only in the morning.'

'No way. It was all done in consultation with the Home Department. The Home Department said it was Mia's birthday. If you got late, it would have been over. Perhaps you might want to verify the facts with the Home Department itself.'

The Home Department is, of course, my wife Shadia. The food chain is like this: I am Baiju's slave; he is *Hunthappi Bussatto*'s slave (*Hunthrappi Bussatto* is an allegory I stole from the great poet Vaikkom Muhammed Basheer to describe my life partner).

A surprise birthday party had been planned for my youngest child Mia. Unfortunately, I landed up at the police station that night, because the police thought it was easier handling me than an entire excited crowd.

But all said, this rogue of a manager has his uses too. He has saved me in some dangerous situations, when he would assume the role of a Protocol Officer. One such instance occurred soon after the Mumbai fiasco. I was told that a massive family gathering had been organized in Kerala in honour of my Oscar conquest.

I was a bit lost. Massive family gathering? What family was this?

'That's the northern clan.'

'What's this northern clan? That should be my mother's family, no?' I asked.

I felt irritated. Where had all these other family members been all this while? I had not seen any of them before; how come suddenly they emerged? Why should I meet them now? Simple—there won't be any such gathering; I have no time; I am going; pack up!'

Babukka, my eldest brother, cleared his throat.

'Huh… But… oh… but… can't you just wait only for this?'

I asked my manager, 'What's happening?'

'It's just a matter of showing your face there once in the morning; it'll be on your way.'

I couldn't defy my manager. So I went.

Now, while I had been lauded for my achievements by people across the country, I received no such praise from anyone in this family platoon. They had another agenda. The whole thing turned out to be a character assassination campaign. I barely survived the inquisition! The general verdict of the court martial was in the lines of, '. . . should have received the Oscar in the name of Allah . . . should have behaved like a good Muslim . . .'

I felt a familiar sensation—the itch of annoyance that starts from the tip of my toe and spreads up, suddenly billowing into full-blown rage.

Immediately, Baiju warned me (in a voice that boomed

like one of my childhood film heroes—where the hell did he suddenly get a voice like that?):

'You should not get angry like that . . . your image has changed. Don't display your old self.'

This is the kind of problem I am faced with these days. I can't yell at anyone, no matter how angry I am. The manager had also set up a code of conduct for me; if I violated that in any way, there was a fine that I had to pay him! He had made quite a bit of money when I lost it with someone over the phone at the Kozhikode airport. What does he do with all this money?

'Listen, there are all Malayalis around. They can all understand what you're saying. It's okay in Mumbai. Don't start it here in Kozhikode. This is Kerala, your home state.' Saying that, he dipped into my wallet.

The family gathering really started to get on my nerves. 'Let's get out of here,' I told Baiju.

He got up and promptly announced: 'It's time for Resul Saar to leave.'

My eldest uncle told him, 'You step aside. This doesn't concern you.'

This uncle had no idea who Baiju was; he thought he was probably one of my sycophants. But, knowing that he was my uncle, Baiju respectfully stepped aside.

I shot Baiju a laser look. Motioning for him to come closer, I whispered in his ears, 'If you start listening to all these guys, nothing is going to happen. You should insist that we must leave. You just call me; I will get up and go. Be strong!'

That's how he discovered the power of the word 'protocol'. He stood up and delivered a dialogue: 'We have heard everything that you have had to say. We have only five minutes left here now; I am in charge of protocol. You might be his family and all, but that doesn't concern me. It is a matter of my official duty. I will lose my job if I don't do what I have to do now. I can't wait any more. Sir, we have to leave.'

I got up to leave. The uncle's face went through some colour correction. At least we should have lunch, he humbly requested.

'No time for lunch and all. We will eat on the way somewhere,' said my new Protocol Officer.

Uncle came down further: 'Sir, at least a little bit of rice, Sir...'

A little bit of rice, *Sir*! I was having trouble trying not to laugh. They had clearly assumed he was some bigwig official from Mumbai. Had they figured out his true identity, they would have handed me something when I left—a heavy sack with neatly diced pieces of Baiju Kalluvila. They would have said, 'Son, just throw this in the public dustbin on your way.'

The prospects of finding something to eat on the way were not very bright. So we made a big show of agreeing to eat something for *their* sake.

Instantly, a desk and a bench materialized, and we were seated ceremoniously. But nobody knew where the food was. The Protocol Officer asked: 'Where is the biryani?'

Nobody knew. My long-lost relatives panicked at being caught on the wrong foot. They had no idea where the food was being prepared or even by whom.

That was one of the situations where I was rescued by my Protocol Officer's commendable cunning.

Babukka, my eldest brother, even addressed Baiju in front of the entire clan: 'Hey, Baiju . . . I must admit that you have earned my respect. So for the sake of Biju, till the day Biju leaves from here, we shall all do exactly what you tell us to do, promise. We have now started getting an idea about the whole thing . . .'

This surprised me a great deal. For one, it was unusual for Babukka to speak like this. Secondly, I was convinced my family was out to get Baiju. You see, before this visit to Kerala, Baiju made it impossible for anyone to contact me. Having learnt from the fiasco at the Mumbai airport, we made it a point to make some systematic arrangements for the Kerala visit. To start with, I decided to stay put in Mumbai for the first few days till the initial frenzy died down. And if there was a phone call from home asking for 'Biju'—my pet name—my manager would simply say: 'No, can't give him the phone.'

Most of the time, he would say I was being interviewed by some newspaper or TV channel. Once, my third sister Zeenath managed to get me on the phone. She told me exasperatedly, 'If we ever catch him, we will make mincemeat of him and give it you. We don't want you. We want him. Is it possible to send him here, please? We are all waiting for the moment.' As far as they were concerned, he was single-handedly blocking their access to me.'

So now, I thought: okay, it's just revenge postponed; they will deal with him once I leave. But my manager managed to reach Mumbai even before I did. And he wasted no time in citing protocol left, right and centre. With the help of this one word, he has been able to hold on. He even makes people think that there is something like a protocol around the Oscar.

For instance, the Pune Film Institute gave me a reception for the Oscar. Pune is not like Mumbai. Eight o'clock is never really eight o' clock; it can easily become eight thirty. I reached on time. Some news reporters came late and missed the photo session of me holding the Oscar statuette. They appealed to the manager: 'We want to see the Oscar'. Then the Protocol Officer in him took over. He explained to the media guys: 'We had to sign an agreement to carry the Oscar. We can't show it around just like that. At one go, we are not allowed to expose it for more than eight minutes max. Then it has to be kept back in the locker.' Of course, he was giving them utter bullshit!

The next day's newspapers carried Baiju Kalluvila's photos and a report. The protocol was explained in great detail.

I asked him, 'Where did you get this thing of eight minutes from?

'I just made it up to deal with that situation Saar, the thing is, a lot of people have major respect for this thing now!'

What should I do with him? Shouldn't he be finished off?

*

When I was first asked by the respected publishers to narrate my story, I remember being far too busy shuttling between recording studios and reception halls; and that too, under the Manager Raj. Shadia encouraged me: 'Write, it will be good fun.' I didn't know where to begin or how to go about it. It wasn't until I visited the actor Mammooty's home that my resolve strengthened.

Mammooty invited me home after a reception in my honour hosted by a cinema workers' organization in Ernakulum. I accepted happily. His home was filled with all the heavy-duty Malayali directors—Sibi Malayil, Lohitadas and others. Mammooty saw me coming in with a whole army behind me—eight family members and their relatives, and lots of kids and cousins. It was a mob of about thirty that was invading Mammooty's house. Mammooty looked a bit uncomfortable—he wouldn't have expected these many people.

I surveyed the proceedings: there's Babukka checking out Mammooty's wall finish; Kunjumolitha is staring at Mammooty, then looking at her husband; Lahurumacha is into some heavy discussion with Lohitadas; the Protocol Officer is bringing in Nazarumacha and Ponni who were waiting outside (Nazarumacha had refused to enter initially); my doctor cousin and family from Trissur are examining Mammooty from a safe distance; Zeenath and Sherafumacha are giving Mammooty red salutes; Mani is intensely studying Mammooty from a corner; Samadmacha is deep-breathing and puffing his chest out while taking a stroll on Mammooty's fancy wooden floor; Kochumon has stiffly planted himself at one spot; my sisters have placed themselves in strategic locations to prepare an inventory of the things in Mammooty's house; Shadia is at the dining table talking to Mammooty's wife; while all the kids are running around wildly. Everybody is excited to see Mammooty in person. This is not something any of them could have anticipated even in their dreams—but now, they were right inside Mammooty's house, clicking photos with him! Some of them—when no one was looking—are finding excuses to simply be near him. Meanwhile, the Protocol Officer has lost all control and is standing there, agape. Then my brother Saif asked him, 'So, we are having dinner here only, no?'

I experienced a profound peace. I was in the presence of a bigger and brighter star. Everybody's focus was on him. Nobody needed me. A brief spell of freedom! In that momentary bubble of calm, I felt a vague narrative of my life begin to take shape, a kaleidoscope of struggles and triumphs, of the people and experiences that have shaped me and the isolated memories and recurring dreams that continue to haunt me. In short, all the varied things that have made me the man I am today.

I suddenly felt restless to have my story told.

Then I slowly looked at Mammooty's face. He had not completely recovered. He couldn't have expected more than seven or eight people. Already very tempting smells were coming from the kitchen. But, determined to maintain a sense of decorum, I gathered everyone and tricked them out of the house.

That was my post-Oscar entourage—a mother goat and countless little lambs following—would flit from one reception to the next. One journalist from *Kerala Kaumudi* said this was absolutely great. When I pointed out the inconvenience it created for others, he asked me if it was not for this that I had worked so hard all these years. 'These are the components of our happiness. Being able to do this is great. Seeing you doing this makes us also very happy.'

Now, I'm going to patch together the story of these people and of the cinema world where I have finally landed up.

I have been through many hardships. But this is a phase of my life where I am indeed very happy. And it would be very rewarding and satisfying for me if my memories and experiences could delight and inspire others as well.

The memories of my childhood are entwined like noodles: the school, the countryside, oil palms and home. Those memories are not at all organized. So, how could I write an autobiography? But then, what matters more is that I tell the truth.

One of the truths is that I have no clue about when I was born. I don't celebrate my 'Happy Birthday'. When I had asked Umma, she said she was very sure it was either before or after the rains. Then she said, 'Actually, it was a couple of days before Anthram Kochappa's death.' The only official document regarding my genesis is the school certificate. For the convenience of admission procedures, the headmaster Krishnan Nair Saar gave me a suitable birthday: 30 May 1970. The astrological guidelines I follow in life are based on this date.

PART 1

DREAMS AND MEMORIES

1

FAMILY SNAPSHOTS

I used to have some recurring dreams. Terrific visuals coming from deep within. I have always wanted to use those images in films some day. One of them had a red dirt road that led to a hill. The hill had a huge dried-up tree at its top; and there was a man walking towards it. Another one: a man standing behind a hillock, facing the other side. I could never make out who that was. Sometimes I have seen it as the silhouette of Bappa. This was before he died.

I used to have many nightmares about Bappa's death. Many late-night telephone calls have woken me with dread because I would immediately assume that those phonecalls meant news of my Bappa's death. At one level, this constant fear of his death had become some kind of an ulterior wish. Then came the rude blow of Umma's death.

She used to say she would die at the age of sixty-three. We would tease her, 'As if it's all written down for you; are you by any chance Allah's private secretary?'

It was only after Umma's death that I started believing that Umma did indeed have the gift of foresight. She had predicted many things, although she lived a very ordinary life and was not someone who wondered about the self or existence or things like that.

In all senses, it was she who gave me my core identity as a Vilakkupara boy. Bappa and the Communist Party were the other influences.

My Bappa, Pazhaya Theruvil Thambikkunju Pookutty, was a 24×7 dedicated Communist Party worker. I remember not seeing much of him in my early years. There was a transport corporation called KCT, a co-operative set up by the communists in Kayamkulam. Bappa was one of the founder members. We used to call the KCT bus Bappa's bus. The realization that he was just an employee who worked there for a salary dawned upon me only after my childhood days. Bappa's work required him to spend most of his time in Kayamkulam. He came home only when he could take leave. He always came just before the schools opened. The material he got for his uniform from KCT became our school clothes—khaki shorts and shirts.

Those days we were completely in awe of him as we never had enough of him. We never sat in front of him when he was around; never used his bath towel; never slept on his sleeping mat (he had a special softer mat; we all slept on regular straw mats. When he left, this mat was rolled up and kept away). The feelings I had for him was a mixture of respect, love and that special joy of seeing someone whose stature was much higher than ours.

Bappa was a very kind and caring man. He didn't want anything for himself. His general attitude was that nothing really belonged to anyone; this was an attitude that irritated Umma no end. Bappa never did much for the family in the conventional sense; a common, bigger goal for the society was more important for him. When the Communist Party split, he was deeply upset. He was very worried about the future of communism. My Umma, Alikkunju Nabizabeebi, had no trace of communism in her. Her Bappa was a hard-working man and pretty well off. He was in the timber business in the forests up the hills. She was the only sister to six brothers. All six of them had their own businesses in Anchal, and lived well. Theirs was the first family to buy a car in that area. People of Vilakkupara called her 'Anchakkari Umma', the mother from Anchal.

Umma and Bappa lived in Kayamkulam for some time after their marriage. Bappa's was a joint family, which was mired in utter poverty. If my guess is correct, by that period in her life, Umma would have had some conclusive opinions on the necessity of private wealth. She must have been over twenty. One fine morning, she just left Kayamkulam—not because of any fight or anything. She didn't go to her brothers' or relatives' place. She went to Vilakkupara, where she had a piece of land in her name. She built a house on it and started living there—a hard, farmer's life. It was with great difficulty that she raised her family.

However, our higher education was Bappa's department. After tenth standard, we all studied in MSM College, Kayamkulam, Bappa's town. As kids, this place was paradise for us—electricity, tubelights, sweetmeats, biryani, loudspeaker songs up the coconut tree . When coming back from there, we were always given sweet flattened rice and lots of fried stuff.

Umma belonged to a very orthodox Muslim family, while Bappa of course was a stainless-steel communist, who refused to even enter a mosque. How these two characters met, mingled and came to marry is still a mystery to me. But they were together for fifty years. They had ten children, including the two who died later.

Those were the days when Bappa and Umma were caught in a situation where they could neither live together nor live without each other—a lot like how Shadia and I live today. Umma could never be punctual. She never could get ready on time. Ten always became ten-thirty for her. By the time she was ready, the bus would have started moving. Bappa would probably be ready by nine and grumble at her throughout: 'You're not ready yet? The bus is going to go.' She would get very angry: 'What the hell is wrong with this man! Ready at six in the morning! Just to irritate others!' Things are more or less the same in my married life too. With Shadia, it's always a miracle how we don't miss a flight.

*

I think a lot about Umma and Bappa.

There are many endearing tales about Umma; memories to smile about. When the cellphone came, I showed her one. We were travelling somewhere by car. I asked her, 'Don't you want to call Saarumama?' He was her dearest brother. She called and said to him, 'I am now calling from a mobile phone, sitting in a car. You don't know what a mobile is; we can talk like this even while travelling.' Email also came around that time. I would go to the BSNL email centre whenever I was in Thiruvananthapuram. Sometimes, I took Umma along. If there was an email from London, I would read it out to her, saying, 'It's an email from London.' And she would ask innocently, 'What does that mean? How did it come here?'

That was Umma. She would say the most unpredictable things in any given situation. She harboured very interesting views on the ways of the world. Once I was taking her to Kayamkulam in a luxury bus. It was plush, with cushioned seats that one could sink into. When the bus started moving, I asked her, 'How is it?'

'Oh, feels like sitting in a *kabaristan*,' she replied. A graveyard.

Once when we were leaving a restaurant after a meal, I asked Umma to keep the bill. Inside the car, she asked, 'But, why did you want that bill?'

I told her that we needed to show the government the account of our expenses and pay taxes based on our income.

'What kind of government is this?' she asked. 'You have no job, so it's the government that should be giving you money. Why are you paying the government instead?'

I had most certainly started working by that time. But according to my mother, since I did not have a 'government job', it meant I was an unemployed youth. Which meant that the government should be paying me! That was Umma's logic.

I told her this was about income tax. She knew what income tax was. All her brothers had business. She had seen sales tax guys coming and checking accounts and taking bribes. When

I mentioned income tax, she said, 'I know them very well. They are thieves. You have no idea of how much money they had taken from your uncles' shops!'

With Bappa, it was very different. I came to really comprehend who and what Bappa was only when I grew in years and was doing my pre-degree course. Later, we started and continued writing to each other regularly. In these letters, I could be very open to him about everything.

Although the Communist Party split killed Bappa's spirit, he continued to be a CPI supporter till the end. At some point during those days, he started working on his own. Those earnings went into our schooling and some household expenses. I recall that he read and wrote a lot. I have a lot of mental snapshots of him sitting lost in whatever he was reading.

Later, when Bappa retired, my brother Saif had a bakery shop called Appu's, in Anchal. Bappa sat there as the manager, but was wholly immersed in books and magazines; so, he was completely oblivious to the sweets and puffs being lifted off by smart kids. Umma used to get very angry with him for this, and she would ask, 'If you have so much to study for your exam, why don't you go and sit with these college boys!'

Bappa was very close to Thoppil Bhasi whose writings had a crucial role in the development of communism in Travancore of Kerala. When the police were looking for Bhasi, he had gone into hiding in Bappa's house. He had mentioned that in his famous book, *The Memories in Hiding*. He was arrested in a week after he shifted from our house. I vaguely remember reading, in *The Memories in Hiding*, about Thoppil Bhasi, Bappa and Bappa's brother hatching a plan, sitting in our house, to bomb the Kayamkulam jail when M.N. Govindan Nair was held there.

Umma would tell us stories of Bappa marching through Kayamkulam town, reciting his own poems. When Umma was staying at Bappa's house in Kayamkulam, he was fully involved with party work, sometimes even going into hiding. Bappa's brothers were also communists. The men of the house were never at home. Bappa's sister, Valyappachi, was a tough woman. Kerala women are usually a bit subdued, but Valyappachi was of a different sort altogether—she was very strong. And those were the days when Muslim women never ventured outside their homes. When the police would come home in the night looking for Bappa and his brothers, she used to terrorize them, shouting, 'Who the hell are you, what the hell are you doing here, barging into a house full of women in the middle of the night?'

There is an interesting story about the two finally going to the Ajmer Dargah. I was the one who made it possible.

Umma's ultimate wish was to go to Ajmer Dargah. Once, Bappa had made a wager: 'If ever I go to a mosque, it would be the Ajmer Dargah.' That was because of his deep interest in Sufism. Umma didn't know anything about Sufism, but on hearing Bappa's pledge was quite encouraged—'Okay, if that's the case, I am going to take him to Ajmer.' From that day, on she started putting coins in her terracotta money box and started sending offerings to Ajmer.

In 1998, I returned home to find that the whole thing was getting slightly out of control. People were making fun of Umma's Ajmer plan. I decided that they had to be sent to Ajmer as soon as possible. I had some money with me from whatever work I had done. I wanted them to fly, but the money I had was not enough. To go somewhere in a flight was another great ambition of Umma's. She never did. I can't quite forgive myself for not being able to do that for her. Anyway, I booked train tickets. My parents didn't know Hindi, so I also sent my eldest brother with them. Umma was an extremely social woman who found it next to impossible to sit quietly anywhere. After the train left Kerala, language became an issue. It was like a serious solitary confinement for Umma. She sat for some time gritting her teeth and finally resorted to sign language. The stories from Umma's Ajmer trip always guarantee a good laugh from all of us. What was commendable was her determination—she did manage to take Bappa to a mosque!

There is another snapshot of Bappa that still lingers in my mind. We were all very young. The setting was a rainy night with thunder and lightning. We were all studying in the light of a kerosene lamp. Bappa arrival was usually announced by the sound of him clearing his throat while he scraped the mud off his chappals on the granite slab at the entrance to the veranda. I looked up and saw Bappa standing there even as vertical lines of rain water were falling from the roof edge. He was soaked and water was dripping from his clothes. He was holding a bundle of books and clothes close to his chest. It's an image I can never forget. There was major excitement whenever Bappa came like this once in a while. He would bring some things to eat, some books and new clothes for us. But after the first day of his arrival we waited for him to leave! Our freedom shrank considerably when he was around. Once I got a thrashing from him for addressing my brother Kochumon by his first name!

Kochumon and I are almost the same age—just a difference of one and a half years. We called each other by first names or worse. Bappa wanted me to call him *ikka* like all Muslims in Kerala called their elder brothers. But addressing Kochumon as *ikka* was unimaginable for me. I didn't even call Saif *ikka*. At the most I could address Babukka as *ikka*. But Bappa was insistent: 'You must not address elders by their first name. He is elder to you, you should call him *ikka*!' One unfortunate day, I forgot this commandment. And got rewarded accordingly— Bappa hit me with the *klanjil*, the long and knotted stem that attaches a coconut to its bunch. An unforgettable sensual experience on the bottom! Terribly painful.

Kochumon was very happy. Bloody rascal! I don't remember Bappa beating me again. But the sting of that lashing still lingers. However, that didn't make me address Kochumon with any more brotherly respect.

*

Our house in Vilakkupara was, at first, mainly made of mud and had a conical thatched roof. The walls were plastered with a mixture of charcoal, cowdung and the special mud that came out of earthworms, which we collected from all over the countryside. The house in Vilakkupara was built by Umma's determination and resourceful nature; she was the one who pooled up the money. Bappa hadn't shown much interest in the whole thing. His most immediate concern was about helping others, a trait that irritated Umma the most. 'Irresponsible man!' she would say.

My elder sister's wedding took place in Kayamkulam because our Vilakkupara home was just a mud house. Besides, Bappa's whole clan was in Kayamkulam. I still remember how the bull for the wedding biryani was walked all the way from Vilakkupara. Somebody was brought from Kayamkulam to walk the bull, and Saif had to accompany him. The long march blistered Saif's feet badly. The whole thing was Umma's idea to save some money, but she started crying when she saw the state of Saif's feet.

Not only that, a thief broke into our Vilakkupara house after we all left for the wedding. There was not much to rob in our house. But this incident accelerated Umma's plans to build a new house in Vilakkupara. Ours was the first concrete house in Vilakkupara. Over time, it also came to acquire the rare distinctions of being the first house with a TV, and the first one with a phone. Umma had made several attempts to build the house earlier too, after saving up from wherever she could. The first time the plan had to be aborted because I had a paralysis attack. The next time I had jaundice. 'The paisa I saved up to make the house all went into the hospital for you,' she had told me. It was not something she said seriously; still, it stayed in my mind. And the guilt never quite left me.

I also nursed a similar sense of guilt about my eldest brother's wedding.

Babukka was my childhood superhero. From Kayamkulam, he would come to Vilakkupara on a Rajdoot bike, wearing what we animatedly called 'cooling glasses'. Bappa wanted him to be a doctor. But he went for sociology or something after his BSc. He was involved in college politics and thus his career went nowhere. Later, my brother became a teacher in a tutorial college. Then he started a tutorial of his own and became famous in Kayamkulam. In the meantime, he started seeing a cousin, Masiniyitha, and decided to marry her.

When Umma heard about it, she exploded. She had hopes pinned on him as someone who was capable of looking after the family. This out-of-the-blue wedding plan was more than she could tolerate. She got really upset and left home. We were all very small. We didn't know where she had disappeared. But then, how far can a mullah run—only till the mosque, right? Umma went straight to her dear brother. He came and spoke to my Bappa. Bappa quoted an old Malayalam saying which compared children to cattle, 'If they don't go the way you lead; lead them on the way they go. If he wants to do this, what can we do?' With such arguments, Bappa somehow managed to convince Umma and the wedding finally took place.

I still clearly remember the day she left home in anger. She cried holding us kids close to her, especially me. She lamented about her eldest son leaving our family and how he was not even thinking about his sisters who had reached a marriageable age. She said he first destroyed his future running after politics and now he's running after a girl. That day, at my tender, immature age I took some hard decisions about my life: I won't have a love marriage; I won't enter into politics. Because all these things would hurt my Umma. I still remember her tears falling on my head and face. I couldn't believe that Umma was crying, because, she was always such a strong lady.

After Babukka's wedding, his wife came to Umma's house to stay and study. It was amusing how quickly Umma's heart melted and she forgot the rage that took hold of her before Babukka's wedding. Babukka and Masiniyitha became her favourites. She would even give Masiniyitha milk and eggs without anybody seeing, especially her daughters.

When I think of Umma and the others, I get carried back to old Vilakkupara, where Umma would be wearing a lungi, blouse and scarf, carrying rice gruel for the workers in the paddy fields, and me accompanying her; or all of us grinding rice all night for the big Eid and small Eid, and Umma sending us with sweetmeats to all the neighbours . . .

Vilakkupara is an 'expat' village. Everybody there had come from somewhere else. Each one was known by where he or she came from. Like Anchakkari Umma, Perigallur Acchayan, and soon. Mine is the first generation of people who were actually born in Vilakkupara.

Vilakkupara was built by a bunch of free and spirited people; a spirit that still lingers in the lives of these hard-working villagers. The occasional law-and-order situation came chiefly from the wild elephants coming down from the forests. British rule, army rule, police raj or the World Wars all came and went without finding any reference in Vilakkupara's history. The most luxurious lifestyle article those days was the extra earthen pot we kept—the portable urinal into which we pissed so that we did not have to step out into the night where wild elephants lurked. The villagers would beat old tin cans to scare away the elephants. I sometimes joke about how this special sound design compelled the elephants to flee—an early indicator of my strong audio lineage in Vilakkupara.

In my early memories, Vilakkupara was a tiny settlement lying somewhere on a narrow, twisted dirt road from Eroor to Ayiranalloor, a village even more remote than Vilakkupara. Eroor was better; one could go to Anchal from there, and anywhere else in the world from Anchal!

Vilakkupara's business establishments began and ended with the tea shop of Samuelachayan and the paan–beedi hole of Balakrishnan Channar. There was a weekly bazaar at Maravanchira. People walked all the way there to buy and sell things. I have gone there myself many times. Vilakkupara's own market only came into existence when I was in high school. The first bus service also started around that time. It was a very active village. You could hear the village waking up. A bus load of people would get down in the morning. They all worked in the oil palm plantation. They walked energetically in a line to their workplace and in the evening would come back in a similar long procession. There were lots of pretty girls and handsome guys among them.

Vilakkupara had some interesting characters. One of them was Peringallur Acchayan, a giant of a man and ace hunter who nobody messed with. He had only one advice to the world: don't send anyone to school. His youngest two sons went to college and came back spoilt. Other noteworthy characters were Odakku Rajan, Acchayan's hunting protégé (and, later, his rival) whose skills in the forest were matched by his appetite for getting into *odakku* or fights; Kochukulam Kochannan, the neighbourhood drunk who would contest elections with his trademark burning torch; and Azhathi Kovalan, the resident madman who served as a constant warning of the social disorder that our community could fall into if it weren't careful.

The east–west road takes a 320-degree turn in front of my house. The place was called Kochukulam Junction in the beginning, and when the market came, it was renamed Market Junction. (Now it is called the Oscar Junction!) A memory that stands out vividly is that of the circus which came to Market Junction. I was in the eighth standard. On the way to school, our bus used to make a fifteen-minute stop at a place called Alancheri. One day, when the bus reached there, I heard a sound, 'kada-kada-kada' . . . I looked out of the window and saw a guy on a cycle with a contraption attached to its wheel—this was making that sound. Another guy was breaking tubelights on his bare chest. The sight was unbelievably spectacular for a boy my age. It turned out that these were circus folk. I half jumped out of the window and shouted to one of them: 'Come to the Market Junction in Vilakkupara.' I was dying to see the show. I gave them my house address, and told them that it was not difficult to find as the house was right at the bus stop.

I had completely forgotten about the whole thing, never expecting them to turn up. But they did. It was on a Saturday or a Sunday that these guys landed up and started looking for me. I knew the situation was going to get tricky. Umma was sure to thrash me if she heard about it. I tried to slip away but they caught me, saying, 'Ah! Here he is!' Right then, Umma stepped in, asking what the commotion was about. If I told her was about the impulsive invitation I had extended to the circus people, I would never be allowed to step into my house again. But I so desperately wanted to see the circus. Peringallur Acchayan had given land for setting up the market. He didn't mind the circus folk camping in the market. I was very thrilled: a whole circus troupe was going to camp right in front of my house!

By evening, they started blaring songs on loud speakers. *If the neighbour's chicken laid an egg in this house, whose egg is that*—those were the kind of songs that were being played. Everyone turned up to see the show. Entertainment of any kind was a weakness for us Vilakkupara folk; we wouldn't let a spectacle like this pass us by. There would be a 'cinematic dance' by Ms Gracy Rodriguez, the announcement said, but Ms Gracy was actually a man in woman's dress. Some of the viewers got suspicious and peeped into the green room to check. But then some others intervened, saying that it was not nice to disturb an artistic enterprise.

The most entertaining item in the circus was the auction. The items being auctioned varied from chickens to coconuts. Sometimes Umma also came to see the circus; sometimes with a coconut or a chicken egg for the auction. Just when Umma would start the bid, someone would put money in her name, triggering an instant announcement: 'Pushing down the Anchakkari Umma (Our Lady from Anchal) into the deep pit of failure, Rajan is forging ahead . . .' Umma's instinctive reaction would be: 'Get lost, you dirty son of a fraud.' Umma couldn't take snubs like 'deep pit of failure'. The circus went on for about a month in all its festive fervour.

*

My family nomenclature follows Bappa's lineage, with our house carrying the same ancestral name of Bappa's home in Kayamkulam—Pazhayatheruvil. My siblings are scattered around Kayamkulam, Kollam, Anchal and Vilakkupara. Of the eight of us, my brother P.T. Shamzuddin (whom we call Babukka) is the oldest. I have two other brothers: P.T. Saifuddin (hadn't given him any brotherly suffix,in the event of a fight he would be addressed as Thomman) and P.T. Baiju (also called Kochumon and sometimes even Poriyan). My sisters are Nazeema P. (or Kunjumolitha), P.T. Sheeja (or Ponnumolitha), P. Zeenath (or Zeenathitha), P.T. Sheeba (or Mani).

I share the closest bond with Kochumon. But I spare no brotherly honorifics for him. I have given him enough and received enough from him—blows, I mean. In fact, I grew up bearing the brunt of his blows. These days he also writes forewords to books on me.

He was a rogue right from his primary school days. Once, he carefully broke a corner of his slate so that he could put his finger through it and carry it in a casual style. The slate originally belonged to Saif. Mani had inherited it from Saif; and Kochumon from Mani. But I never could inherit it from Kochumon. He carried the slate in this particular fashion for the convenience of hitting other kids with it.

He got into a lot of trouble because of this aggressive streak. When we started using fountain pens, in the upper primary classes, the fountain pen became his favourite weapon. He would stab kids with the pen's nib. One such classroom case became a village-level issue and Umma's brothers had to come from Anchal to sort out things.

Kochumon was the leader of our brigade. Although he later became an intellectual of sorts, as a child, creating social disorder was his main agenda. We have had many scuffles with the madmen of our area. I suppose he had issues with the crazies who, too, had a similar agenda.

Once, he got into a fight with Azhathi Kovalan, saying that there was something seriously wrong with the madman. He pelted stones at Kovalan who duly returned the favour. I went and hid behind a tamarind tree while Kochumon found a place behind a coconut tree. Kovalan had a stone ready in his hand. Kochumon was restless in his hiding place; he wanted to come to my defence. Finally he got up and ran to where I was. The sequence still runs very clearly in my mind, almost like a film reel: Kochumon darts from the coconut tree to the tamarind tree; Azhathi Kovalan throws the stone; the stone hits Kochumon on his spine; he falls. All in slow motion. I remember this episode whenever Kochumon complains of backache.

This was not the only injury he had suffered. He would climb the breadfruit tree behind the kitchen and do gymnastics there; sometimes he would even climb the cashew tree and shit from there—especially when a wind was blowing! One day, during his acrobatic session at the breadfruit tree, he lost his grip and fell. He lay still on the ground for a long time.

There was no question of reporting such events at home—we would only get thrashed. After a long while, he crawled back into the house. This injury, too, went untreated.

He used to take me to the forest to bash me up. His resented the fact that Umma seemed to have that extra love for me. I was the feeble kid in Umma's eyes. Besides, I used to do all the spy work for her. When my second sister Ponnumolitha was staying at home, sometimes there would be a bit of friction between her and Umma. I would fill Umma's ears with what Ponni had to say about her. (Thus, Ponni, too, couldn't stand me.) For such good work, Umma would secretly give me some milk or an egg. Kochumon wasn't necessarily a recipient of such goodies. But he knew what was happening. And while Umma would excuse some of my mistakes, Kochumon would regularly get thrashed.

It is true that Kochumon was perhaps my biggest tormentor in childhood. But at the same time, he has protected me the most too. Outside the house, he was my bodyguard. In fact, the incident of him stabbing someone with a pen, which became a big issue, was all part of defending me. Of course, this never stopped us from fighting.

I remember when Kochumon had to leave for further studies. Unlike everybody else who went to Bappa's place in Kayamkulam, Kochumon went to Kollam after the tenth grade. There was a reason for this. Saif didn't pass the tenth standard. He wanted to start earning because he could not bear the sight of Umma's hardship. He went and joined a workshop in Anchal to learn welding, for which he received a daily wages. The idea was to support Umma by giving her some regular money. (I wanted to be a singer those days. I used to ask him to buy me film-song books. I would inquire every day whether he had bought me one, but he never ever did.)

These were the circumstances that prompted Kochumon to go to Kollam—where my sister was alone—instead of Kayamkulam. (That's how I got separated from him; later, on my request, when I was studying for degree in Kayamkulam, he too joined the same college for the degree course.)

Kochumon went through his dramatic transformation in Kollam. In two years, he turned into a major intellectual, which he still is. He would deliver heavy discourses on serious things, leaving me wondering how the person I grew up with could spout so eloquently on such major matters. I just couldn't believe it! I remember him reading the biography of Ram Manohar Lohia. The guy also had Maxim Gorky's biography—the first time I saw a copy.

He had lost a lot of his aggression. But he increasingly started quarrelling with Umma. She didn't understand anything he said any more. I was torn—I couldn't stomach Kochumon's opposition to Umma, while at the same time, I couldn't really disagree with him either when he explained why. My emotional bond with Umma was very strong. I never really had any problem with anything that Umma said, even if I didn't necessarily agree with her. But Kochumon didn't have that kind of patience. Umma worried a lot about him. She thought he was immature and wouldn't be able to do anything properly.

By the time I finished school and went out into the world, he had plunged into pure leftist stuff; his worldview was being shaped by the Socialist Unity Centre of India. He was on a different philosophical plane altogether. Now he is into general politics and runs some business for a living. My relationship with him remains very strong. Such a terrific bond, I guess, can only be forged after many spats and fights!

Vexed by the constant fisticuffs between Kochumon and me, my parents put us in the Aylara school. My age was raised by a year for the official records. On foot, the school was two and a half miles from Vilakkupara. I started walking that distance, to and fro, when I was four.

How was a four-year-old able to walk five miles every day? In another time, would I be able to make my son Monu walk that much? How could my Bappa and Umma think of sending me that far on foot? Sometimes, I ask myself these questions. Only one answer would come to mind: the power of education—it's this power that drives all parents in Kerala to surmount the limitations of their times and send their children to school.

But that said, what did I ever learn in my ten years of schooling? Zilch. It was all about blows, punches, slaps, fights, climbing trees, somersaults, karate, songs . . .

But then, all of that has made me what I am today.

2

SCHOOL DAYS...AND BEYOND

My memories of my school have nothing to do with what I was taught there; all I can actually recall are vacations, the walks to the school and getting caned.

The primary attraction of the summer vacations was the setting up of one's own shop. It only required four poles and some coconut-leaf thatch for the structure. These leaves would be collected from the ones discarded during the re-thatching of our house. The shop roof and walls were all made with that. We would borrow five rupees from Umma as capital. Three bottles of butter milk, a bunch of bananas, one jar of peanuts and some puffed rice sugar balls comprised the merchandise. There was another item, a lucky draw, called the 'prize'. It was a sort of calendar with lots of tiny stamp-sized envelopes stuck on it. For a very nominal fee, you could pluck one of these to check your luck. The winners got combs, mirrors, plates, and so on. But if you happened to pick a joker, you lost your money. I used a torch to check and pluck off all the non-jokers to ensure a successful business.

During the temple festival, we would set up a coffee shop. Ginger coffee. The capital for this venture was ten rupees, from Umma again. One cup of coffee was twenty paise. The temple committee provided the space. Saif was the chief of this business operation. One day he put me in charge and went somewhere. He returned to find me fast asleep and all the money missing from the box. In a rage, Saif gave me a sound thrashing—he started beating me even before I could wake up. Saif's main concern was how we would explain the stolen money to Umma. Four rupees of profit along with the ten rupees of capital had to go back to her; only the rest was ours. I was unanimously elected to face her wrath. I made a confession and swore to return the entire amount the next season.

Once in a while, Umma used to go to her Anchal house for a general visit and would sometimes even stay there overnight. It was on such occasions that we became the kings of our own home. We would invite over a dozen of our friends—altogether a sizable gathering of various age groups. Mani handled the cooking. The cow was the boys' responsibility, but the herding of the cow would be reduced to just tying the poor thing to various coconut trees in the course of the day. After all, our main preoccupation was to play and create a general ruckus.

Another favourite activity was to perform plays. The stage would be set up around the breadfruit tree with straw mats as curtains. Sword fights were most popular—farm knives and ladles stood in for swords; idli steamers became the shields. By the time all the eighteen steps of *Kalarippayattu* were performed, most of Umma's utensils would get dented and twisted, and strewn all over the place. Of course, this swordplay paled in comparison to the real fireworks that would erupt when Umma returned home. Even the most accomplished warriors and knights stood no chance against her fury. Once I hid myself under a cot. Everybody got really worried and started searching for the missing boy. The search party finally discovered my hideout. But I refused to come out. Umma brought me a glass of milk and, in a voice dripping with love, cajoled me: 'Sweetie, come out, have some milk, come, come out . . .' Unable to resist the invitation, I reached out for the milk. Once she got my hands, she pulled me out and thrashed me to pulp.

Sometimes, I simply ignored the things she asked me to do and just loafed around. She would keep track of this. In those days, there would be tapioca with lunch. The chunks of boiled tapioca would be crushed with an improvised pestle— a coconut-leaf stump. I enjoyed eating the tapioca bits that stuck to this pestle. Knowing this, Umma would call out, 'Come, sweetie, eat the tapioca mash.' But even as I reached for the spoon, she would catch me and say, 'So you are not *that* busy to miss the tapioca, unlike when I asked you to do something a while back . . .' Two lashes!

*

There was a rural version of nursery school called Ashaan Kalari all over Kerala at that time. Translated literally, it means the Master's Arena. Here one learns the ABCD of writing, on palm leaves. I remember the Ashaan teaching us letters from the palm leaves which we would inscribe on the sand with our fingertips. I remember holding on to the hand of Vijayamma *akka*, Baiju Kalluvila's elder sister, while going to this school. Those days are largely a blur. But one thing I remember is the fourth standard. I fell in love with a girl in my class. I won't reveal her name. In fact, I was in love with almost all the girls! My dream was to make a lot of money, buy a Fiat, again make more money, and gift these girls things that nobody could ever give them—a car, a big house, the stuff of dreams that I didn't possess myself back then.

We walked to school every day on a road of loose gravel. Our feet were always in a state of wear and tear with most of our toenails badly chipped, sometimes hanging loose altogether. The current nail of my left foot's second toe is its fifth generation. Sometimes we would improvise transport with the steel wheel: to procure one you gave the blacksmith fifty paise, and he welded you a steel ring about the size of a cycle wheel; this had a long rod with a hook at the end of it to guide and propel the wheel. One wheeled this thing everywhere with oral sound effects of gear shift and all. As a thrashing was inevitable from Umma if I asked her for the fifty paise, I would go and squat in the cycle shop till the shop guy took pity on me and donated one of his old, worn-out cycle tyres. With minor improvisation using a tree branch of appropriate shape, I would have my own transport ready.

There was no fixed timing for going to school: one generally left home in the morning with no particular instruction from anyone. There were six of us from the neighbourhood—Santhosh, Radhakrishnan, Kalyani *akka*'s son Biju, Baiju,

Sam Babu and me. Santhosh's father had a paan–beedi shop. He would put his son to man the shop and go for a bath. We timed our arrival right at that time. Santhosh would give us twenty-five paise or some peanuts and channa; mostly it was money. We were equal partners in the crime. I have never seen anything like the kind of equality that was displayed while sharing the spoils. On the way back from school, we would stop at Unnichayan's shop and exchange the stolen money for peanuts and gas candy (a primitive version of the mint with a hole); then we would mix them up and eat—oh, it was really tasty!

Other fragments filter in. I recall how, on our way to school, we would collect certain round leaves on which the free lunch at school would be served. The school lunch was plain-wheat *puttu* (a dough steamed into little cylinders). We ate this with the sugar (taken from home without Umma's knowledge) and chillies (it was a test of manhood to see who could eat the most—a test I passed with flying colours).

I also remember how school would always reopen right at the onset of the monsoon. The new set of shirts and shorts would lose its colour and turn into a wet mess perfect for mushroom farming. During this season, Umma dried our clothes on a line above the kitchen fire. We would just pull out the driest one to wear and go to school; no one cared who was wearing whose clothes. We would even carry our bundle of books inside our shirts—you could get wet, but the books had to be protected at all cost.

Once in a while, someone would carry a razor blade. It would be broken into four and shared. In case of heavy rains, we would get into some banana plantation and cut leaves with this. A banana-leaf umbrella could cover up to four of us, till the leaf was completely torn. From above, in a top-angle shot, we must have looked like a procession of banana leaves. Yam leaves also made good umbrellas, but we often got chased with sticks when we sneaked in to cut these leaves. We would run and even fall into puddles, but wouldn't let go of the leaves.

Streams and trees were all such an integral and immediate part of our days. We climbed the fruit-laden trees like monkeys, and when some fruits would fall into the stream, we would jump right into it. Some days, we would get into the stream and have four or five baths. Our only worry was being caught by a teacher. How did your shorts get wet, oh, aren't you the son of so and so? A thrashing would inevitably follow. On the way, we sometimes made knots on rice plants, a lucky charm to not get beaten up in school. If we got thrashed, the plants were to blame. Then we would just smash them. We also believed that if you stepped into cowdung by mistake, you would have to quickly go and touch someone, and that person would be beaten up.

A lot of time went into all these activities. It was only when we saw that the other groups had all reached far ahead, we would know that we were late. We usually reached when the first period was well under way.

There were some eighteen or twenty steps up to the school entrance. Sharada Teacher would be waiting there with a cane. We knew we were late and we knew there was a beating for that. So we would walk up, extend our hands, get the caning and go to class—no questions asked. And if you pulled away your hand to dodge the cane, more would follow—sometimes on the bum. She would wait at the gate till about eleven thirty to catch the latecomers. Still, we would engage in a bit of stealth to find out whether she had left her sentry post or not. Later, they started taking attendance for every period. It was easier to catch us that way. I would get late more than three or four days in the week.

*

Those days I was mesmerized by the Malayalam superstar Jayan. Once, during one of the Friday class meetings, I even broke into a song from one of his films. These meetings were mainly an occasion for extra-curricular activities, and were held during the last period. After that sudden bursting into a song, I became an artiste; I sang regularly after that. It was then that an idea of the self started emerging.

I often fancied that I was Jayan himself. In the long walk to school, I would often see senior kids fighting. They were a different group with some real villains. Though I was physically a nonentity, while watching the fight I would become Jayan. I was completely into this notion of a hero. Somebody who could knock down at least ten guys at one go. I had heard of Bruce Lee. I got my hair cut like his and started learning karate secretly. Baiju Kalluvila was my guru. Hee! . . . haw! . . . shaaa! . . . shooo! . . . those were the sound effects. Kids respected the guys who knew karate. Another good thing about karate is that one needn't be very big and muscular. Kochumon used to beat us up quite a lot those days. Later, we started striking karate poses when his gang passed by. Those days, Baiju and I were study mates in home. Baiju would be on the slab in the kitchen, giving me karate instructions; if someone came in suddenly, he would read the textbook in a karate pose.

While I was in school, completely out of the blue, I became *Kalathilakam*, a prestigious title given to the best student in performing arts. The title came to me overnight. What followed was an intense period fully dedicated to the arts— from singing songs to storytelling.

This happened while I was in the sixth grade. Dineshan was the reigning school star then. (He is now in the Navy. After the Oscar, he has become a crazed fan of mine, a victim of Resul-mania.) He was a very talented guy—good at acting, singing, dancing; quite an all-rounder. I had gone with him for the taluk schools' art festival as a general supporter. There, it turned out that only two names had been offered for participation in mono-acting and mimicry. Without a minimum of three contestants, the competition would be called off. Dineshan was our prize talent and a sure-shot winner. Our teachers, who were part of the organizing committee, gave my name as the third contestant.

I gave the performance of a lifetime! First prizes in all categories! Dineshan got two second prizes. I came back with a lot of crockery—plates, cups, saucers. These were the prizes those days. Umma was very excited: 'What are all these? Where did you get these from?' I said these were prizes for doing mono-acting and mimicry. She appraised the porcelain plates and kept everything away safely, saying, 'Very well, now we will serve food in these when guests come.'

The next day I was congratulated at the school assembly. Our school, which was a complete nonentity till then, had come second in the art festival with around thirty-four points. This made the school quite famous in the taluk. But Dineshan was very pissed off that I had become the star.

Life became rather hectic thereon. How much I walked carrying the harmonium on my head! That was for group songs. Our troupe comprised Yeshumati (who sang very well), Anil, Dineshan and myself. I really didn't know how to sing; I just sang along. A teacher had once advised us that our performances would improve if we enjoyed ourselves more while singing. After that, we really started letting ourselves go—lots of laughter and merriment; the singing turned into a major interactive performance. We didn't have any rhythm, but we would just belt away. In a couple of places, we even managed to get the first prize—perhaps for the element of fun we infused into our performances, but certainly not for the music!

My most popular mimicry act those days was the about the predicament of a pregnant woman in an autorickshaw. It was a satire on the deplorable state of roads. The rickshaw would go 'tur . . . rrrr', the sound varying according to the state of the road, and at the end you would have the cry of the newborn inside the rickshaw. I would get bookings for temple festivals—it was all service, no money. For mono-acting, I would present the death of Veluthambi Dalawa, the Travancore braveheart. When surrounded by his enemies, he shut himself up inside a temple and stabbed himself to death. I wrote up his last speech without knowing much about the historical facts. I was unable to pursue formal training in music because it was an expensive proposition. Instead, I discovered storytelling—more precisely, the popular storytelling form of *kathaprasangam*, which is narrated through songs. It often has instrumental accompaniment too. Ours was a small affair put together by a couple of friends. We had one guy who could play the tabla. He had six fingers on one hand—two thumbs. I remember him when I see the actor Hrithik Roshan. (After my Oscar win, during a function in Thiruvananthapuram where they were unveiling a wax statue of mine, a man shook hands with me and asked whether I remembered him. I only did when I noticed his double thumb!)

By the time I reached the tenth standard, my life in arts came to a halt. I could revive it only after joining the law college. There, I concentrated on mimicry. The teachers were the main targets of imitation. My take on Sathyasheelan Saar would receive hearty cheers. A lot of the mimicry was based on Marxist party stories. The speech of a comrade at a party congress was particularly popular. 'So, that's the thing', was his characteristic reaction to most things.

I also mimicked the Marxist leader V.S. Achuthanandan. Most of the material for this came from Jayachandran, whom we used to call Annan. I have now completely forgotten those V.S. numbers. There was another one I got from Annan, of a roadside quack selling an ayurvedic remedy. His sales pitch to the crowd started with: 'Suhrrthe . . .' means 'Fffrrrriend . . .' The preparation of one of his medicines involved the very gruelling process of 'first spotting, chasing, then catching the white fox, which fearlessly roamed the Gir forests of Assam'. The distillation process is, unfortunately, not printable here. This was a huge hit during my Mumbai bachelor days. Murali (K.K. Muralidharan), Ramu (Ramu Aravindan) and all still remember me in this quack's avatar. Murali still calls me 'Fffrrrriend'.

At the Film Institute, Madhu and Rajiv Ravi were my juniors. Just the two of us, Rajiv and me, had once staged a strike against the Dunkel Draft. Madhu, Rajiv and I used to talk to each other in the style and voice of Jayan, the Malayalam star who had passed away by then. We were sure that Jayan would return one day. Even now, when we meet, Rajiv and I talk in Jayan style: 'Chettaa . . . means "Bhroder" . . .'

Another crowd-pleaser, which I also developed at the Institute, involved a discussion on Tarkovsky's films. Doordarshan used to show some great movies those days. I saw Soviet filmmaker Andrei Tarkovsky's *Solaris* and other films on Doordarshan even before I joined the Institute. The film was followed by a discussion. The participants all looked the same: bearded, greying and armed with cloth bags. They were the most intense kind of intellectuals, the kind who smoked Dinesh beedi, drank black tea and ate *daal vada*. Four or five such people would sit and conduct extremely deep discussions about the film. There was the possibility that you might be able to understand the film—but not the discussion. It was loaded with heavy words and long pauses between the words and, sometimes, even between the syllables—making it all unnecessarily serious. But all the same, it provided ample fodder for my mimicry.

After I shifted to Mumbai, whenever Rajivan Ayyappan, Ramu Aravindan, Manoj Nair, Satheesh P.M. and I got together, Satheesh would always pick this one up: 'But Resul—can we just . . .that other thing! You know which . . .'

And I would clear my throat and start: 'Actually . . . if we are . . . going to talk about . . . the . . . use of imagery in Tarkovsky's . . . films . . . that actually comes from . . . a combination of the . . . effort . . . and the ability . . . to . . . explore . . . a journey that leads . . . to . . . the ultimate realization, or to the peak of such a realization . . . of . . . one's own . . . self. One can see . . . that . . . the usage of certain . . . images . . . which repeatedly appear . . . throughout, in his films, like for example . . . the horse . . . the dog . . . the visuals of . . . turbulent water surfaces . . . entangled in a series of such images are . . . or in the metaphoric levels of those . . . images are . . . the particles which . . . tell us the . . . nature . . . of . . . time itself and such . . . infinite possibilities . . . or the visual possibilities . . . of a medium that . . . or the techniques of the medium which Tarkovsky . . . explored, analysed and applied . . . with a very deep understanding . . . that evoke in us . . . a certain kind of . . . awe, an existential emptiness . . . all should be part of the . . . systematic . . . decoding of . . . our approach when we consider . . . what is this man . . . as an . . . artist . . . trying to tell us . . . which should also be the underlining thought of our . . . point of view . . . is what one . . . is trying to . . . say.'

This was a big hit—especially among young expat Malayalis used to life outside Kerala. You know, mimicry is still something that I won't hesitate to do, if you ask me to.

*

In my life, I have tried to run away from only three things: geography, mathematics and Hindi. I managed to escape from them for a time, but eventually, they returned to chase me.

It was much later in life, when I was working in Mumbai for the first time, that my friend Satheesh P.M. cured me of my geography phobia. We would often travel together, and Satheesh would be the one who constantly referred to maps wherever he went. At first I thought this was an unnecessary quirk on his part. But in time, I came to depend on maps myself as a sure way to travel without any major hiccups. It was while travelling with Satheesh that I began to reconcile myself with geography.

As for mathematics, I dropped it after the tenth standard, choosing a pre-degree option called Second Group which put you on the road to becoming of a doctor, zoologist or botanist. But for my degree, mathematics returned, this time as a subsidiary subject. I scored 2 marks in the first year—not a nice thing to mention anywhere. I secretly applied for an improvement examination, worked very hard and scored 68 out of the 70.

But Hindi has been the most persistent problem. In school, we studied Hindi in Malayalam. Learning a language entailed reading aloud from a textbook in the class. A cane would swing in your direction and command you to read. And you read. With Hindi, it was always a problem. So we would get the Hindi text written down in Malayalam by someone who could read Hindi and, keeping that piece of paper at our feet, we would refer to that while pretending to read from the open book in hand. It was terrible if you were caught. I once saw Kochumon getting thrashed when the incriminating piece of paper was discovered at his feet. The reason I was privy to his humiliation is because I could see Kochumon's class from mine. It was a time when education had no walls. Your classroom ended where the other began—back to back.

My Hindi scores were terrible—in my tenth standard Onam exam: 2 marks; Christmas exam: 8 marks. But I somehow managed to scrape through in the finals: 32 marks. How? I don't know. The thought of not having to deal with Hindi after the tenth standard was surely very motivating. I took Malayalam as my second language for my pre-degree; and later for my degree too. But then I landed up at the Pune Film Institute. Stepping out of the campus, even for the most basic interaction with people, you needed Hindi.

Inside the Institute, I kind of managed the situation with English. But outside? My friend Satheesh P.M. would instruct me the night before: 'You should reach the location on time in the morning.' He would give me the location name. I would write down all the details, then frantically call some friends and ask: 'Need to go to 3 C in Juhu in the morning. I am going to tell you the way to that place in Hindi. Just listen and tell me whether it sounds all right.'

In the morning, I would get to the road and catch an

autorickshaw, telling the driver—'Bhai Saab, I don't know the way to this place; take ten rupees more if you want, but please take me there before nine o' clock.' I could manage this much of Hindi for the auto guy after learning the line by heart the previous night with someone's help. But that's the great thing about Mumbai. Quite the opposite of the popular notions created by Malayalam films: that Mumbai is all underworld and Dharavi; everybody is hacking and killing all the time; the dialogues the actor Mohanlal taught us (like 'I have grown up in Dharavi . . .'). Nonsense. The Mumbai autorickshaw guys are the best in India. They will take you safely and precisely to your destination and charge you according to the meter.

My first film was supposed to be dubbed in Hindi. I told the director that my Hindi was zero. He said that this was by no means a fresh piece of news at all for anyone on the set, considering I had been with them for all these days

When we were doing *Gandhi, My Father,* director Feroz Abbas Khan had only one instruction for me: 'Don't ever speak in Hindi. Do everything else; you are a good man, I trust you a lot, but don't speak in Hindi. You know, we Hindiwallahs, we respect language a lot, so don't speak in Hindi.' So I am very reluctant to speak in Hindi when I work with Feroz.

*

Now for some memories of romance from my school days.

On one of the post-Oscar days, I got a phone call from the Gulf. A female voice said, 'Huh . . . Is that Resul? This is (so and so).'

'Aha!' I exclaimed. 'Isn't this my love from the tenth standard!'
She was astonished. 'You still remember me!'

'How can I ever forget you?' I said. 'How many songs have I sung looking into your eyes!'

She laughed.

The memory took me back to the tenth grade in Anchal High School. Boys and girls were in separate batches. But after school, we all went for tuitions to a tutorial academy, where we were allowed to sit the same class.

I was a very small-built boy, she was quite tall—no match in physiques at all. But as they say, love has no eyes. Or even a nose or ears, for that matter. I was in love. And that was that.

The tuitions were over by five in the evening. My bus to Vilakkupara was at quarter to seven. I would have an hour and a half to spare. I would hire a cycle and pedal furiously to her home. The excuse was 'to exchange class notes'. I clearly remember the lily pond on the way. I hung around there. Sometimes, I would give her younger brother—a fourth standard boy—a ride on the cycle and chat with him, buying time. She also had an elder brother who was doing his pre-degree. I was slightly daunted by him, but the supposed academic nature of my relationship with his sister gave me courage.

Finally, the process matured into *I Love You*, gallantly expressed within the confines of a chemistry textbook. Isn't it all about chemistry anyway?

My memory doesn't serve me too well, but the catalyst was a long letter that was skilfully hidden inside the dustjacket of the book. I handed the book to her with a short instruction: 'Look inside the dustcover.' She saw, read the letter and returned the book after two days. I dug behind the cover and found nothing; looked again, and there still was nothing. Big frustration! I just couldn't figure out what had gone wrong. I had to know whether this romance was going one way or both ways.

I told her in the evening, 'You didn't give me any reply.'

She said, 'Oh, I did write something.' I ran back to the book and frantically searched for her message. In the end, I discovered it on the title page, where you write your name and class; she had written *I Love You* under my name *Resul P.*—and the page was cleverly shoved inside the dustjacket. I still remember her handwriting. This was my first official romance. But after the tenth standard, it all dissolved and melted away. By that time, I was busy trying to figure out all those big questions about my aims and objectives in life. I also had to leave the place to pursue my further studies.

It was only this telephone call that finally brought us in touch again.

So while my first real romance was floundering, I was occupied with the distant goal of becoming a doctor. I applied to St John's College in Anchal for the pre-degree course. Umma wanted me to remain with her at home. But I didn't get admission there. So I headed to Kayamkulam for my pre-degree.

The Kayamkulam college was another world altogether. There everybody knew my family because all my elder brothers had studied there. Moreover, Zeenath was also studying there. The loss of anonymity was kind of limiting.

When I came to Kayamkulam, I knew I had to be serious
about my studies. My cousin sister had recently become a
rank-holder in a prestigious scholarship exam and had
received the award from the all-time superstar of Malayalam
films, Prem Nazir. I had attended the function, which, for me
at that time, was a mega event of incomprehensible scale. So
I was duly inspired to become an earnest student—no more
romance, no more artistic activities.

*

Bappa's younger brother, Taha Kochappa, lived in the
Kayamkulam house. Taha Kochappa didn't have any regular
work in particular. Most of the expenses of the household and
our education were met from my Bappa's insignificant salary.
All this I realized only after moving there.

Kochappa and Kochumma (Bappa's brother and sister-in-
law) were very fond of me. In many ways, Kochumma was like
a mother to me. Kochappa was a great character. Kochappa's
bath and meals were events in themselves. He came home
only once in a while. When he came, before a meal, he had
a bath—an outdoor ritual performed right in front of the
house. I had to draw buckets full of water from the well and
empty it over his head while he sat as if in meditation. After
about ten buckets, he would raise his hand as a signal for
me to stop. Then he would violently soap himself till he was
completely transformed into a froth ball in human shape.
On the days of this bathing ritual, the girls from Babukka's
college—which was located opposite the house—never came

anywhere in the vicinity of Kochappa's house. It was very embarrassing for me.

When he finished his bath, he would sit to eat. Kochumma was a bit forgetful. So she kind of never finished serving—she would go back and forth to get the forgotten dishes. Even after the last dish was brought, Kochappa would wait.

'What?' she would ask.

'Nothing, just waiting to make sure that you have not forgotten anything else.' Then he would attack the food—squash everything into one homogeneous pulp. At this juncture, all the crows and cats of the locality would present themselves. One handful for the crows, another for the cats and a third for himself—that was how he dealt with his meals. What he did for a living is still a mystery to me. But somehow he looked after his family and even managed to build a house.

*

Looking back, I now realize how fortunate I have been in having teachers who have guided and inspired me at practically every juncture in the course of my education. This is evident as far back as my school days—Soman Saar, who taught biology; Sahadevan Saar who taught Malayalam; Balan Pillai Saar and Sharada Teacher; Suni Teacher who taught music. These are some of the teachers I shall always be indebted to for helping me overcome my difficulties in school and for fostering in me the desire to learn.

And luckily for me, this didn't stop at school. The ensuing years brought into my life many other mentors.

When I went to MSM College, Kayamkulam, there were Rashid Saar and Jabbar Saar for more inspiration. The change in the medium of instruction from Malayalam (in school) to English (in college) was quite a tough deal for me. When the language—our medium of expression—changes, our thinking, too, changes with it. Rashid Saar was the one who cracked this concept for me.

Under Rashid Saar's guidance, even the most complex theories of physics became simple things of day-to-day life. Even the paradoxical quantum physics would be related to life experiences in his illustrations. In Kerala, we have this tiny object that we call *allu*—a small metal spike in the shape of a tetrapod. No matter which way it falls, it will always have one sharp spike pointing up. This was extensively used, during the post-Emergency strikes in Kerala, to puncture the tyres of government vehicles. This thing was used on coconut trees as well to discourage thieves from stealing the coconuts. It was with this familiar object that Rashid Saar explained some of the most complicated electro-magnetic concepts. I may have forgotten the formal name of a particular theorem, but I can never forget the theorem itself—it will always be associated with that tiny thing, the *allu*.

Rashid Saar helped me cast away my fear of studies. This is what helped me in becoming a topper. I would go to his house after classes, where he would patiently tackle my queries and dissolve my doubts. He would explain everything, even touching on matters that were not part of the syllabus. I used to help him with the evaluation of class tests. He trusted me that much. By the time I was in my final year, he had brought me up to a stage where I was as knowledgeable as he was, and could do my own research. He had no insecurities about his students learning too much. After a point, we forged a companionship in exploring new areas of knowledge where he was also a seeker like me, often consulting advanced books to understand and explain further. It was an amazing sensation for a student, to be at that level with a teacher where he needed to refer to books to explain things to you. But whatever he taught you, you would never ever forget.

Once I was in such difficulty that I had no money to pay his tuition fees. That was in my final year of college. I never told him about it. Had he known about my hardships, he would never have taken money from me. I sold Bappa's watch to pay his fees. If Rashid Saar comes to know about this, I am sure it will make him cry, even now. He was such a loving and caring man. Although he was a strict disciplinarian, he was very close to his students. If at all a teacher ever needed his students' backing, Rashid Saar was one who could always count on tens of thousands of students supporting him.

After his final class with us, he cut a cake for the entire batch. It was an emotional moment for me since I realized that we would be parting ways here. Crying, I stayed rooted to the spot even after everybody had left. I went home to dump my books and then rushed back to his house and told him I didn't want to leave, that I could become a teacher and stay on in the college.

But life had other plans for me. I enrolled at the Government Law College in Thiruvananthapuram. While studying there, I developed a similar deep intimacy with Sathyasheelan Saar. Like Rashid Saar, he was a brilliant teacher who taught extensively from outside the syllabus—a rare exception to the ways of the general teaching fraternity. He introduced me to the works of Nietzsche, Osho, Jiddu Krishnamurthy and Gurdjieff, and was responsible for changing my outlook on life in fundamental ways. I have no account of the number of times he bought me food. Almost every evening, he took me to a place in East Fort, where we ate fish fry and tapioca, the taste of which I will never be able to forget. Another teacher who went out of his way to care for me was Thaha Saar. Some friends told me that Thaha Saar was from some big-time influential family from Varkala. I wondered if there was some nice girl in that family whom I could marry. It should be worth a try . . . years later, it turned out that he was in fact my mother-in-law's first cousin!

Inspired by the mentors in my life, I even became a part-time teacher at Babukka's tuition centre while at college. These were the special people I was referring to while expressing my sincere and deepest gratitude to my teachers in my Oscar speech.

3

THE LOVE OF ANIMALS, THE LURE OF CINEMA

Some of my most vivid memories are of sound. The cows' hooves scratching the floor on a quiet night; the sound of them getting up; the distinctive rhythm of their breathing . . . Umma knew the meanings of such sounds. Some meant that there were wild animals nearby. Then Umma would get up and light the lamp. Sometimes, the goats suddenly cried together and then would fall into an equally sudden silence. That meant one of them was gone. Umma was the one who explained to me the meanings of these sound signs. I have a lot of memories of a time when goats, chicken, cows and people all lived together.

All through my life I have watched animals. I have spent a lot of time with them, very closely. As a kid I talked a lot—to animals. I used to have very long conversations with the cows. We, the children, were the main attendants and midwives when they gave birth.

At the birth of a newborn—whether a calf or a goat—its hooves are very soft. They have to be broken first to make them strong and hard so that the animal can walk. The process takes two to three days. The calf can't walk during this period, so we would carry it everywhere. Vilakkupara was close to the forest. Wild dogs and wolves would come in the nights; so for the first few days, the newborn was kept inside the house. It was great fun to have these creatures inside the house at night. It was completely my scene. My monologue to the infant cows and goats went late into the nights.

I used to carry the baby goats like we carry human babies—across the shoulder—and take them everywhere. They would happily settle on your shoulder and try to bite and eat your ear with their pre-molar soft mouths. Over the next few days, things would improve dramatically. After the morning feed, they would come out into the early morning sun and frolic like crazy—intoxicated by a potent combination of happiness and energy. We would get excited seeing this and run towards them; they too would run and oh, it was an amazing experience!

I would make these infant creatures wear my old shorts. Later, as rebellious teenagers, they came to lock horns with you. Then you would give them a couple of tight slaps and ask them to get lost. Through them, you got to see the entire process of life in fast-forward mode. A newborn that could hardly stand on its own legs would transform into a majestic lady and mother in just two years.

There was an ash-pit in a shack next to our kitchen, a place that gave you a special feeling. The hen would sit there brooding over her eggs. She also laid the eggs there. I spent a lot of time inside there. The moment the egg was out I would shoot off with it to Umma in the kitchen. She would boil it for me. If tapioca or rice was cooking, she would just wash the egg and drop it into the pot. I would wait, looking at the boiling pot. That was one way of earning one's boiled egg.

Sometimes the hen didn't lay eggs, and I would lose my patience. I would place my palm under the hen and wait. Most often, it would get very irritated and lay the egg just to get to get some peace. All these operations were carried out in partnership with Kochumon. In fact, most operations those days were our joint effort. Later, when I read Van Gogh's letters to Theo, I found a similarity between my relationship with Kochumon and the one that Van Gogh and Theo had shared. I imagined him as my Theo. We grew up fighting like cats and dogs, which only strengthened our bond. We haven't exchanged that many letters, though.

At the time Kochumon was a complete villain and a tough guy. I have lost count of the number of salamanders and insects he would routinely kill. He would even mistreat the hens and my pet cat, which he would fling into the air, saying, 'Now let's see how it always falls on all its fours.' It really depressed me. But now, believe it or not, Kochumon has become such a gentle soul!

The cat used to wait on the road outside the house for me to come back from school. Then she would rub herself on my legs and run into the house before me. After I had washed up and sat to eat, she would sit there watching me eat. After a while, she would lift her paw, as if to ask: what about me? I always waited for that moment. After she would lift her paw like that a couple of times, I would give her one ball of rice. She would look at the rice and then at me, only touching it once I gave her the go-ahead.

One day when I came back from school, the cat wasn't there at her usual spot. She had been run over earlier that day. I sat where she was buried and cried. I made a little tomb and grew a plant there. I watered it for months.

There have been other pets that I remember fondly. One was a squirrel that came into my care while I was studying law in Thiruvananthapuram. It became my hostel roommate until an unfortunate accident ended its life. It was crushed under a writing board in my hostel room. I buried him in the college compound. That was a very painful experience.

Another pet that I got very close to was Mojo. That was in Mumbai. Mojo, a Great Dane, was P.M. Satheesh's dog. Whenever I stayed over at Satheesh's house, I would sleep with him; or Satheesh and I would sleep with this guy in the middle. He would casually throw one enormous limb around me in his sleep. The day that Mojo died I was in a Madhya Pradesh village on a shoot for a film called *Mathrubhumi*. Satheesh was working on some other film. He had fed Mojo and left for the day. When Satheesh came back after work, Mojo was very excited to see him. He ran to Satheesh and clambered over him and collapsed. He died in Satheesh's arms. Apparently, that's how it is with pure-bred Great Danes. You are not supposed to let them run when their stomach is full. What happens is that on a full stomach, if a Great Dane suddenly stops in its run, his intestine gets pressed against the diaphragm and chokes him. Mojo was someone who left us after giving us a lot of love, a victim of his own intense affection!

These three deaths have scarred me deeply.

I have seen a lot of animal suffering. I have seen goats and calves struggling for dear life after getting poisoned by eating the leaves of rubber trees. Many of them I have saved by handling them with mature calm. This was a pretty routine affair in my school days. The treatment was to somehow get this stuff out of their stomach. One technique was to choke them with beedi smoke. You would blow the beedi smoke into the snout of the animal. When thus choked, they would vomit the poisonous stuff out. Or you could make a deadly combination of pepper, strong ginger and other spices and shove it into the animal's gullet.

A common affliction of cattle was the extremely painful hoof infection. The treatment for this was a brew of centipedes stewed in castor oil. After washing and cleaning the hooves, we would apply this country medicine. I was very good at all this. When I nursed the animals, they quietly complied. They understood I was trying to cure their problem. I really know animals very well.

*

I have pondered over animals a great deal—particularly goats, pigs and donkeys, which have exerted a strong influence over my life. These animals have featured prominently in world literature and cinema, especially the donkey. The donkey is a very docile creature, but one who has seen the world.

When you ponder over the riddles of existence, you attain certain qualities that become part of your visible personality, like humility, soulfulness, a sense of depth and such like. I think donkeys have attained those qualities. We just can't call them idiots and dismiss their whole being. There's more to a donkey than that.

Then there are the pigs that scavenge around in groups and clean up an area. But we consider them appalling creatures. In Islam, the mere utterance of the word 'pig' costs you forty days' loss of faith; you can't take the animal's name, or eat its meat. I don't know the real reason behind all this. Christians happily eat them. For the Hindu, he is God's avatar. I can't understand why the pig is looked down upon in Islam. It also didn't find a place in Noah's ark. A species of fish too was denied admittance in the ark. The people who speak of the scientific basis of Islam say it is because of the tapeworm in pork. Islam has a lot of dictums connected to hygiene: what to say before and after taking a leak; what *surah* to chant before having sex; and so on. I am not an expert on religion, but I know a reasonable amount of things about all religions. The point here is that I still haven't understood the reason behind the sad status of the pig in Islam.

At the same time, Islam perhaps has helped me in understanding goats. I have a lot of memories about goats. In my early childhood, I used to be woken up early in the morning by Umma's shout—to hold the goat's legs while she milked the animal. I would be barely awake, without having even taken the morning leak. I would go and hold the goat's legs and nod off. In that drowsy condition, I would wrestle with a grave moral dilemma: the mother goat's milk belonged to its baby, who was a very close friend of mine. So, humans should not be allowed to milk it. But then, I would appease myself with the thought that if I held the mother goat's legs till Umma finished milking, Umma would then be letting the baby drink its mother's milk.

The goat's agility is a thing of wonder. It's always wandering around, eating, biting and eyeing things—a goat tastes everything in life. And it gives you whatever you want, whenever. There's no particular time to milk a goat. Sprinkle some water on the udder and give it a couple of knocks, and the milk would flow. That's a major thing. You don't need a fridge or things like that to keep the milk. The goat is a walking fridge.

And it's one pet that Muslim households keep; it's like a member of the family. One handsome male goat with its head held high, a few female ones and the kids—that's the scene.

In Islam, the goat is a sacrificial animal. It's also sacrificed in Hindu *yagna*s. The goat is important in Ayurveda too. It's the one who eats up all kinds of leaves. The meat of the black goat is a major ingredient in the Ayurvedic remedy for rheumatic arthritis as the goat eats up all kinds of medicinal herbs. We often think of Ayurveda as a vegetarian thing, but goat meat is indeed used in the medicines of Agasthya's Ayurveda, in mainstream Ayurveda and in the Unani system. There are many references to the goat in Christianity and Buddhism too. However, that's nothing compared to Islam's relationship with it—for Muslims, goat is food, friend and sacrifice. A major being indeed.

I read Basheer's *Pathumma's Goat* in one sitting. I was so overwhelmed and thought there must be some serious connection between the author and me. There was no one else who had done such thorough goat watching. I thought of him as someone like me, who grew up with goats; who knew the mind of a goat. I wondered a lot about him—what kind of a man would he have been? He had travelled a lot; he had had many romantic affairs and was someone who had attempted to understand women. In fact, in my estimation, Basheer was someone who completely understood women. Otherwise, how could he have written a story like 'Hunthrappy Bussotta'? A woman is a Hunthrappy Bussotta—an unpredictable phenomenon of many things that we can't comprehend! The word doesn't mean anything, just go by the sound of it! I have often felt that about Shadia. The Creator's tool to muddle up mankind, to always remind you, *'Hey, idiot, thou shall not forget me!'*

I have wondered about many of Basheer's love affairs. There is a book of his called *The Walls*. The book ends with the question of the purpose of freedom. The whole deal is of a dry twig going up and down, on the other side of a prison wall. That is all what the writer sees of the heroine. Maybe he met her after he was released from the prison, going by practical logic. But Basheer never says anything about that. We are left wondering—what happened to her, who and what was she? Did they ever meet? The mystery bothered me for a long time. In Basheer's *Childhood Sweetheart* and some other works, he has touched upon certain incidents of his life, but there's no further mention of this lady of *The Walls*. There must be something to it, I was sure. When I went to Calicut after the Oscar, his son Anees Basheer came and met me. He invited me home, saying, 'Ikka must definitely visit our house; it's a house that many great men have visited in the past.'

But I was in Calicut only for a day, and I couldn't make it. The son looked strikingly like the father—maybe a bit fairer, but the lips and all were exactly the same. I really wanted to go and see that umma and everyone.

I have often compared Bappa and Basheer. Basheer had suffered a mental breakdown at some point. He would have conversations with birds and animals. I have never thought that's insane. I used to ask my goat—the mother goat whom I used to call the 'elder goat'—to show its teeth and it would promptly raise its upper lip. And if I saw a snake ten feet in front of me, I never panicked; I knew it would carry on to wherever it had set out to go. (The snake won't bite you just because you spotted it; it will bite you if it's scared.) For me, this is actually what spirituality is. It's a sort of communion— with all the beings of the world. You don't need to visit temples or mosques to achieve that.

I have heard many stories of Basheer scolding animals. One day, when the writer M.T. Vasudevan Nair went to his place, he saw Basheer yelling at a cobra, 'Rascal, fold up your hood, can't you see who is coming . . .?' It's said that the cobra indeed wrapped up its show and went home.

Once, my Bappa was lying down reading something. He usually never got up before finishing whatever he was reading. He was in his lungi, lying on his special soft mat. A big rat snake came into the room. Bappa lifted his head from the book and looked at the snake. The snake too lifted its head and looked at him. Bappa returned to reading and the snake returned to his crawling. But from the outside, what we saw was a massive rat snake going into the house. It was on the lookout for rats. We rushed in with a stick and chased it off. But what would always stay in the mind is that image of Bappa and the snake lifting their heads and looking at each other and then returning to whatever they were doing. That was quite a Basheerian incident.

In so many ways, especially when it comes to goats, Basheer is always present in my mind. In Calicut, when I came back to the hotel after meeting Basheer's son, there was a young man waiting for me. 'I have come to meet you. I don't have an appointment and all. I would like to ask you something . . . I have a film script with me; I would like to read it out to you.'

I asked him to tell me what it was about.

He said, 'My film is called *Beyond the Walls*.'

Interesting! The story about what happened to the heroine of *The Walls*!

I heard only that much and I declared that I would do the film. 'Give me the script. This is a sign, a good omen!'

The lad couldn't believe himself. He had taken a chance and come to see me; and his film was now being okayed! He couldn't control himself and held my legs and started crying. Oh, how Basheer keeps coming back to my life! I had this idea for long and now somebody has written it all out and brought it to me!

When I look at my life, I see a lot of such returns, revisits and circular journeys—all very significant indeed.

PART 2

PUNE AND MUMBAI

1

NEW JOURNEYS

I wasn't always called Resul Pookutty. Back home in Kerala, my name was officially Resul P. Things changed after I left for the Film and Television Institute of India (FTII) in Pune.

This story begins when I came to the Institute for the first time for an interview. The application form contained a separate column for surnames. But I didn't have one. Then (going by what the other applicants were doing), I saw that the surname could also be the expansion of one's initials. So I wrote 'Pookutty' in the surname column.

When I came to the Institute, I was addressed as R. Pookutty or Mr Pookutty. Naturally, I found it difficult to respond to this name—Mr Pookutty was my Bappa, not me! I had never been called Pookutty by anyone before. Moreover, I was this guy who had never sat in front of my Bappa, or wore his clothes, or used any of his things—all as part of a serious protocol of love and respect. And here, people were forcing his name on me! *Mr Pookutty, please come here!* This was something I had never imagined would happen. When I applied the next time, I decided not to put a surname. I just put my initial 'P' in that column. When I landed up, the guys behind the counter looked at me suspiciously. *Isn't this one the same Pookutty of last time?* However, I became Resul P. once again.

After the Institute, when I started working, I thought this name Resul P. didn't have much of a punch to it. No *chimittu*, as Sathyasheelan Saar would put it. I don't know what it means. It's a complex mixture of elegance, crispness, personality and such stuff. To me, it also sounds a bit like the burst of a cracker.

So I decided to add this little *chimittu* to my name. This was for a serial called *Margarita*, which I didn't complete. I gave up after the first schedule since the sound in that serial was terribly boring. But in the credits of *Margarita*, I put my name as Resul Pookutty. I took a VHS copy of it and showed it to Umma at home. When she saw it, her face fell. I knew what was going through her mind. She was always of the opinion that all her children were Bappa's babies and that there was no one to support her. She said, 'Everybody is with Bappa. Even the name is Bappa's.'

'What are you saying, Umma?' I asked her. 'So what shall I do? Shall I change my name to Resul Nabeeza Beevi or what?'

She didn't insist that I should.

That's how I became and remained Resul Pookutty ever after. But the journey that led me to this began elsewhere. Let me start from the beginning . . .

*

I had applied for the Film Institute without really planning to do so. I originally wanted to pursue a masters in physics after my degree. But the seats were too few in MSc Physics and I didn't get in. Considering Bappa's scruples, there was no question of paying a 'donation' for a seat. Umma was quite the opposite. She thought that if we could sell some land for a couple of lakhs, I could get an MBBS admission.

My personal philosophy is a blend of both my parents'. I have inherited my Bappa's integrity and my Umma's capacity for hard work. This combination is a gift.

I applied all over for MSc admissions, including the Farook College in Kozhikode where I went with Babukka. (After my Oscar, this was the first place I visited; I got a fantastic reception there—see where all life's currents can take you!) When the MSc didn't happen, I went to study law. I didn't want to waste time. And law had some professional possibilities. That's when a couple of friends saw an ad in a paper and told me about the sound engineering course in the Pune Film Institute; the basic qualification was graduation in physics or electronics.

Ting! It was as though a hundred-watt bulb suddenly lit up inside my head.

You see, when I was a boy, a newspaper advertisement had appeared calling for child artistes for a Malayalam film by a well-known director. I don't remember which film it was. The aspiring children should send three photographs: full size, profile and close-up. The rest was up to your fate. I cried at Umma's feet. The photos had to be organized. A matter of a hundred and fifty rupees! That was a huge sum, but we managed to arrange for the photographs.

Everyone could see that I was utterly consumed by dreams of seeing myself in films! While carrying home bundles of rather sharp blades of grass, Kochumon would often remind me, 'Hey, be careful about your face; don't get any scratches. You're going to act in a film.' (Mind you, this bit of advice was coming from the brother who otherwise wouldn't hesitate to slap me to the ground on a daily basis.)

One day, I read in the newspaper that some other kid had been selected for that role. I sank into deep depression. My second brother-in-law noticed me hanging around, looking pathetic and not eating at all. He told me, 'Don't worry, son, one day we'll send you to the Poonafiliminstitute!'

The name sounded odd. Poonafilminstitute? What was this thing? And was there an acting course there? But the name stuck in my mind. And so all those years later, seeing the ad in the papers, the memory of my childhood cinematic obsession returned. *Ting!*

The Institute offered only four courses: in direction, camera, editing and sound. Direction wasn't my scene. I had no idea about cameras. Editing? I didn't even know what it was! What I knew was physics. There was sound in physics. Yes, that's what I would try: sound! And so I applied.

I appeared for the all-India entrance test. When the results were declared, I found that I had been selected for an orientation course at the Institute. Now, the FTII selection process had two parts. The first was an entrance test conducted simultaneously at various centres across the country. People shortlisted from that were called for the orientation course. The philosophy of the Institute is that while people from the remote villages of the country might not have had a great exposure to the film medium unlike their big city counterparts, they could otherwise be equal, in terms of the attitude and aptitude required for a career in cinema. That's what the Institute figures out.

So all are brought on a common platform and shown several films. This would be followed by serious discussions. The emphasis would be on how a movie was interpreted. These discussions and interactions help in assessing a potential student's capability and motivation. The first stage involves a series of interactive sessions from Monday to Friday. Then a written test is held based on the sessions, with an interview at the end of it all. I didn't know all this at the time and would only learn the intricacies when I reached FTII.

But, to get back to my story, the euphoria of being selected was dimmed by the realization that I had to still find a way to get there! I went and fell at the feet of the principal of the law college, begging him to certify me for a student's railway concession ticket to Pune! The ticket was three hundred rupees then. A princely sum! And there was no way I could ask my parents for the money. With persistent pleas, I finally found myself aboard the Jayanti Janata Express, heading from Thiruvananthapuram to Pune, on a student concession ticket that cost me a hundred and thirty-five rupees.

That was the opening shot of my Pune journey. I had just completed twenty years then and was stepping out of the Kerala state border for the very first time. I didn't even know the basic dos and don'ts of a long train journey. I wondered about things like how to get food in the train. Someone told me I had to get out on to the station platform to drink water.

I had asked around to find out if anyone else was also heading to FTII. There was a Mahesh from Thiruvananthapuram and a Hari from Kollam. Luckily, our seats were together. Mahesh had already had an interview before. I had met him earlier: a serious guy; not very interactive. He buried himself in a book the moment the train started moving. Hari was going through a railway map. I had no idea what use a railway map would be. But at least I could talk to Hari.

The train pulled into Kadappa station. It was massive! Until that point in my life, the biggest station I had seen before was Ernakulam station, while here was something far bigger, of astronomical proportions! But the place was incredibly filthy. I thought, what's the point of making something so big if it stinks like this! Then we reached Pune station and I was astounded by the expansive sea of humanity! It was two in the morning and bitterly cold. Despite the late hour, huge crowds were rushing around in all directions when we reached there.

'No point in landing up at the Institute in the middle of the night. We can sit in the waiting room till morning. There is a bathroom and all here,' Mahesh suggested.

Mahesh was an experienced traveller. He got out of the train, found a corner for himself and in no time was fast asleep! I wore a sweater and sat there waiting for the dawn.

I couldn't sleep. I was still overwhelmed by the profusion of people. To keep myself busy, I decided to do some people watching, trying to figure out the subject's socio-economic background from the body language and attire.

I noticed a young guy: smart, short and handsome. He walked into the waiting room very confidently, found a place to sit, and started talking to the woman next to him in Hindi. I was very impressed. This guy sure knew a lot, I thought. I should be like him.

I often wanted to be like someone else who was better or smarter than me.

This guy got whatever information he wanted from the woman and did a 360-degree scan of the surroundings. He saw me looking at him. He paused for a moment, then came and sat next to me. He introduced himself.

This guy was Raman. We were to become great friends. He was also going to the Institute. He had been in some other train. To my amazement, this fluent Hindi speaker turned out to be a Malayali. He told me his background: the eldest son belonging to a Brahmin family from East Fort, Thiruvananthapuram. He was very focused; his sole purpose in life was to get into the Film Institute and learn everything there was to know about wielding a camera. But his parents didn't think this ambition lofty enough. He had fought with them before coming. He knew cinematography was going to be a life or death issue for him.

I was very impressed. An ideal man, I thought. For starters, he knew Hindi! He quickly found out the bus number and route to the Institute. Under his leadership, things moved fast and we reached the Institute with all our bags and baggage.

The list and names were all put up right at the gate. We were led to the hostel rooms, two people sharing one. I don't remember who my roommate was.

When I reached the gate, it was as if I was about to enter a glorious new empire. A black pathway extended from my feet through the gate into a vanishing point on the horizon. There stood a majestic tree right at the gate with innumerable roots hanging from it. More trees stood alongside the path, like some philosophical milestones. And there was a mango tree opposite the canteen—this was the famous Wisdom Tree of the Institute. I felt I was walking on a red carpet leading into another life. This was the place where the film-maker John Abraham had studied. How many luminaries must have walked this very path upon which I was now treading with the rubber slippers on my rustic feet! That walk, that very first walk into that magnificent place, shall never be forgotten.

We had landed up at the Institute on the early morning of a Sunday. I washed my clothes, took a bath and went for lunch at noon. Hostel food was only from Monday onwards. They would give us food coupons during the registration procedure on Monday morning. The whole orientation course was absolutely free!

On day one, lunch was served outside the Institute. Hari and I went together. The sum total of our knowledge of Hindi amounted to a big fat zero. We went through the menu at one place and couldn't comprehend anything of the cuisine of this new world. *Alu-gobi* didn't exist in our dictionary. We tried making an inquiry in English and failed. Finally we settled for veg-pulao. When we finished, two stainless steel bowls of water arrived with lemon slices luxuriously floating in them. Must be lime juice, we decided. I tried to drink it and thought why they would want to heat up lime juice. It created a spectacle, with everyone showering us with a lot of instructions in Hindi, which of course we didn't understand; but I noticed that the rest of humanity was not drinking the mysterious concoction—they were washing their fingers in it! Though the purpose of the bowls finally dawned on me, I couldn't help thinking, what kind of guys are these; they don't even wash their mouths and hands after eating!

The good Malayali has a pretty in-depth hand-washing ceremony before a meal. And after the meal, it's nothing less than a good Kathakali performance—one's fingers probe inside the mouth for bits of food stuck there; polish the teeth; massage the gums; wipe the tongue clean to its original pink . . . And the whole show is accompanied by a range of sound effects—from guttural grunts to violent gargling. Our whole notion of hygiene is inseparably associated with the physical performance of washing. And here I had landed in the middle of a culture whose entire post-lunch personal hygiene consisted of just a twist of fingertips in a tiny bowl which was only half filled! At Pune, I also noticed people's paan habit—at the bus depot, there were a number of people chewing paan and spraying their immediate environment with rich scarlet spit. The Malayali in me was disgusted.

*

I had no idea about what to do for the interview. The only thing that I was clear about was that I should impress the

board at all costs. I had to get an admission! I held many
discussions with friends on what I should say at the interview.
I also sought inspiration from the memoirs of Malayattoor
Ramakrishnan, the Malayali bureaucrat-turned-writer. So, I
generally decided to sound a bit heavy and philosophical at
the interview.

In one of the group discussions, I was asked, 'Why are you here?'

I let it rip: 'Cinema is a major social medium. It can be a
very powerful agent of social change.'

'But isn't sound a technical course?'

'Yes. But I want to do such things while doing sound!
Meaning, I would do sound specifically for films that are
powerful agents of social change. That is my prime motive.' I
passionately argued my points.

They agreed. But my passion didn't help. I didn't get in.

Later, I thought about the entire process and came to a
conclusion: you need an original gut feeling, something real
and sincere that springs from within. You shouldn't dwell too
much in the realm of thought; it's when you go overboard
with thinking that you fail. Really, my advice is: as much as
possible, try not to think. When we do something without
thinking, at least it has some elements of truth in it; maybe
it's your own truth, but it's truth nevertheless. That truth
should sustain you.

I used to read quite a bit in the college days, a habit I had
inherited from Bappa. Malayalam literature was a particularly
favourite diet—from *Second Turn* (M.T. Vasudevan Nair's
interpretation of the Mahabharata, narrated through the eyes
of Bhim) to *Delhi* by M. Mukundan (one of the foremost of

Malayalam literature's existentialists). I had lots of idealistic notions then. I was pretty confident, and focusing on how to handle the tests and interviews. I now feel that my answers were rather studied and readymade.

I also realized how I had tried to be too clever during the discussions rather than observing closely and responding with my gut feeling. The discussions held during that orientation course had opened another world to me. I sat stunned watching *Rashomon*. If this was how movies were made, I decided, I had to get into this place. Unfortunately, in my eagerness to prove that I was a connoisseur of films, I made the mistake of sounding pompous by talking about cinema in philosophical riddles. Clearly, that was unwise. All told, I was very upset about not being able to get in.

The only thing that upset me more was the food I had there for a week. The food was a sheer culture shock—like the dried-up thing they served as chapatti! I tried not to eat at all for a couple days. I even thought of going back, leaving it all. I really had a tough time with food.

Raman, Suresh Pai (a fellow I became very good friends with) and I returned on a bus headed to Mangalore. None of us had made it. We were all pretty depressed. Mahesh, however, had made the cut. Another guy who made it was Vinod Sukumaran. He got editing. He tried to cheer us up, saying we'd surely make it the next year. But what really did cheer us up was the delicious meal we had when we reached Mangalore! The memory of that meal clouds the disappointment of my failed first attempt to get into FTII.

*

Those five days of intense interactions at the Film Institute certainly did open my eyes, however. It also opened the doors to a bigger world. I decided on my way back: *this is what I want to do!* At the time, my family had no idea of these grand plans. So as not to upset anything, I had to continue with my law studies.

My law college friends knew that I had been to the Pune Film Institute for an interview. There was a girl called Anita with whom I was sort of close. She was very smart, and would always score well in tests. She came from a well-to-do family and had studied in an English-medium school, so her English was impeccable. She was also disciplined and organized in her studies. She kept meticulous notes which I excessively copied. There was also some competition between us. If I happened to score half a mark or something more than her, she would burst into tears. The crying always happened in the library, and I often wonder what the onlookers must have thought! They would see a girl and a boy—Anita and me—sitting face to face across the library desk and the girl suddenly breaking down! But one area where I truly scored over her was in the realm of political ideologies and theories.

I ended up sharing her lunch on a regular basis. I ate her lunch more out of necessity than as a rite of a campus romance. You see, I received about three hundred rupees as a scholarship. There was a small sum coming from home as well. This was just about enough for college and hostel fees.

Not that this was something new for me. While studying at MSM College, Kayamkulam, there was another lunch box I frequently partook of. It belonged to a girl named Lekha, who was also studying there. She brought omelettes for lunch every day, which I would promptly polish off. Later on, she started bringing a supplementary parcel of lunch. Lekha's lunch had a very prominent role in my growth. In jest or otherwise, I used to tell her: let's elope and go somewhere far away. This was during the first or second year of my graduation. But by the third year, I was madly in love with a girl called Salina! I was quite popular in college: a smart, energetic young man.

Incidentally, Lekha called me when the Oscar nominations were out.

'Resul! Have you forgotten me or what, man!'

I said I hadn't. I asked her whether she remembered us.

'Of course, man! You used to tell me, let us run away, let us run away! What a pity! I should have just run away with you!'

'Now you know!' I joked.

But I digress. When I returned from the FTII orientation course, Anita gave me a book she had issued from the library—*Cinema and I* by Ritwik Ghatak. I then immersed myself in the subject of cinema throughout the following year. I even read up loads on art and culture. Both Sathyasheelan Saar and Anita helped me a lot during my second attempt at getting into the Institute. Whenever I got disheartened and gave up, saying, 'Okay screw it, I might as well continue with law', it was Anita who pushed me relentlessly, always reminding me of my original goal. We were very close and in love, but never accepted or acknowledged that fact! (Once she bought me a book, *Our Film Their Film*. Interestingly, when I sat for the FTII entrance exam for the second time, one of the questions was to name the author of *Our Film Their Film*? I immediately remembered Anita.)

Those days she was preparing for the IAS. I was considering doing the same myself. After all, joining the IAS was not a bad idea—actually it was quite a big thing—so perhaps the Film Institute could wait and I should give IAS a real try. But I had no money to attend the coaching classes. I even asked Anita to attend those classes and then come back and coach me.

But then appeared Raman, with his hardcore determination to get into the Film Institute, and he re-ignited my passion to get into the world of cinema. We started to pursue with renewed vigour a life infused with cinema. We regularly watched movies at the Tagore Theatre and walked back to the hostel at night. The heavy cinema discussions that followed often turned violent. Later, I became a member of the Chalachitra Film Society. I saw the entire retrospective of Zanussi there. I also got familiar with the works of film-makers like Aribam Shyam Sharma.

Raman's father was working with the Bank of Baroda. He had a Soorya Film Society membership. We stole his card and watched the Soorya film festival. Those days, three films a week was my diet. Raman used to do a bit of photography. Whenever he earned some money from his photo assignments, he would bring me *porotta* and beef. There was a small restaurant across Ragam Theatre. You got some damn good beef there. Despite being a Brahmin, Raman knew the places where you got good beef!

Somewhere around that time, Raman's father suffered a stroke and fell ill. Raman now became unsure about his Film

Institute plans. Even I became disheartened and was in two minds. On the last day to send the application, Raman came and blasted me for delaying the whole thing. He rushed and sent my application through the railway mail service, which was much swifter than the regular mail. Were it not for Raman's intervention, my application wouldn't have reached Pune in time.

Raman has been miraculously present during all the significant events of my life. He would somehow appear from nowhere, like a good omen. He popped up at my wedding too. There was no news of him till then. And when I bought my house, again Raman was there. I needed a witness to sign on the agreement. Strangely, Raman appeared that morning and signed on my papers.

On the day the list of Oscar nominees was announced, I met Raman. I told him, 'Raman, they are going to announce the nominations, do pray for me! What if they make a mistake and I get nominated!'

'Man, you'll get it,' he assured me.

I had already been nominated for the BAFTA and CAS awards. And yes, that day I did get the Oscar nomination. Raman was jumping up and down in joy. I told him to break a coconut for the Ganapati of Pazhavangadi temple. Later, I was in a London hotel, getting ready to go for the BAFTA awards ceremony, when I got Raman's message that he had gone to the Pazhavangadi temple and broke the coconuts: BROKE COCONUTS AT PAZHAVANGADI. NOT ONE, BUT THREE. SURE YOU WILL WIN.

That evening, I won the BAFTA. The first person I called was Raman.

After his father's illness, he was not sure about his Pune plans. He was the eldest son. His biggest ambition was to learn cinematography. I spoke with his parents about supporting his plans. Raman's sister, Sujata, who sang very well, also strongly supported him. Finally, Raman did make it to the Institute. But he has not been able to concentrate on his career because of many family-related difficulties. He has done a couple of films. But in the decade or so of his career, he hasn't got the break he so deserves. However, I am sure it's going to happen very soon. He is a cameraman with an incredible sense of narration.

*

For the Institute interview the second time, Raman and I travelled together. All of us from last year's interview had kept in touch through letters. We met up with Suresh in Pune, before proceeding to the Institute. I felt like a veteran. I was not tense or anxious at all. Furthermore, I had watched many more films and had become far more knowledgeable about cinema. In any case, I was thinking that if FTII did not work out, there was always the IAS! And, if worse came to worst, there was always the law college to complete and be a law-abiding citizen! So I felt very confident and at ease.

But this time I was not saying anything in the group discussions, remembering how I messed things up last time. I maintained a golden silence for three or four days.

One day they screened Ritwik Ghatak's *Meghe Dhaka Tara*, and the next day the dean came to inspect our group discussions. John Shankaramangalam was the dean. He asked us about the difference in the soundtracks of a regular film and the film that we had watched the previous day. The group comprised some intimidatingly bright guys from various IITs and other engineering colleges. They spoke fantastic English as well. All of them were waxing eloquently while I sat there with my mouth shut. But when the question about the soundtrack of the film came from the dean, the group fell silent. No one had anything to offer. As the silence lingered, I lifted my hand.

The dean asked me, 'Okay, Resul, what is your opinion?'

I said, 'If you close your eyes and listen only to the soundtrack of the film, you'd never guess the story of the film; it would evoke another image track that works on a completely different level.'

The dean said, 'Fantastic! At least one person has understood this.'

The IIT dudes all turned around to see who this enlightened one was, and saw this small thing sitting quietly in the corner.

The discussions eventually culminated in a written test. And then came the interview. I told myself there was no reason to get stressed or worried and create disasters like the last time. Play it cool, and even if you didn't get in, go back with a smile—a clear plan of action was in place!

The turn for my interview came on an afternoon while I was having a cup of tea after lunch. I walked into the interview room and found everyone very happy and in a light mood. They smiled and asked me, 'Why are you here again?'

'I gave the test, you called me.'

'Oh . . . interesting. Are you confident? What'd you do if you don't get in?

'What would I do if I don't get in is not a question that I ask myself. I'm very confident, as confident as I should be at this stage.'

Then the dean asked me, 'What if I fail you?'

'Well, there are seven others on the board; what if they all wanted me to get in? Then what?' I asked him.

They all burst into laughter. They said, 'Okay, okay. Anything else?'

I said there was nothing else.

'Okay then, the interview is over.' And the interview was indeed over!

What! My interview over in a matter of just two minutes! Other interviews had taken much more time.

I gulped and walked out.

Shit! I've screwed it up. This is a disaster. Why the hell did I say things like that? I was acting too cheeky for my own good. I had a small chance, and now I had thrown it into the dustbin, a bloody idiot I am!

I went straight to Prakash Kutty and told him, 'Man, I screwed it up; there was a chance, but it's gone. Never mind, I will survive. I feel bad about it, though.'

He just looked at me and said, 'Come, let's go watch a film.'

So we went to Alka Theatre and saw a Hollywood comedy, *A Fish Called Wanda*. It was damn funny—we laughed all the way through. We were walking back after the film and somebody said the list was out. We met Subhash Sahu on the way. He said, 'Hey, you got through, man!' I got worried—did I really get in by mistake?

I ran to check the list. I started scanning it from the bottom. I was sure I would be somewhere at the bottom of the list. The tenth number wasn't me, nor the ninth, nor the eighth. Even the seventh number was not mine. So I glanced further up and found myself perched right on the top—first rank! I was above everyone else. Direction, sound, camera—in everything I was the topper! That got me both central and state government scholarships.

I calculated quickly—that's eight hundred rupees a month. I could manage on my own. That meant I could break the news at home now. There would be nothing more idiotic than not joining here after topping the selection. *I must join, no matter what!* Moreover, Raman, Prakash and Suresh Pai had also made it to the list. I felt terribly happy. I had to come back to this place. It was out of question not to join. But there was going to be some problem at home. I told Prakash that there was a chance that I might not be able to come back here. Prakash said, 'Come, let's go to Mumbai.' I looked at Raman. He said, 'Man, yes, let's go to Mumbai and come back!' I agreed.

We went to Mumbai—then called Bombay—and stayed in Prakash's house. My ideas about the city were limited to the propaganda spouted in Malayalam films. I knew of two places in Mumbai: Kamathipura, the red-light district, and Dharavi, the slum. The other thing I knew about Mumbai was that it was a dangerous place. I told Prakash that we must go to Kamathipura. Prakash, quite a firebrand, got very angry: 'This is the bloody problem with all you Malayalis! Do you think the whole of Mumbai is about Kamathipura? You're all a bunch of bloody voyeuristic perverts.'

I had to back down. 'Okay, baba,' I said, 'I don't want to see Kamathipura. So then, where is this Mumbai? Take me there and show it to me.'

I saw Mumbai—and got terribly depressed. People, vehicles, beggars, stink and dirt . . . I was especially dejected seeing all those beggars. I felt that the whole place was in distress. Everybody seemed to live on the roads. It was all very dirty, unhygienic and smelly. That stink of Mumbai is still there in my nostrils; the city smelt of chapattis and shit. I decided instantly that this was not a place where I was ever going to come back to or stay in.

That evening, I sent a telegram to Umma: WON FIRST RANK.

Just before leaving home, I had told two family members about my FTII plans: Umma and my elder sister Mani. It took some convincing, but eventually, both of them supported my endeavour. Umma had always understood and empathized with my gut feelings. She said if this was what I wanted to study, I should go for it. I borrowed hundred rupees from her. Mani broke her money box and gave me thirty rupees.

But the telegram I sent created a bit of a furore. When Umma was told her son had sent her a telegram from Mumbai, she panicked. Why was her son sending a telegram from Mumbai? He had gone to Pune, not Mumbai. In villages, a telegram invariably meant one thing—bad news, usually a death. She was on a bus, on her way back from a routine check-up at the hospital, when she met the postman who gave her the news. She agonized for the entire duration of the bus journey home, even breaking into tears. On reaching the village, she started bawling, '*Aiyyo,* everyone please come over, there is a telegram from Mumbai . . . please find out what it says . . .'

The postman, who had done nothing to ease the situation so far, also appeared and now told her the news was nothing to cry about. 'The telegram just says your son got a first rank.'

When I finally visited home after my trip to Mumbai, Umma came up to me and gave me a tight slap. She didn't like it that the telegram came from Mumbai. I told her that I had gone to Mumbai with Prakash as it was a chance to see Mumbai. She started crying. She told me how much I made her worry with one bloody telegram; but then she conceded everything turned out all right, owing to Allah's kindness.

Eventually, I presented my case at home regarding joining the Film Institute. Bappa got angry. He was completely against me dropping the professional course I was already doing. 'Why are you jumping like a monkey from branch to branch? Why can't you concentrate on one thing properly? Aren't you already doing a professional course? What is wrong with the lawyer's profession; if you want you can try IAS also, no?'

I knew my case was not moving very well. I then concentrated my efforts on Umma. I managed to brainwash her.

Fortunately, Umma didn't think much of lawyers. She called them crows. She was convinced that these guys in black overalls were frauds who lied all the time. She once had to deal with lawyers. The experience was anything but good. And so she didn't want me to turn into one of them; she would be rather happy if I dropped the law studies altogether.

I was still a bit worried. I told Mani that I was really interested in a career in cinema and that she should try to make Umma understand this in detail. My lobbying worked; Umma and Mani supported me strongly. Umma supported me loudly too. 'If this is what he wants to study, let him,' she announced at home.

To bolster my case, I told her, 'Umma, I will get something like twenty-five thousand rupees salary if I become a sound engineer!'

'Oh! You'll make twenty-five a month?' she asked me, lowering her voice.

'Surely,' I said.

Umma was happy. 'Okay, son, then you do it.'

*

There were another two months left to join the Institute. So I went back to the law college. I had one more round of discussions with friends in the college on the pros and cons of joining the Institute. Sri Prakash, Siraj, Radhakrishnan (who was called Crow then)—all have become top-shots now—all said I must go. Anita and Sathyasheelan Saar had no doubts either.

Bappa kept quiet. I wrote him a letter from the hostel. I don't remember the details of it; generally, it explained at length why it was important for me to go to the Film Institute and study. Though we used to write regularly to each other, he didn't reply specifically to that letter. But he never expressed any opposition to my plans after that.

I packed up my stuff from the law college, got it home and started packing for the Pune trip. I packed one big red box with the basic survival stuff and some books. I then returned to the law college, carrying the red box in tow, because the train was going to leave from Thiruvananthapuram. I had managed to accumulate a disaster fund of sorts for myself. A small amount came from the earnings of Saif's bakery in Anchal, opposite St John's College, which was the family's lone source of income at the time. My sister Zeenath, who had finished her Teachers' Training Course and had got a job in faraway Palakkad through the Government Employment Exchange, sent me two hundred and fifty rupees. She had assured me that I didn't need to worry and that she would do whatever she could to help. Another two hundred rupees came from Umma. There was also some scholarship money from the law college. Altogether I had three thousand five hundred rupees with me. The fee was two thousand rupees, while the hostel would cost another six hundred. If I took into account the scholarship also, I thought I could just about manage.

On my last night at the hostel, Thaha Saar, who was the hostel warden, called a general hostellers' gathering, where I explained why I was leaving the law college and what I was going to study in Pune. It was a touching farewell party. The party went on all night, spiced with obscene parody songs.

I was walking out of the hostel the next morning after the eventful and emotional farewell night. My friend Siraj came and deposited a hundred-rupee note in my pocket. After the Oscar ceremony, I found out his number and called him. He said he couldn't believe that I was calling him. He wanted to listen to the conversation again and again. He asked me whether he could record it all.

I told him to go ahead and asked whether he had forgotten me. He said he could not forget me ever, but that he couldn't believe that I was calling him. I asked him whether he had forgotten about the hundred-rupee note that he had put in my pocket.

He started crying. He was overwhelmed that I remembered his gesture of friendship. He had thought it was only customary for people to forget others when they climb up in life.

But how can I ever forget?

Indeed, my years at the law college were great fun! I recall how we used to play pranks on unsuspecting folk. For instance, we would change the name of our hostel every year. One year, it became the telegram office. A signboard with words 'Telegram Office' was written on its façade. An old man had come to the nearby post office to send a telegram. The poor man made the mistake of asking a law student for directions to the post office. The student found out that the old man wanted to send a telegram and directed him to the hostel. The old man spent the rest of the day walking up and down the hostel corridors looking for the telegram office. It was certainly a cruel prank to play on the poor old man. But we were young and foolish. And in search of harmless fun.

*

Anita and her friend came to the Thiruvananthapuram railway station to see me off. There were also a couple of my friends from the law college. Raman had also reached. We had adjoining seats. When the train started moving, Anita turned her face away and started crying. Raman saw this and asked me, 'Man, is your Bappa that progressive or what? How can you leave a girl who loves you so much?'

I said, 'Never mind! It's a new journey from here on. Let's see where it takes us.'

That's how we left Thiruvananthapuram. The train reached Kayamkulam station. My sister had made some food for us and sent it with Kochumon to the platform. I had written to him earlier that the train had only a minute's stop at that station. I had instructed him to find out where the S2 compartment would come on the platform and wait there. But he had gone and waited somewhere else. When the train started moving, he came running from out of nowhere, and somehow managed to give me my food parcel. But Raman's vegetarian parcel fell down and was lost. I felt really bad. Kochumon also felt terrible. Poor Raman had to make do with the vegetarian morsels of my meal.

On that journey, I marvelled at where my life was taking me. There was no looking back now.

2

THE MAGICAL WORLD OF FTII

We arrived at the Institute in a festive state of mind. We felt like victors. Suresh Pai had arrived; Prakash Kutty had reached from Mumbai. Everybody was very excited. I was unprepared for how cold it was—freezing, practically. I didn't even have a blanket. But the Institute provided everything—bed, blankets and all.

We were only worried about the ragging. My previous experience of ragging at the law college was quite terrible. There, the manner in which the seniors ragged their juniors was very physical and crude. A bunch of people would come in the dead of night, switch off the lights and terrorize the new students. I remember a blur of shrieks and screams; students were pushed around and beaten; clothes were ripped to shreds. It was all unnecessarily violent.

I wondered if the ragging ceremony at FTII would be much worse. But I wasn't too anxious. I believe that if you start thinking too much, you're bound to develop anxieties about various things and, consequently, create problems for yourself. Also, hadn't I already got a PhD in ragging from the law college back home? Suresh was really scared. I told him there was nothing to worry about. 'Just do what they ask you to do. If they ask you to take off your clothes, take off your clothes. Big deal!'

However, as it turned out, I really enjoyed the ragging. And since I was this first-rank holder in the entrance tests, my seniors were keen to pay particular attention to me as far as the ragging was concerned!

There was this scary guy—an unforgettable character. He came and asked, 'Huh, who's Resul amongst you?'

There were only about thirty-five or so of us. They knew everyone's name and all the relevant details.

'First rank in sound! . . . oh, you? Okay, come here. Sit . . . now tell me something. Can you define infinity?'

It was like being invited to sit on the sharp end of a spear. I was sure to be brutalized if I tried to hazard any sort of a definition of infinity. But the story would be the same if I didn't define it. To cut a long and unpleasant story short, I shall just say that I was raped—yes, no other word could possibly encapsulate the sheer humiliation of that episode!—that day. For the first time in my life, I felt as if I knew nothing about anything. That's the state of mind ragging brings you down to.

This was very different from the kind of ragging we usually hear about. This was an intellectual affair. The main objective of the exercise was to completely destroy you—intellectually. We became nothing at the end of it all. Nothing would be left of what you were or where you were from. Your culture, your identity—everything would be demolished.

The guys who came from metros like Delhi were a spoilt bunch. Most of them were arrogant. They generally thought they knew it all. But such attitudes and notions suffered serious casualties during the ragging. The campaign lasted twenty days. If you managed to go along with it, without fighting it or resisting it too much, there was nothing more enjoyable than this ragging. Once the entire ritual was over, there was a great feeling of brotherhood and fraternity—as though we were all part of a family. Come to think of it, I miss the way seniors and freshers bonded through the ragging ritual at FTII. And I must admit that from the second year on, I myself became quite an expert at ragging.

At night, all of us were summoned under the Wisdom Tree. That's where it would all begin. The Wisdom Tree is a huge mango tree. Everyone was made to sit in a line on the road. The Institute has an anthem that we were made to sing. I hadn't been able to understand a word of it. I had memorized the whole thing after writing it down in Malayalam. In fact, even if someone were to abuse me to my face in the choicest of Hindi words—'arrey behnchod' being a particular favourite— it wouldn't have any effect on me. The words that did make my blood boil were all from the Malayalam language: mai, poo, ku, re, lee. Sometimes my seniors tried to learn these Dravidian words so that they could use them on me—but it always made me laugh to hear them abuse in a language that was so alien to them.

Another bizarre ragging ritual was to make us sit in the open in the winter cold, freezing and vibrating like generator engines. It ended there; there was nothing more to it. The freshers were seen as a bunch of regular guys who went to sleep at ten and woke up seven in the morning and our seniors felt that such bio-rhythms needed to be broken! That was the objective of the freezing exercise. You can't make films if you live a seven-to-ten kind of life; sometimes, you shot all night. So we were often left shivering out in the cold till four or five in the morning! But there was one important thing. When we stayed up all night in the cold, we were not the only ones going through it—the seniors too were around, staying up. This exercise was not about someone's sadistic pleasure, since our seniors too were losing sleep. By the third day, we could sense some kind of a trust developing between us and our seniors. There was definitely a method in the apparent madness. In three days, we figured out the higher and altruistic purpose of this procedure: our routines had been broken!

Then there was a strict no-no to cultural clans. The general tendency was for two Malayalis or two Bengalis to pair up and share a room. This was strictly banned. The two people who occupied a room had to have different linguistic and state origins—this was an unwritten rule. Any anomalies detected were sorted out during the ragging. Of course, it took a little more effort to share a room with someone from a different culture, but eventually, it was more rewarding. There was also no segregation between the sexes—the guys and girls were always together.

During the ragging season, it was common to find exhausted freshers dozing during class lectures. The teachers were aware of the rigours of ragging, so they took it easy for the first three weeks—nothing substantial was taught in those days.

On the last day of ragging, the seniors gave us a party that went on all night long. It began at sunrise with the declaration that the ragging had ended. Apparently, we were now free to do anything to the seniors—beat them, abuse them or rag them back. It was the time to settle some scores. We woke up those seniors who were sleeping and had tea with them that morning. No classes took place that day. Everybody slept soundly instead. The teachers also came for the fresher's party in the evening. Usually, it would be a Friday evening. Now that unity and brotherhood were established, further bonding of souls were explored and decided this day. Units—a director, a cameraman, a sound man, an editor—were formed. We even abused all the seniors we hated while many brawls broke out.

A new world opened up before me. It was only in films that I had seen people drinking and dancing this way. The mainstream media usually portrayed partying as an immoral activity—too modern, decadent and Western, where people drank and kissed with wild abandon. Suddenly, I was seeing the real thing, and it was far from vulgar. It was just another facet of life and its celebration.

*

The Film Institute illustrated one very important point. One can't achieve much merely through individual pursuits. Film-making is all about managing a group of people. To do that, you need to know your people. Film-making is, after all, a collective effort.

When someone writes a script, it doesn't automatically become a film. When you give the script to the cameraman, he devises a visual language for the film based on his knowledge about the camera, life, art and all. One guy takes this written stuff to another guy to take it to another level. Then you should be able to evaluate the other, give in to the other. You have to take him in. Whether it's an editor or a sound man, you have to take them all in. You have to let them flourish and bloom within the project. Professionalism in cinema is not about giving someone money to do something in some time.

Of course, there is a fee involved in professional work. But that's not the point. In the field of cinema, everyone must realize that they are part of a larger whole. Individual egos do not matter. Everybody must work towards a unified goal. If various individual technicians and artistes don't collaborate and cooperate together to make the film, then nothing will get done. Unity is essential. This is something I learned over the years in the Institute, but I think it was the ragging process that first laid the foundation for this conviction. After that, we became true students—ready to deal with anything! We were like men bearing torches, on the threshold of an entirely new phase of life.

My outlook changed entirely. I found it difficult to relate to the old patterns of my life. This transformation happened in a very brief period, in an environment that was vary far away and insulated from the world I grew up in. That's how I became a student.

*

It was to learn sound engineering that I came to FTII. But the training I received covered far wider ground. It wasn't only confined to learning what sound was or how to produce and capture it. Instead, every week we handled different disciplines of film-making. One week, I learnt only direction; next week only camera. In a cycle of four weeks, I came back to the first. This continued to rotate. And every evening, there would be film screenings at the main theatre. We had to watch all of them. The screenings were followed by discussions, fist fights and drinking. In the thick mix of all these, the education progressed through interactions of all kinds.

On the first day, there was an incident that I consider important. We were all put in a vehicle and dropped at the Maharashtra Bhulai Bhandar, a large marketplace in Pune. This was an actuality trip—an excursion to understand the essence of a place. We needed to have a first-hand experience of what the place was all about, how it functioned, what the people there did, and so on.

How do you go about making a documentary film about this place? The visit had to be developed into a script. The experience was a complete shocker for me. I just couldn't function. I couldn't talk to anybody there. I didn't know a word of Hindi. English . . . well, yes. But they didn't. How would I communicate with these people? I felt as if I was in water and drowning.

Suddenly, the truth of language dawned upon me. All my notions of education took a dramatic diversion from this point on. That's one reason why I think of the Institute as this towering monolith that melted, reshaped and transformed me into something new. The very first academic exercise made me realize that what I had learnt so far was completely worthless. That wasn't education. Because I wasn't learning language! Real education is in learning language, language at all levels. This was a major insight.

The government is supposed to reduce the differences between the rich and the poor and introduce some kind of material equality among its people. At least, that's what is said to be one of the goals of the government. The only equality we seem to currently have is the political equality wherein every vote carries equal value. It's a symbolic equality. The real equality, in my opinion, is an unattainable ideal. Giving the poor a lot of money and making them rich can't solve this.

I often think that the communist ideology is a baseless construct. I think it can't operate at basic human levels. It works at a philosophical level. And for it to work beyond that, the society needs to be precise and controlled like a laboratory. But then that kind of control would lead to autocracy and dictatorship. Within the limitations of our times, a practical kind of equality is possible when the rich and poor speak a common language. We can experience a kind of equality when a common language is available for all so that complete communication is possible at all levels of expression and comprehension. Currently, that is all we can hope for. Education should be a tool to bring in this common language to the entire society. The time to completely dismantle our education system has long passed. We need better human beings, not just a bunch of doctors and engineers.

So I sat down at the marketplace wondering what to do. I looked at all the people milling around, buying vegetables. I noticed their clothes. What they wore and how many of them had worn it in the Marathi style, etc. I got immersed in my observations of the surroundings. At that time, I didn't realize that what I was making were anthropological observations.

One thing that makes cinema different and more beautiful from the other arts is that through cinema, we can get a lot closer to other people and cultures.

Reading and writing are much more personal and private experiences compared to cinema. A book triggers different sensations and thoughts in different readers. The experience is directly related to the knowledge base of the reader. Cinema also has this quality to an extent, but the collective character of cinema is more powerful. A film is watched by a group of people. In the two hours we spend in the theatre we are part of a group, sharing a lot of common sensations of emotions and excitement. Cinema unites a group of people in certain ways.

I had come from a science background. Suddenly, I was in the midst of new kinds of theories. I was being thrown into the water to learn swimming. I was slapping around in the water trying to stay afloat and learn swimming. Who are these people at this marketplace, why are they doing what they are doing? You see, finally one had to weave a story out of all these questions?

That was the objective of the exercise. You have to narrate a story. Bring in the interactions you see in this place. Then you start thinking about how to introduce visual space into the story. That's what the camera does. Then you bring sound into that space. Then your story becomes something that can be seen and heard. It also brings the element of time into your story. Sound lives in time. This is the essence of transforming a place into an experience—break it down into its audio and visual components that progress in time. Fantastic concept, isn't it? I beat around in the water quite a bit; drank a lot of water. That was the first experience. But I started swimming. Eventually, I started diving under water and enjoyed the experience thoroughly.

Then I was given a video camera and asked to take a shot. The place you saw the previous day looked completely different the next day through the camera. The reason: the camera sees only one angle at a time. In real life, we experience the entire environment at the same time. The camera always asks you: what do you want to see, what do you want to show? You are faced with a tremendous choice. Where to point your camera is a serious political decision. People are going to see what you want them to see. That is power and that is political. Do you have it in you to handle this power? There arises the need for you to develop into an individual who is capable of exercising such a power. At that time, I didn't feel capable of it. I thought I couldn't handle it. I needed to learn a lot more things; I needed to become a new human being. I must. I must enrich my life. That's the thought that came to me. And I decided to go ahead and do that. This realization helped me to start learning a whole lot of things I didn't know till then.

So the studies took off into many fields: music, art, painting, literature, architecture . . . come to think of it, the whole thing was quite mind blowing. Cinema is not something which you can start doing after you finish learning something. With a camera in your hands, you learn to see space; when you notice that the scene changes with your angles, you wonder about exposition; when you think of exposing, you think of architectural space, then compositions, then of painting . . . you can't do anything without studying all these, especially if you have a science background.

I maintained a basic notion that if an idea is not backed by a proper theory, there is something wrong with it. That's from physics: theorize all phenomena. Analysis follows reason. In fact, politics and philosophy are also based on reasoning . . . everything is intermingled. I was entering into a tricky place—a long dark tunnel with a faint promise of light at the very end. I wasn't sure how I would get out of it. I am still not sure about it.

After I won the Oscar, people have been asking me why I don't direct a film. I am sceptical because I am aware of a lot of things—especially my strengths and my weaknesses. If one is not aware, then there is perhaps no problem. After all, one can just go ahead and make a movie. The vice-president of a major production company recently told me the reason why they don't hire me. In his words: '*Resul, it's not the money, the fact that you know what you can do works against you sometimes; we don't need you in Bollywood.*' The schools help you in being aware. But what to take from what you know is your own personal exploration. You can't do everything in one life, can you? Even the things I managed to do were not based on just the knowledge gained from my three years at the Institute. I am saying all this fourteen years after I came out from there. In fact, the Institute was one place that confused me the most. The linear progression of my thoughts comes only now, or I recognize the order of the past only now. Nothing was presented to me like how it is narrated here. I relentlessly struggled with the realities outside the Institute. In fact, that is what helped me the most.

*

In the Institute, you face a dilemma: you watch all major world films and cinema movements and feel intensely about it all; then you come out to have a cup of tea and you have to deal with the people on the street who are way off from your world, your thoughts and your feelings. Physically, you are among them, but your mind and soul are somewhere else.

You will be so affected by some films, like the films of Tarkovsky or such intense masters; then you usually stop talking to people and end up walking around with a heavy heart. I would look at all the regular people in the street busy going about their regular lives as if nothing had happened, and think: 'These guys have no idea of the kind of things I am seeing, studying, or of the nature of life itself. They don't have a clue about their own situation. What ignorance!' That's how I saw the outside world from inside that place, the Institute—a powerhouse of intellectual vitality and a beacon of light. We were a bunch of people, walking around fully charged and radiating electricity out of every pore, like creatures from some other world. The Institute was a big culture shock right from the beginning. Like, back home, how we kept the tiny chicks under an upturned cane basket, a bunch of us had been brought from all across the country to be kept inside this campus. There was nothing in common in our backgrounds and experiences or in what we knew. Then suddenly, what do you see? You are in the middle of the best of all art forms of the world—architecture, painting, music, cinema, literature. It is not a gradual exposure or introduction. It possesses you and holds you like a paralytic seizure. An intense flash of light scorches your eyes. Then you walk around blinking like a firefly. That's when you take pity on the common folks outside and sigh: 'Poor things, they have no idea!' The whole of the first year, that was my state of mind.

For a while I kept in touch with Anita, my law college sweetheart who had insistently pushed me to join this place. Sometimes we wrote up to eight letters a week. I could write to her from here about exactly what she was feeling there. We were intensely connected, emotionally and intellectually. I even went and met her during the vacations after the first semester. But I just couldn't say a word to her. There was no communication taking place between us! We just sat in silence for some time and I came back. Clearly my life had changed completely.

Relationships didn't mean anything to me any more, even with my own parents. It was all worthless. I was going through a major negation of my past. For the next two years, home disappeared from my mind.

Those days we watched two films a day. They were mostly European films—not much to do with our culture or lives. A film could be about a single emotion. But when we watch the film, we feel it as a life-long experience. It's an illusion. Cinema has that power. The emotions of an instance, a day or a week in a film is felt as a life-long experience. We identify with the main character through the perspective of the incidents in the film—as the most important event or set of events in the life of the character.

I had felt that way with many Malayalam films earlier. We never really ask what happens to a character after the story ends. Cinema has that power that makes such questions irrelevant. But this power can turn dangerous unless recognized and used wisely.

Many of our film-makers go about their business of making films completely oblivious to all these factors. For them, film-making is something that happens on an emotional high. But abroad, the film-making craft is more calculated. In their film-making, where, how and when to manipulate the emotions of the audience are well worked out and planned in great detail. I got into the whirlpool of all these and went on a turbulent trip that took me to new mental terrains. I let go of my relationships. I was in a peculiar psychological state. It was very depressing. Take John Abraham films, for example. Watching them, you get into the state of mind of the characters. Then you start to believe it as real, that that's how things are. That's also what Mukundan's and Franz Kafka's works can do to you.

At some point, the boundary between art and reality dissolved. Everything became real for me—authentic. This was not a simple delusion. I had lost my boundaries through hard observation, and was authenticating every strand of fiction that I saw, heard or read.

The fact that I came here from a place called Vilakkupara where Umma was struggling hard, Bappa had no work, and there was no money to marry off my two sisters, all became completely irrelevant. When you are battling with a new-found reality and that too at a new level, it's inevitable that some other branches of reality will completely disappear into a mist. The problems of reality that you saw in Tarkovsky's *Stalker* became your own problems.

I guess I could say that those three years, I didn't have much to say to anyone. This transformation took place after the first semester. I felt that all my elderly relatives were fools and that they had no idea about what I was going through. How could they know anything! I was not telling any of them what I was going through nor were they watching any avant-garde French cinema. Although they were elder to me and had seen much more life than I had, I completely dismissed them.

In a period of a year and a half, I watched some 350-odd films. I watched that many lives and cultures. When you see *Rashomon*, you feel you are living in another era. I was convinced I was getting supremely enriched by these cinematic experiences. But what about someone like Kochikkamama who knew nothing about these things? His concerns were totally different: why didn't I at least give him a call when I came home? When I heard of such things, I would wonder—what this is, what is the big deal about a phone call? That was not something very relevant to my reality. So there was a conflict in the reality show—between mine and everyone else's.

I had only one thing in mind: cinema. I was prepared to do anything for that. I was ready to manipulate people; I could even kill. It was all justified. The singular, supreme concern of life was the shot you were going to take. That shot was life and death. The film that we all had to make for our diploma was something that you constantly kneaded and nursed in your mind, frame by frame, for three years. There was nothing else to life. And so in my first year, I terminated my communications with Anita. I rejected almost everything—behaved as if nothing could touch me except cinema. Relationships, women, Umma, Bappa, brothers, sisters, all meant nothing. Friendship meant nothing. It was a terribly selfish trip. Actually, such a trip can be powerful and useful if handled well; but if you mess up your sorting and analysis, this can slip into delusional behaviour.

Perhaps every film-maker goes through such a process while making a film. It is a completely selfish trip. I never had any relationship to speak of during my Institute years. Yes, I had intense friendships, but those were all developed around cinema. Those friendships are much diluted now as our ideas of cinema have changed.

At one time, I just couldn't imagine my life without Suresh Pai in it. We were that close. We ate together and slept on the same mat. We stayed together even after coming to Mumbai. Years later, we are not that thick any more. It's much the same situation with Prakash Kutty. We used to walk the streets of Pune hand in hand. We would jump into each other's arms whenever we met. We behaved almost like a gay couple. And now? Now it is just a phone call once in a long while. This has got to do with the fact that our bonding was all about cinema; when our ideas of cinema changed, the intensity of these bonds, too, underwent a transformation.

The Institute has a magical quality to its world that makes you want to stay and live within the campus walls forever. There have always been people who dreaded the end of these three magical years and continued to study there for five or six years. There is a French guy, much junior to me. Everyone calls him Pyare Mohan. He is still at the Institute even after six or seven years. He is studying direction after finishing his camera course. There are a lot more like him.

At the same time, it must be said that many students at the Institute found it extremely difficult to deal with the rigours of their professional training. It was common for many to break under pressure. One of my batchmates lost his mental balance. Another one tried to commit suicide. Some of them took the escape route of alcohol and dope, instead of dealing with the harshness of reality. Such instances were often sparked by small incidents which then got amplified out of context purely because they couldn't comprehend the dynamics of their professional situation. As I've said before, a campus can be an unreal world—a cocoon of sorts. It's quite tough to come out of it. Once you have read a lot of philosophy and all that, you might slip into a state where nothing really matters. You will be convinced that everything is meaningless and that the whole show is quite absurd. You need a lot of counselling to get you out of that terrible state. This counselling should be part of the curriculum. I think all art schools should have in-house counselling services.

Luckily, I have never needed any counselling as I have had enough occasions in my life that kept me in constant contact with my reality. What has kept me anchored to that reality is the boundless love that I've received from Umma and Bappa. Still, I have had my share of intense conflicts, often between the sense of duty that came from my love for my family and the rebelliousness that came out of my intellectual awakening at the Institute. These battles have left many wounds and scars in my mind.

In fact, it was my family's love that grounded me back to the real world at a critical point in time when I was dithering over what to do next in life. Like many others, I was also seriously tempted to prolong my stint at FTII. I wanted to study direction after sound, but it was not financially feasible for me. I was then contemplating the idea of pursuing another fine arts course elsewhere—perhaps painting. I finally deleted these plans altogether during the trips home in my final year. Those trips were powerful reality checks. Returning home from the magical cocoon of FTII and seeing my parents, brothers, sisters, my original surroundings and people, I started wondering all over again. And it hit me like a sack of bricks: *this* is the real world, *this* is reality.

Here is an incident. I had once visited home during the vacations because my sister Mani was getting married—the last girl in the line. A girl's wedding is an expensive affair. Umma didn't want to send her daughter off to another household without a minimum of fifty sovereigns of gold, along with half an acre of land or its equivalent in cash. I had previously asked her why we were even considering giving dowry—nobody would marry her without it or what? Umma brusquely told me that I could do what I wanted with my own marriage, but Mani was not stepping out of the house without the dowry. That was the reality of the situation. And there I was, questioning this reality. It is these constant attempts of mine to bridge these two wildly different realities—of what I believed in and what the circumstances dictated—that have given me the greatest counselling in life.

On the night the wedding decisions were being finalized, Umma and Bappa had called everyone in for the decision-making process—including me. For the first time I felt like an adult. Until then, I was a small kid—albeit with a beard and moustache. I had never even sat in front of Bappa before. But here I was asked to sit and participate in the discussions.

My second sister's husband Nazarmacha was in the Gulf then. He was reasonably well off. But our finances were in a bad shape. Nazarmacha and Moothamacha are the eldest brothers-in-law. They always supported the family in times of need, immeasurably and lovingly. The excess funds needed for this wedding were also to come from these two gentlemen. My second sister had already promised to give ten sovereigns of gold. The rest too was expected from my two elder sisters' side. But the deal needed to be formalized. To give them land in return was what everyone had in mind. Land was all we had.

But when the deal came out in words, Umma felt very bad. It arose from a typical complex created by financial difficulty and ego. It is often so for the person at the receiving end of any sort of charity. So when it was decided that some land should be given and that there should be a written agreement, Umma got very emotional and angry. It was obviously a reaction that came from the helplessness of being helped.

'Do you really have to spell out things like this, as if I wouldn't give anything to my girl?' Umma expressed her angst.

Bappa got very uncomfortable. He kept sighing the rest of the time as if something had gone hopelessly and embarrassingly out of control. I don't know how much I cried that night—at my inability to do anything to help the situation. *What was the bloody point of seeing Tarkovsky, Bresson and Ghatak? Does it solve anything in life? Look at how upset my Umma is! Look at how my Bappa is sitting—so helpless he is.*

The situation became so emotionally complex that Umma became completely silent. A decision had to be taken by the next day—otherwise there wouldn't be any marriage.

This was one of those situations that gave me a much-needed wake-up kick. This was the bridging process I was talking about. Then I could understand what my duties were. It was not about making a world-class film; it was about being a good son, a good brother—as simple as that! What you knew, studied and understood is one thing—something that's useful for your knowledge and growth. But none of that is the real thing. The real thing is the lives of the people who live outside the walls of the Institute, because that's your life too.

This was the hard-won realization with which I returned to the Institute.

3

CRUMBLING CONVICTIONS, THRESHOLD TIMES

Two film-makers came to teach us in my final year: Krzysztof Zanussi and Jean Claude Carrier. They dealt me a blow each, to guide me back into reality. Especially the one that came from Zanussi hit me real bad.

I had thought of Zanussi as someone who lived neck-deep in cinema, someone who had cinema for breakfast and lunch and a little bit for dinner; someone who, late into the night, 'spread a cinema' and slept on it. That had been my idea of Zanussi. And as for myself, cinema was the very spinal cord of my existence.

Those days, going to the main theatre at the campus was like going to the temple. It was a spiritual experience. Even today, it's a bit like that. My earliest concepts about sound were formed inside that theatre. My thoughts about the phenomenon of hearing were shaped inside that theatre.

Hearing is an important perceptional tool for the entire human species. At the same time, this is also one species that knows so little about this faculty. All other animals have completely figured out hearing. The dog chasing you to give you a bite probably has more working knowledge of sound than you possess. These days, humans are able to comprehend hearing only after attaining a level of spirituality.

All movements of our life are connected to our respiratory or breathing process. We hear our breathing all the time without realizing it. The movie theatre is one place where you can notice this. When we sit in the dark and focus our attention on a place in front of us, watching a film, our breathing strikes a resonance with the rhythm of the film. That's when we hear the sound of our own breath. This resonance we experience in the theatre is the reason why even the minor details in the film affect us strongly. Even a pin that drops makes its impact in your ears. In that state of being, you can even see a light that shines deep inside you. It's an experience similar to the one that you get while standing in front of the deity in a temple.

There are a lot of people in cinema who have recognized this phenomenon and worked on it. Robert Bresson believed that through cinema, it was possible to attain something similar to the state of grace in Christianity. So, cinema has even been used as a medium to attain spiritual enlightenment.

I remember my first movie-watching experience; it was at Jayamohan Theatre in Anchal; it was a Malayalam sentimental, romantic film called *Shalini, My Friend*. I screamed in fear. The popular actors of that time like Sukumaran and Jayan became my heroes. Later on, Mammooty and Mohanlal appeared and impressed me with some of Malayalam's most enjoyable and hard-hitting films.

When I entered the last phase of my studies at the Institute, I stood paralyzed in front of the staggering possibilities of cinema in human life. As part of the curriculum, there were two screenings daily at the main theatre, a short film and a feature film. There would only be students in the auditorium. It was an atmosphere of complete silence.

A lot of my theories about sound were formed inside this auditorium. Some of the products of these thoughts I tried out later in the film *Saawariya*. But you see, the many things you have intellectually worked out, don't really work as planned in practice. The things I did in *Black* were more instinctive rather than intellectual. But it worked amazingly.

What one needs is an emotional conviction more than intellectual calibre. That's what makes Shah Rukh Khan a superstar. Kamal Hassan is lost somewhere between a thinking film-maker and a superstar. That's because he is a man who tends to think a great deal; his work shows more intelligence than necessary. Remember the daredevil Kamal Hassan of old? The dancer, the trapeze artist, the stuntman! Now when you see him doing the stunts, it doesn't touch you. It's not convincing any more. Instead, we wickedly wonder when he is going to make a film called *Kauravas* and do all the hundred roles himself. He is someone who tried to do things differently, but could only come up with indifferent products. His problem is that he thinks too much.

One more thing about breath and cinema—this has got to do with the difference between television and cinema. Television functions on beats. The cutting pattern on television is based on the beats, not on rhythm. That's why television fails to deliver experience. Television is passive. Remember the days we kept a radio on while working late night? Another source of sound among a lot of other sounds. Television is like that.

So, one fine morning, the great film-maker Zanussi arrives on campus to conduct a workshop on film-making. This fine morning is in the second semester of my final year. We are all waiting for pearls of wisdom from one of the great masters of cinema, someone who must be breathing cinema. He comes in and announces: cinema is not such a big deal in life!

Cut to: interior. Hostel room. Evening. Resul Pookutty is crying at his table. A film-maker from Poland has come and smashed his entire belief structure into rubble. 'There are more important things in life than cinema!'

I wanted to know what could be those things, things that are more important than cinema.

Till then I had thought that cinema was my life. Like the old communists for whom the Party was everything. In my scheme of things, the role of the rest of the world in my life was to help me take, in its maximum effectiveness, that shot I have been so painstakingly planning. I was sort of convinced that the world at large didn't have many other functions.

Zanussi showed us one of his films and narrated an incident that had taken place during its production. It was a film about a music composer. His last performance is shown in the film. The music piece for that scene had been composed by a very close friend of Zanussi. The piece turned out to be much longer than the scene. But if the scene was extended to match the length of the music piece, the drama would be lost. He could cut and shorten the music piece. But that would not be fair to his dear friend; it would be like cutting him. Finally, he found a way out. The character in the scene, the composer lying in the hospital, is watching his own performance on TV. Then the scene jumps to the flashback of the performance. So, to maintain the integrity of his friend's music piece, Zanussi added one more scene to the film. As if cinema was meant to solve such practical problems. This added ten whole minutes to the film.

I was flabbergasted! Is cinema meant to solve issues like this? Isn't cinema the ultimate thing where everything else was changed and rearranged around its artistic integrity? Then I realized that was not the case—even for the master film-makers. The ultimate thing is to live. Live as the best human being you can possibly be. This was the starting point of my next transformation.

It doesn't mean I started thinking that cinema is nothing. In fact, I had told Shadia before our wedding: look, my first wife would always be cinema, you come only second. I have no idea in what state of mind one can say such things. But during my first baby's circumcision ceremony, I wanted to spend a few more days with him. I was working on Rohan Sippy's *Bluffmaster!* at the time, so I went and begged him to postpone the film's mixing for another two days. I promised him that I would finish the work no matter what, working two or three days without sleeping, if need be. Obviously, that was a huge change for me. It was one of those moments when I realized that there were other important things in life than cinema.

I now see that in my three years at the Institute, I was living on an island of sorts. But it gave me rock-solid experiences.

*

It suddenly dawned on me that it was 1995, and my course at the Institute was coming to an end. In those days, I had two strong desires. One was to do sync sound and the other to create a sound archive for Indian cinema. I did a preliminary assessment of the possibilities of accomplishing these two projects, but found out that it would be impossible. I checked out Thiruvananthapuram and Madras (now Chennai): there was no space to work in the Malayalam movie industry. Forget about creating sublime sounds for a film, I would not even be able to do basic work from there.

Those were threshold times for me. I needed to figure out my next course of action. So I arrived at a decision—I would complete my unfinished law course after the Film Institute and then practise law somewhere near home. I would also help out Umma and Bappa. In the last semester, just before getting my diploma, I packed up my books and stuff and dumped everything at home. I told myself that this was no big deal; that nothing was lost. For three years, I had studied what cinema was. Okay, it was a good learning experience; now I would go back home and work. I could still appear for the IAS—I hadn't crossed the age limit. I came home with such a resolve—that I would do something or the other, but from home.

But once I got back to the Institute, my resolve slowly started evaporating. I started thinking about cinema again. It was a vicious circle. What could I do if I couldn't do films? Maybe I should write about cinema and become a cinema journalist. But whatever happens, I would live with cinema, make a living with cinema. These thoughts started taking roots. But deep inside my heart, Umma, Bappa and the whole reality of my life outside FTII were always present like a stone inside one's shoe.

We usually don't forget the moments that make us cry. Happy moments disappear fast and don't leave much of a residue. The details of the whole Oscar episode and its euphoria have begun to fade already. But sorrow is not like that. I guess that's the reason why sorrow becomes a constant accompaniment in life. Maybe that's why we love melodrama.

I went back to the Institute and finished the course. But the thirst to see more films wasn't finished yet. I hung around there for a few more days. Finally, one of my professors blasted me. He pushed me out of the campus, telling me to go and find some work. There was a film festival happening in Mumbai, in December–January, which I decided to attend. My plan was to head straight back home to Kerala immediately after the festival. But a film guy is always ambitious,he would try things till the very last moment. I had studied film but hadn't become a film-maker, and my ambitions were firmly in place. So I had asked friends like Arun Nambiar and Mohandas, before heading to Mumbai, 'Is there any possibility of work?'

Arun had said, 'You can assist me if you want to.'

And so I decided that once I reached Mumbai, I would assist Arun. It was quite a decision, considering I hadn't taken a shine to Mumbai on my previous visit. It still remained, in my mind, as the dirty city that reeked of chapattis and shit; I had sworn that I would never live and work in this city. And I now surprised myself by returning to do just the opposite.

At the festival, I was watching the *Three Colours* of Kieslowski. It was showing at the Metro. After seeing *Blue* and *White*, I was watching *Red*. Then suddenly I heard a voice:

'Resul Pookutty, please come out!'

It was Prakash Kutty. Once outside the theatre, he introduced me to someone, saying, 'See, this is Arvind Dave, a senior of ours. They are shooting a serial called *Misal*. Their sound recordist hasn't turned up. Can you handle it?'

I was a bit taken aback. 'Well . . . but . . .'

'What but? Anyway you were going to assist someone. Why can't you do some recording then?'

'All right, I will go.'

The shooting was at Uran in Raighad district. Two weeks' schedule. During the festival, I was staying with Suresh Pai in Andheri. I didn't have the keys to the house. There was no phone to call him either. Anyway, there wasn't enough time to go and pick up my clothes and things from Andheri; it was already seven in the evening.

'You just need some clothes, right? Come with us.' They took me to the famous Fashion Street of Mumbai. I went to work carrying a plastic bag containing the clothes I had bought there. That was my first professional project. It was directed by Ajay Karthik.

How does one work in a commercial industry? I had no idea! How does one interact and behave with people? No idea. How's a production unit controlled? I wasn't smart or mature enough for that either. All I knew was sound. As in what was correct and what was not. I fought and threw out all that was not correct. 'This mike is not good; this thing won't work; this needs to be changed; I don't want this; I want new stuff, you can pack all this junk and take it back . . .'

Everyone was in a state of shock. 'Oh look at this boy who just passed out from the Institute yesterday and he's giving orders as if he runs the show!'

'You want to do this thing properly? Listen to what I say. Otherwise, please pack me up too.' That was my stand.

The third day their recordist was supposed to join back. The director told him he needn't bother. 'The replacement will do fine. The replacement is pretty good, very loud and clear.'

In two days, I changed this, that and the other. Changed the crew and later changed the unit too. Everything fell into place. Everything went smoothly after that.

All this was done purely based on the strength of my conviction. This is how I am, how I think and operate. If you know one thing, do that thing properly. It could be sound, camera or anything, but do decide that this is what you are going to do henceforth in life.

During that shoot, one day I was on the verge of hitting the production executive, right in front of the director. What had happened was that he had taken me to the location where the shoot would take place next day. I told him if the traffic couldn't be controlled, we could dub the scene. He said it wasn't a problem and that he would see to it that the traffic was controlled. In the night, I went with him and marked out the spot where the generator should be parked.

The next day I noticed that the generator had not been parked at the spot specified by me. We started rolling. There was no one to control the traffic. This sort of a thing I just can't handle: not doing the things that you promised to do. I can't tolerate it, whoever it is. It's being dishonest; it's cheating. If somebody is working with me and he finds that he can't do something, he should let me know, then I can find out other ways to get it done.

I removed the headphones and switched off the equipment. The shooting came to a halt. I called the guy over and caught him by the collar. I raised my hand and asked him what had happened to my instructions. The director, who was also the producer, came running and pulled me back. The production executive in question was Gurudas Pai, a very nice man. I feel bad about that incident now. He still is a bit scared of me.

But my actions were based on my convictions. It's the strength of my convictions that drives me—whether in being repetitive, friendly or quarrelsome. Recently, I started a sound studio. The first project I got was Ajay Karthik's second feature film. I fought with him too! During the mixing, we had a difference of opinion about the panning of sound. He was not willing to agree with my arguments. I told him he was absolutely wrong and that the sound should be in the right speaker at a particular point, or else we should drop the sound. Later, during a lunch break, he told me: 'It is impressive that you still maintain your convictions, right from the days of our first shoot. As a film-maker, I will say it's better to agree with a technician if he is so firmly convinced about something that he knows. He will definitely change the product.'

While I was shooting for *Misal*, news came that my Umma was unwell and had been hospitalized. My first thought was to send her some money immediately. I told the production guys. It wasn't much. It was six or eight thousand rupees. The production team sent the money. It was a big thing for me. You know, I was this guy who used to think 'I am cinema' while wandering around with a distant look in my eyes. And when it had come to the occasion of my sister's wedding, I had shut myself inside a room and wept. Those were two extremes of my self. The day I sent money to Umma I was convinced that now it didn't matter if I didn't make the most magnificent film in the history of mankind or anything. As far as I was concerned, I had bridged a seemingly impossible gap—one that connected the two divergent paths: dream and reality.

There was another reason why I had done that serial. I was very keen on doing sync sound. Only television had sync sound in those days. It was the boom-time for satellite TV. For a programme to go on air on time, there was no time to waste on dubbing and all that. That's also the reason why Indian TV sounds so bad. Anyway, I got quickly tired of this frantic pace of work. I returned to Mumbai after the first schedule, deciding not to work in this medium any more.

Being unfamiliar with the layout of the city—in addition to the fact that my Hindi was very poor—I had no idea how to get back to Suresh Pai's house. I begged one guy from the unit to get me back to the place and he dropped me there. It was already two weeks since the festival was over and there was a bunch of seven or eight people sitting in Suresh Pai's room. No one had any work. They would sit there, looking at each other. There was a Shetty's tea shop nearby. These guys would go and have countless cups of tea there. For lunch, they ate rice with curd and daal. The rest of the day would be spent in the shop, sitting and discussing cinema and life as if they were sitting under the Wisdom Tree in the Institute. Once in a while, someone got some work. It was a ten-or-fifteen-hundred-rupees-a-shift affair. The wages would be disbursed right at the end of the shift. Their livelihood was entirely dependent on that.

I was shocked at this state of affairs. I decided not to give up the work that I had in hand. My general thought process had also undergone some alteration since sending Umma the money for her treatment. If I continued working, there would be a little money. It would be useful for someone or the other. I could even become a dependable family member in case of an emergency. So I went on to do the second schedule, too, and completed the project.

I did one more serial—*Margarita*, its chief significance being that it gave me the name I am now known by everywhere: Resul Pookutty.

4

LIFE IN MUMBAI

'But, Resul, although you claim to be a major Bollywood sound man who does proper sync sound and all, nothing seems to be in sync in this! By the way, the girl—A, B or C—who you said is your close friend seems to be now deeply in love with X, Y or C!'

After saying this, he would wink at whoever happens to be present there—or even at an imaginary person at the door—before looking at me. Then he would say the same things to this A, B or C at some other point.

'But, A, weren't you the one who told me this Resul is a very loving character, has lots of ideas and all? But it seems he is sharing all his ideas and love and all with C, D or E!' Then the wink would be put to work again.

The whole thing would also be accompanied by a charming smile. I am talking about Satheesh P.M. He starts all his sentences with a 'but'. When I asked some linguists about this, they said that opening a sentence with words like *but, no, if, once* is actually an established strategy in debates and that the man I was referring to must be a great debater. That's a fact. Even if a dream project landed in this man's lap, he would still ask: 'But, Resul, we have worked so hard on this; what if these guys refuse to pay up at the end?'

For my wedding, Shadia and I had bought a brand-new car; we brought it to Mumbai. Then our man says, 'But, Resul, you spent five–six lakhs and bought this car, but people are still eyeing mine which costs only a lakh and a half!'

The first time I saw Satheesh was at the Institute. When Satheesh and Manoj Nair—they are very close friends—came to the Institute a couple of times, they had stayed in my room. You see, mine was the cleanest room in the hostel!

Satheesh is a mentor in my life. A mentor is very essential for anybody. Even Spielberg and George Lucas say they have mentors in the industry. In my case, Satheesh has been my mentor in everything. He has influenced me positively in my social life as well as in my general outlook on life. I am fortunate to have had someone like him around right from my formative years. Satheesh, Manoj Nair, Vikram Jogelaker are all acquaintances from the institute. We became close very soon. Vikram has given me a lot of guidance.

Manoj is honest to a fault; he is an uncompromising professional. During the time when he was about to leave India to settle in London, he had paid all his taxes before he left. Indeed, he was very stressed about whether he would be able to pay these taxes before he left. He wouldn't lie, ever. All this has influenced me intensely. Tell me, does anyone even blink while telling a lie in this land! I have lied to even the most respected of my teachers—to save my skin. That such things are totally at odds with a certain kind of lifestyle was revealed to me only when I could closely view the behaviour of people like Manoj.

It's significant that I could meet, work and live with these people during my formative phase in Mumbai.

Satheesh has been a mentor to me at many levels; as a friend, he has stood by me in all the crises in my life; and in my professional career, he has supported me throughout—together, we have done things no one had done before in the Indian sound scene.

As I mentioned earlier, Ajay Karthik's serial had come my way right after I came to Mumbai. It was only after that project that I started being in regular touch with Satheesh. He would say, 'But, Resul, come along!'

I would go along with him to the shoot, hang around and help him. He started trusting me. I had with me some literature on stereo microphone technology that I had Xeroxed from the library. I gave him all that. This technology was very new to India at that time. Together, we figured out the whole thing. Satheesh has played an important role in formulating my concepts about sound.

In Mumbai, during this period, I was staying in a tiny flat in a housing complex called PMGP (Prime Minister's Grand Project). Apart from me and Suresh Pai, there were five to six guys staying there. We used to call this concentration camp of ours the Poor Man's Grand Project. And we had to shell out some two thousand five hundred rupees as rent. I was mostly jobless. Those days the first thing I did after getting up was to call him. 'Satheesh, are you home?'

'But, Resul, what? No work?'

'No.'

'But then do one thing. Come over.'

I would bathe and dress up and get into a bus that would drop me at the Pump House stop. Then I would walk to the Apna Ghar Society. By ten sharp, I would be at Satheesh's door.

He would greet me with his usual line: 'But, Resul, I haven't seen you being so punctual even for a shoot!'

Satheesh and Manoj have fed me more times than I can remember. They are absolutely unforgettable characters in my life. That was a time when Satheesh, Manoj and Vikram Jogelaker were intensely involved in affairs with foreign girls. But. in a way, I was the one who enjoyed the fruits of their amour—I got to do my first film because Vikram could not be available owing to his romantic duties.

Manoj took off to London for a month pursuing his passionate romance. Satheesh followed shortly after.

So I could enjoy the luxury of a house where I didn't have to pay rent and which had a phone connection. The conditions they set were liberal; I was to take down the messages meant for them from the answering machine and relay the same when they called. It was an easy life. I was completely broke those days. Walking up and down was all that I was doing, in expectation of some work; but such a thing was nowhere to be seen on the horizon.

By this time, Satheesh's love life had reached a critical stage. He looked like someone who was standing on a red-hot stone. As the writer Basheer would have put it, the boil was about to burst. All it needed was the touch of a woman's lips. An international documentary project came to him at this stage. But if he stayed back to do it, he might as well kiss his love goodbye. So he asked me if I could do it and I said yes. That was a major break for me.

Plentiful monies! I worked for thirty days and got ninety thousand rupees. This much money I was seeing for the first time. I took a flight and went home the very next day after the project. It was my first plane ride! At home, I spread the bundles of currency notes on a table in front of Umma and Bappa.

Bappa quickly made me put aside some money. Then he called all my brothers and sisters and gave them a share each.

The rest—forty-two thousand rupees, I put in a fixed deposit in my Umma's name. She was ecstatic. Finally, she had something in her own name!

I gave some money to Bappa too. He went and cleared his debts at the tea shop where he would have his tea and beedis. I had put six or seven thousand in my bank account. That would be enough for the next two–three months. I happily went back to Mumbai and once again assumed my duties as the caretaker of the house.

Satheesh came back after a month or so. And with a new thing—the Internet! That was the month when the Internet was declared available in India. Satheesh bought a shell account. But there was no money left to buy a computer. I had made a little more money in the meantime. Satheesh borrowed some thirty thousand rupees from me. We opened a VSNL account and started emailing. That was a novelty then. All of Mumbai had only about two hundred people with the Internet and email. Ah! We were at the cutting edge of technology!

We have travelled a lot together. The first time I travelled abroad was again with Satheesh. The destination was Singapore. Before leaving, he had given me a complete picture about the whole thing—what the immigration procedure is like, what to do and not to, and so on. I have also seen Satheesh speaking from a place he had never been to! That was also when I heard Manoj lie for the first time. It was a hilarious incident involving a common friend named Namita who had also studied sound engineering. Namita is extremely competitive and can get mean and spiteful when she wants to. You really don't want to be around when she gets annoyed.

One day, I saw a major sound set-up at Satheesh's house in Apna Ghar Society. Submarine sound effects were playing. Satheesh then picked up the phone and called Namita. 'But, Namita, how's work?' Then after some pleasant chit-chat, Namita asked him about his work scene. Satheesh told her that the work was tough as he was on a shoot in Antarctica; that it was incredibly cold but it was not that bad as luckily he was inside a submarine.

That was more than enough to shatter Namita's peace of mind. At the same time, she didn't completely believe the story either. She quickly called up Sreeji Apartments, traditionally a place where some sound guy or the other stayed. In our industry, if you need a sound man urgently, Sreeji is the first place you call. It is a hub for sound people.

But the Sreeji 'control room' had been notified and briefed well in advance. When Namita asked about Satheesh, they promptly said, 'Yeah, he is shooting somewhere in Antarctica or something.' Namita got desperate. She called up Manoj. She chatted with him for a long time about movies, the weather and politics, before finally zeroing in on the subject of where Satheesh was. Manoj did a great job hiding his discomfort about lying and told her. 'Satheesh has gone to Antarctica for a shoot. He didn't tell you?'

Of course, after a couple of weeks, Namita figured out that the whole thing was an elaborate joke on her; then she lost it completely and gave everyone a piece of her mind.

Late one night, my phone rang. It was Satheesh. 'But, Resul, there is a shoot tomorrow. I am completely tied up. It's a foreign production. The money is very good. I called to find out if you are free to do it.'

Of course I was free!

I was to reach the spot at seven in the morning. Satheesh gave me the address. I bathed and got ready early. Carrying tons of heavy equipment, I reached the location sharp at six forty-five. I waited. It became seven, then seven fifteen. I started getting very worried. Foreign production teams are usually extremely punctual. I got into a telephone booth and called Apna Ghar. The line was busy for ever! Then I saw another character getting dropped in a rickshaw. It was Namita.

'Hi, Resul! What are you doing here?'

'Hi, Namita. A shoot. You?'

As the conversation progressed, we found out that both of us were there for the same shoot except there was no shoot! It dawned on us that it was 1 April that day, and we were the distinguished fools. Namita was at her abusive best that day. I then suggested to her that there was not much point in thinking about this little incident, and that we should go to the nearby Sreeji Apartments and at least get ourselves some hot tea. We started walking. But Namita said she didn't want to go to Sreeji and that I should not tell anyone about this 'small incident'. So I went to Sreeji alone. Madhu Apsara used to stay there at that time. Madhu opened the door, rubbing his eyes and asked, 'Oh! How was the shoot? Where is Namita?' So clearly the whole thing had been planned in Sreeji itself.

That was a great period. We were freelance professionals but we were living the joyous and carefree life of college students.

*

I had to leave Satheesh's house when he returned from London. I found accommodation as a paying guest in Juhu, at a locality called Esic Nagar. The house belonged to J.M. Wadkar, an income tax clerk. The family was from Satara, Maharashtra.

The rent was two thousand five hundred rupees. Importantly, I could use the house phone for in-coming calls; it was important because people would be able to contact me if there was some work. The other parts of the deal were: tea and biscuits for breakfast; and the payment of half the electricity, water and telephone bills.

It was a government colony, and the rules did not allow paying guests. In case anybody came to check, I would disappear. (Incidentally, this was the theme of a film I did recently: *Pappu Can't Dance Sala!*). This house was what's called a 1BHK—1 Bedroom Hall Kitchen. The terrace had been converted into a bedroom and the landlord's family lived there. The original bedroom was given to me. I accessed my room through a common corridor. The bathroom was shared. The family consisted of the landlord, his wife and son. A relative of theirs would also stay there whenever he came to Mumbai looking for work. There was a TV in the hall, where I never went. I didn't want to get too close.

That's because I didn't have much work at that time. My fear was that if they found out about this, it would lead to my expulsion from the household. So what I would do is take a bath, wear decent clothes and leave home every morning. There were of course friends in Sreeji Apartments and there was also Satheesh to go to. But the problem was that, this being Mumbai, one had to call in advance and find out whether these guys were free or whether it was a good time to visit and soon. You couldn't just land up at a friend's place like how it was back home. If nobody was free, one felt helpless. On such days, I took a bus to Andheri. There was no library or anything in Andheri. All the cultural institutions were in the city and going to the city meant heavy spending. I had no real money with me. So I would explore the footpaths and streets of Andheri. Sometimes I walked all the way from Andheri to Juhu.

Actually, this family was very fond of me, very sweet and caring people with a great understanding of life. They had even become friends with my brother as they would speak to him when he called from home. I realized the depth of their attachment to me only when I was leaving their place, when Suresh Pai, Arun Verma, Manoj and I moved into an independent flat.

That day, the lady of the family looked at me and wept. She couldn't believe I was leaving. I was her best paying guest. She said their next tenant had to be someone I recommended! I want to go and visit her one of these days. In my mind, she symbolizes the goodness of Mumbai.

There are two more women I can't forget from those early years in Mumbai. They were *bais*—female domestic helpers. These bais were the only support system for people like me who were at the nascent stage of their careers. Almost all of them are Maharashtrians except for some from Uttar Pradesh and Gujarat. Sometimes, the entire womenfolk of a family would be bais. These hard-workers are the breadwinners of their family. They usually worked an hour each in many houses and earned a decent income. They are a big part of the Mumbai way of life.

I have had some very caring and unforgettable bais to help me. While at the Institute, the most dreaded work for me was washing and ironing clothes. Not because I thought of it as menial work. It had to do more with a resistance to shift from my all-night, mentally taxing occupation; just one of those things you keep postponing when you are involved in a more exciting cerebral activity. In that context, it was a great relief to know that in Mumbai there were bais to do your washing and ironing. And many of them were very benevolent women who treated me as their son or brother.

I have to tell you about this particular bai who helped me while I was staying in PMGP. She was a big, strong woman. She would walk in to my room like a wrestler, her sari draped Marathi style. The clothes she washed sparkled. There was a cameraman called Vivek staying with me. He had a pair of jeans that he would wear continuously for two or three weeks and only then give it for washing. One day, I saw this curious spectacle of the bai kicking him awake, reprimanding him for keeping his jeans so dirty: '*Aey, pehalwan—kya? Kappada bahut gandha karta hai!*'

Then she showed him a sparkling pair of jeans. His jeans! He was a bit taken aback at the way she spoke to him. Then onwards, if his jeans got a bit extra-dirty—when he shot in the rains, for instance—he would leave it for washing and get out of the home early, before the bai appeared.

This bai spoke with great authority. We gave her the respect and freedom to reprimand us in appropriate situations, like an elder sister would. Initially, I had thought, what the hell, I was the one giving her the salary, how could she talk to me like that! Then I saw the other side of it, the human side, and realized that she was treating us like she would a member of her family.

The real Mumbai—the people who live in it and make a living of it, relate to each other at a one-to-one personal level. Mumbai is also a place with a lot of sadness. I was completely stunned when I sensed this for the first time, this whole thing about its attitude, manner, smell, its people and the way they functioned. A whole lot of people make a living around the traffic lights. They conduct their business when the traffic stops for the red light. During the rains they sold umbrellas; during the school opening time, they sold books and pencils. Otherwise, there were always flowers, toys, magazines, Chinese gadgets and mobile chargers to sell—they were reinventing all the time to survive. There's also a group of people who make its living by exploiting these guys—it's all a complex network. When I had come to Mumbai for the first time, with a villager's mindset, I had found all this too depressing and had gone back thinking I would not come here again or work here.

I returned to Mumbai in accidental circumstances. I started exploring professional possibilities here and the city slowly grew on me—became a part of my life. What really tethered me to the city was the love and care provided by the very same people I had found living a depressing life when I saw them for the first time. It was about their willingness to help someone with the most basic chores of life, not about how much you paid them for it. For me, this definitely was not something that could be limited to the sphere of an employee—employer professional relationship. It had a bigger dimension of human contact and warmth.

In that sense, another bai, Jeejabai, is someone who I owe a lot to—we have a soul bond. When I started living in Saibaba Complex—where I live currently—I used to share an apartment with Arun Varma. That was in 1997, and Jeejabai started coming there as our domestic help. She was a smaller version of the bai I mentioned earlier. An elder son and two daughters and the husband were her family. The husband worked with the municipality. It was to make money to

marry off her daughters that she began working as a domestic
help. In the beginning, she did only the house cleaning and
laundry, but later on, she also started cooking for us.

In Mumbai, even now, perhaps that's the usual pattern
in which bachelor life evolves. First you eat all three meals
outside. Then you think: Ah! Why can't a bai cook for me?
Then you buy a gas stove, utensils, followed by a fridge. It
was through the intervention of such bais that my bachelor
life transformed from being one that was preoccupied with
cinema to one that had some kind of normalcy.

During those days, lots of friends used to land up at our
apartment in Saibaba Complex. They would bring along
some whisky and rum too. Then in the mornings, Jeejabai
would scold me, saying that one shouldn't be drinking such
stuff. I would promptly tell her that it was not me who was
doing the drinking, but my friends. Then she would advise
me to cut off my ties with such friends.

Once she asked me whether we were drinking so much
because we were cinema people. I told her that was not the
case—a lot of people drink in this world. I pointed out the
Jayaprakash Bar across the road, saying that many guys drink
there every day, and they're not cinema people.

'No, they are not. Still, you should not drink.'

'But I don't drink!'

'Maybe. But you could get tempted!'

What I relished in these reprimands was the sense of
security that I got from this kind of love and care.

Jeejabai thus became indispensable. We would exchange
family news and details. My Umma died around that time.

When I came back, I developed a problem in one of my legs. I felt very defeated, physically and psychologically. Umma's death had left me in a void. I didn't want to meet or talk to anybody. I couldn't relate to anyone. In that period, Jeejabai was my only support. She would come in the morning, heat water for me and then massage my leg with Ayurvedic ointments. I even felt my Umma's presence in her when she took care of me like that. Because of the condition of my leg, I couldn't climb stairs and I shifted to a ground-floor place in Saibaba Complex itself. And I turned a vegetarian. That whole experience felt as if the human warmth of the countryside had been brought to this megacity.

Then came Shadia, after marriage. Shadia was a strict and pure non-vegetarian. She gritted her teeth and displayed commendable courage in following me in my vegetarian diet—at least for five or six months. With the healing care that only wives can give, combined with strict medication, my leg improved almost back to its original state. When Shadia started cooking meat, Jeejabai was not very happy about it. She complained that I had started eating non-vegetarian food.

Jeejabai was particularly helpful when our son was born. When I received my first award—the Star Screen Award for *Black*—the first person I went and visited with the trophy was Jeejabai, in her house. I made my son give her a present on that occasion. I visited her often and helped her with money and medication when she was unwell. These are my memories about my Jeejabai. I never got anyone like her ever again. She cared about me so much that in her concern for my well-being she probably matched my Umma's intensity.

I was blessed to have someone like her when I didn't have my Umma near me in this distant land or when I had lost my Umma forever.

The landlady of my paying-guest place who wept when I had to leave; the big, strong bai who had struck terror in Vivek's heart; and Jeejabai—these three women encapsulate the caring spirit of an otherwise harsh city, and I can never forget them in my life.

*

Now, there are some more noteworthy components to the realities of Mumbai. I will tell you about two such situations: Shadia looking for a job and us buying a house. This was when we were at the Saibaba Complex.

We started out on our married life in a small house with minimal infrastructure. As days went by, things started piling up in the house—all kinds of vessels, bottles of various shapes and colours, coconut scrapers, an idli steamer, and more. When I would ask why the empty bottles were still lying at home, there would be a prompt answer: what if you needed one for something? Our place became so crowded that it was not even possible to take an about turn without disturbing something or the other. Our house was smaller than the servant quarter of Shadia's house. But as Shadia had a lot of space in her heart, she didn't complain much. Poor thing! Then my son Monu came into our lives. Now we needed a bigger place to stay.

We started to search for a house in a peaceful area. We

couldn't find anything in the places we liked. Shadia started complaining. Her main point was that we were not getting a house because I was in charge of the search operation. When Satheesh had wanted to buy a flat, he had asked Priya to look for it. His logic was that if women handled such things, it would definitely happen. So I sent Shadia on this mission with an assistant. There were some aspects of Mumbai that she wasn't aware of. I wanted her to get a taste of it.

She had wandered around a lot looking for a job before Monu was born. She was highly qualified and would get short-listed wherever she went, but in the end there was no job for her; others who were less qualified and experienced would get the job instead. Finally, when one more job which she was absolutely confident of getting, slipped through her fingers, I conducted a secret investigation and found out that she was the only Muslim candidate. This was Mumbai's post-riot reality. Shadia didn't know this. I never told her either. So my intention behind sending her house-hunting had also got to do with making her aware of these facts.

I intentionally sent her to a place I was familiar with. It was a Muslim locality. She selected a couple of places and got into a conversation with the landlords. They asked, 'By the way, are you Hindus?' It was because of Shadia's clothes. They also added that if we were Hindus, they couldn't give us the house. She came back very upset. 'What kind of people are these; we don't want to stay in a place like that.' I felt very bad seeing her in tears. I thought, thank God, I didn't send her to a Hindu locality. The Hindus would have told her that they wouldn't give their house to Muslims. Her grief would have been more intense. I told her about these other realities of Mumbai. For a long while after the riots, this had been the sad state of affairs. There is a visible improvement now.

*

Now it is impossible for me to leave Mumbai and live somewhere else. Even at home in Kerala, after two weeks, I start missing Mumbai. You live as yourself in Mumbai; the freedom is reflected even in your thoughts. It is no masked social life. Everyone relates to everyone else at a one-to-one level. All these people I have talked about have enhanced the quality of my life. They brought about the human connections that I thought were only possible in a rural setting. And they were not putting on a show for me—they were being what they were. They had brought with them the core identity of their countryside and replanted it in the city. To a certain extent, cities do accommodate such a way of life.

Movies are just one of the millions of products Mumbai manufactures. The massive infrastructure for all these is supported by the people or communities, something nobody should forget.

The one-to-one experiences at a human level that I have had in this city make me feel that the sectarian attitude can never work as a political stand. It is these communities that have built and sustained Mumbai. In this regard, let me tell you about a Brazilian film that I saw. In it, one fine morning all Brazilians and Spaniards disappear from America. Suddenly, there is nobody to do the housework, no one to man the shops, no taxis . . . everything comes to a standstill. In one day, everyone understands that life cannot function without others. What sustains a city is an intricately connected complex links of lives. So, to view this from outside through a sectarian filter, is part of some other agenda.

In my experience, when you live in a place like Mumbai, the people you have when you need them won't be your blood relatives or anything like that. They will be the people like the bais who contribute a little part of their time to you despite they themselves having very little time to spare. What eventually sustains one's meaningful existence is completely based on how one knits into these lives in terms of relationships and life itself.

It is a huge co-existence. There is a psychological landscape that's alive and breathing behind this co-existence, something that only a culture like India can comprehend.

PART 3

TRIUMPHS AND TRAGEDIES

1

BUILDING A SOUND ARCHIVE

I am not sure whether Amitabh Bachchan remembers this. But this story of building a sound archive has a link to him. This was something I had been meaning to do ever since I passed out of the Institute. We didn't have a library exclusively for Indian sounds then. Interestingly, the first person to have bought a sound effects library for use in Indian cinema was Amitabh Bachchan. He was working on the film *Khuda Gawah* then. Bhagat Singh, the sound recordist of that film, told me this story.

People like Bachchan have also been interested and involved in the post-production part of their films. They sat with the mixing team and generally encouraged the technicians working on it. Yes, stars like Shah Rukh Khan and Aamir Khan do involve themselves in such activities, but only if the film is their own production. Bachchan Saab used to do this in an era much before stars started producing films.

He bought a sound library called Sound Ideas and gave it to Bhagat Singh. That was also a time when technicians were not in a position to travel abroad for the purposes of a film. So, it was remarkable that Bachchan stepped in—as an Indian sound recordist, I doff my hat off to Amitabh Bachchan for showing us a sound library for the first time.

When I was planning my sound effects library, I spoke to a friend about it. She took it seriously and prepared a proposal. That was also the time when Bachchan's ABCL had just started. We submitted the proposal to them. They were willing to do the project. A budget was also sanctioned. But then, their first film, *Mrutyudatta*, came out and crashed at the box office. So they decided to abandon all the commercially unviable projects at hand. My project was one of them.

Then we approached BMG Crescendo. At that point they were doing some amount of non-mainstream work too. They were interested but only if we could slash the budget by half. I agreed and started working within the given constraints.

I started the recordings in 1997. Only when I started did I realize the vastness of the project. The Indian soundscape lay in front of me like an ocean. Just take Hindu religious sounds for example. In that particular area alone, forget India, I wouldn't even be able to cover Mumbai completely with my budget. In Mumbai, the Hanuman *aarti* in one locality is different from another. The sound and its details too vary according to the dialects. I found out that there was more than enough material in each Hindu religious sound for a separate album. How was I going to cover this whole thing? I was faced with a serious anthropological situation. I had walked into an area that needs scientifically accurate documentation. You can't begin it and then opt out.

And if you take just the area of Indian musical instruments, you'll find that there are hundreds of them that are in use as well as facing extinction. I don't know if there is anyone academically documenting this. Even if there are any agencies doing so, I have no idea what they are up to. Ours is a land of great aural traditions. But I doubt whether we have a discipline that documents and conserves our aural history.

I worked on the project for five or six months, within the budget, and recorded the sounds in three parts. I recorded about a hundred hours of various sounds from different parts of the country. I had stuck to a minimalistic plan and concentrated on the sounds typically needed in Hindi cinema: village ambience, religious rituals, public spaces, trains, etc.

But there was no professional set-up in Mumbai then to edit this material. There was only one studio which had a sound software called SADIE. I started editing the first volume in that. Then the money dried up and I had to stop the work. I revisited the project after a year, after Protools was available, and re-digitized and edited everything in a studio and finally released the CD in 1998. It received a tremendous response. I have a royalty on this and the product has been selling for many years, but I haven't received even a single paisa out of this so far. In India nobody cares about royalty, and I don't have the time to pursue it either. I add this to the considerable amount of money owed to me by many in the industry; a three-volume sound library has been another free contribution of mine to the industry. That it is being widely used everywhere is something I am personally sick of hearing again and again. But it also makes me wonder if I should compile and release a few more volumes of it.

Recently, a young man came to visit me. A French director called François Gerard. He and a cameraman were making a film. Some time in the past, he had got excited about this sound library of mine. He had heard a pirated version and didn't know who had recorded and compiled the volume. In the course of our conversation, he realized that he was talking to the very man behind the whole thing. He got very excited and expressed incredible happiness at having been able to meet me. In a way, such reactions are more rewarding than earning royalties. This guy had come to me with a request to do the sound for his film. He didn't have any money but he presented his case. I saw the film—it was just brilliant! His straightforwardness and his spirit were absolutely inspiring. Money becomes immaterial in such a circumstance—it is then a sense of honesty that drives you. I did the film for him.

The Indian soundscape has changed drastically from what it was when I did the recordings in 1997; you see, landscapes and soundscapes change over time. One of the things I am now very seriously considering is to take forward the sound archive project. Now I have a team with me. I also have a tie-up with a big Hollywood company. My vision is to exchange materials with them and finally have a comprehensive sound library—something anybody can access any time from anywhere through our website. Ultimately, that would be one of my largest contributions.

This is something I plan to carry out as a part of my overall scheme to set up a sound design school. My studio, Canaries Postsound, is just a beginning for the entire venture.

My immediate next step is to select about five people. They will be first trained in sound—not in cinema. Then they will be let into cinema. If this works out, we can carry out some revolutionary work in sound. I am not looking at just Indian cinema—cinema as a whole is what I have in mind. There are a lot of youngsters in India who are prepared to do hard work. Discovering them and channelizing their talents are the next steps for me. That would be where I shall be able to give something back to the Indian film industry. Whatever I have done so far has been driven by passion. From now on, even as I retain the passion, I would like to systematize certain things. The coming years will see me putting a lot of my efforts into finding and gathering funds for this venture. For the entire thing to bear fruit, it has to be fuelled by the service motive. Along with this, I will also be trying to convert some of my concepts into workable models. Like, in our country, we don't have a defined concept of a mentor. When Ben Bert said that Walter Murch, Spielberg and Lucas were his mentors, he was acknowledging the fact that these great men had contributed to his growth by generously sharing their work and expertise with him.

But we in India are still far away from that stage where professionals share and learn from each other's work. We are competitive and insecure. Here, when someone does good work, it automatically makes him a rival. Mentorship can only arise from a spirit of generosity. You see, Ben Bert is Walter Murch's legacy. We don't have such a thing in our system. In India, quality is still very much an individual pursuit.

Here, how good you are is completely based on how good
you yourself want to be—it's a measure of your own personal
ambition. In the long run, this will only present us with
failures. There is nothing here to channelize our ambitions.
This is an appalling state of affairs; it can only make things
even more chaotic.

2

FIRST FILM, FIRST CAR

The first feature film I worked on was *Private Detective: Two Plus Two Plus One* as an assistant. Rajat Kapoor was making the film and Rafe Mehmood was doing the camera. They were batchmates at the Institute. The film was meant to be dubbed. I was called in to do the pilot sound, something which is used only as a reference while dubbing the final dialogues. Vikram Jogelaker was the real sound designer of the film.

Jogi (Vikram Jogelaker) knew me. I had had a chance to work on one of his projects while I was still a student. He looks like a philosopher. Like Confucius. His eyes are like Osho's—sparkling, while his beard is long. When you see him for the first time, you may think that he is a major artist, thinker and philosopher. Indeed, his thoughts are deep and he has read just about everything there is to be read. He also has a deep knowledge of music, and an incredible ear—both in size and sensitivity!

Come to think of it, the ear is worthy of a lot of philosophical discussions. It is not just another appendage like the hand or the leg. Wise men say the ear has a philosophy of its own. At least, the ear is the funnel into which people pour all their philosophies. It is the ear that plays a prominent role in the advancement of our culture and civilization.

Jogi has done films of Mani Kaul and Kumar Shahni. He is on a different level altogether. Technically solid and a terrorist in philosophizing about technology and technique, he always leaves you with a feeling that there is a lot more to know and learn.

Though I went as a pilot track recordist for Rajat's film, I considered my brief much beyond that—I would be involved in anything that had to do with the sound recording for the film. Inevitably, there too, I stopped a shoot. Once, when the camera called for the sound roll, I refused to roll. I demanded that the ambient noise be controlled first. They didn't agree; they said that there was no need for all that since the track was just meant to be used as a pilot for dubbing.

I stuck to my guns saying that whether the sound was to be used or not was a post-production decision and that I should be allowed to record.

Imagine someone as lowly as a pilot recordist having the temerity to talk of post-production decisions! Indeed, in my career, I have raised this question in innumerable sets and locations. If some of the better production houses in India have started showing an interest in sync sound, some of the credit for that should go to myself and a couple of other equally crazy guys who fought for it. In that sense, in the Indian context my Oscar also accorded recognition for location sound.

During that film, I was left in tears many a time. In many locations, I couldn't record properly—things like the sound of a car pulling in or braking at the parking lot, absolutely great stuff for using as sound images. Within the constraints of a low-budget production, it was almost always impossible to quieten down the whole area or discipline the entire crew to get a flawless recording. All this made me cry. I have had such an emotional association with all my films.

To cut the story short, I recorded whatever I could. There were some instructions from Jogi as well. We finished the shoot and later started editing the film. In the meantime, Jogi got married and moved to Italy. The circumstances were such that he couldn't continue working on the film.

Having seen my performance and commitment, Rajat asked me if I could take over.

All I had was convictions about sound—which wasn't so bad. In my childhood times, there was a Malayalam actor called Ummer. On screen, he had this characteristic grunt, '*Hmm . . .*' 'Like Ummer's grunt' was a local saying. It sounded serious and loaded, but had no clear meaning. So when Rajat asked me whether I could do it, I came up with Ummer's grunt. This meant I was ready, but I didn't really know how to go about the entire thing. No, this was not a case of jumping at an opportunity; I had the conviction that I could pull it off. I had formulated a clear idea about the film. I used to write down my thoughts here and there. That's when, as fate would have it, the opportunity presented itself.

It also helped that Rajat Kapoor himself knew a lot about sound, actually far more than me. We could discuss and decide exactly what I needed to do.

One of the things that I was unsure about was the decision regarding whether a particular sound was going to be foley or effects or something else altogether which I needed to create. You need to know at what stage you can create a particular soundscape. Jogi is the one who enlightened me on this— that this could be in foley, this part needs to be recorded, etc. They were all there to guide me. Once I got a clue, that was enough for me to figure out the rest. Finally, I was able to record all the sounds for the film: every ambient sound, every little piece of it.

That was also the time when digital technology was becoming popular in India. Protools—a digital sound-editing software—was already in the market. But nobody had tried it in films yet. With Protools, you can work with a lot more tracks than you can with conventional tools. I was certain that this film needed a multilayered sound pattern. Even though the film was in mono, I knew we couldn't achieve multilayering by laying the track through a Steinbeck. The only way out was to go for digital technology. Rajat hadn't used any digital technology till then. He knew only about track laying with a Steinbeck. But he said that if I was convinced about using digital technology, he would give it a try. He also wanted to know the cost implications.

Our budget was pathetic. I did some research and calculated that we could pull it off only if I finished one reel a day. To achieve that, the whole thing had to be conducted like a timed performance. We needed to execute our plans with crystalline clarity. I wrote a scene-by-scene sound script even before booking the studio. I prepared a reel-wise flow chart with counter numbers marked for which sounds came where. Then I marked out which sound was where in which digital tape. In those days, I knew only the analogue method, not the digital mode of working. All I was sure about was the position of every bit of sound in the film.

The first day was a complete disaster. I couldn't even finish half a reel. Rajat said it looked like a bad idea and that this was not quite my area of expertise. I disagreed and asked for another day.

That night, I stayed up and memorized the entire sound of a whole reel. I knew each tape and its counter numbers by heart.

The next day, I went to the studio. I stood like a dictator and commanded: take number one, digitize; take number two, digitize . . . and I digitized the whole reel. Then, like a conductor of an orchestra, I directed which sound went where. The picture was coming in video; I wasn't used to that, familiar as I was only with film. That was a change of technology. I didn't know how to match and sync using time codes. I was learning while doing the job! I went on to finish a reel in eight hours. Rajat was impressed. He was also convinced about the possibilities of the new technology.

The music for this film was composed by Kedar Awati. He was my music teacher at the Institute. He had thought of me as a noisy student who generally hung around without being of any particular use to anyone. After the music recording session, I 'mixed a piece' and came out for a break. Then he told me that he had never thought I would perform at this level. He said my growth was unbelievable. He had also taught me how to play the harmonium.

As I said, I remember sound well. I would remember the performance at the location. Even if I didn't know the language, I wouldn't forget in what way I had heard it. During the dubbing, I would try to get the same performance. I introduced the style of recording with multiple mikes after I realized that by using one mike I was not being able to reproduce the quality of location sound.

Those days the dubbing of major Hindi films used to take place at Aradhana Studio. The guys out there were not very impressed with my experiments. They mumbled: who's this new guy who wants to record with *two* mikes; what's wrong with our single mike recording system that we have been following all these years, with perfect results? The film's final mixing was done by Paddy (Padmanabhan). He was also there at the Institute, as an external faculty member, during our selections.

He came out after premixing the dialogue and told everyone: there is definitely an advantage in recording with two mikes; listen to this and find out for yourself.

'This lad is not so bad.' That was the reputation I earned through my first film.

*

I have never worked with the sole aim of making money; it has always been a by-product. In fact, for many projects I've worked on, the money often never came at all. My early years in Mumbai saw me almost broke most of the time, with usually only about six hundred rupees in my bank account.

Work was also erratic. Of course, those days I could have made a decent living by doing TV serials or something like that. But I was stubborn about the fact that I had come this far to do cinema sound and nothing else. Anyway, whenever I was in a financial crisis and needed money desperately, somehow some work would turn up—as Umma would put it, it was as if Allah was hurrying someone to me to help me out. This used to happen in Umma's case too.

Talking about money, there's an interesting story about how I bought a car. That was when Umma was quite unwell. She was having problems with diabetes and blood pressure. Umma was handling the situation all on her own; none of us really bothered to find out what was happening with her health or treatment. She used to take the local bus to go to the hospital. I decided that the best thing I could do as a son was to buy a car for our home. It was all the more necessary as Umma and Bappa were getting older, and an emergency could crop up at any time.

During this time, when I was back home, a friend landed up in an old Fiat. The car wasn't looking too bad. To cut the story short, I immediately proceeded to buy the car after paying an advance and promising the rest from Mumbai. I had to return to Mumbai the next day. I went to the airport in this car. It managed to run for about ten kilometres before giving up completely. I then had to get help from my uncle, in whose car I finally reached the airport. I cancelled the whole deal and took the advance money back. Umma was a bit disappointed that the entire thing had turned into a fiasco.

In Mumbai, I discussed the car episode with Satheesh. He

said that it had been foolish on my part to buy a used car at that cost; he suggested that the better thing was to take a loan and buy a brand new car. And I did exactly that. In about eight months I organized some money, reached home and, along with my brother, went to decide upon a car. Umma was kept out of the loop of the whole thing.

I had put a fixed deposit in Umma's name a long while ago—some forty-two thousand rupees. She had been very thrilled about that. Now I told her that as I was in need of some money, and that she needed to break her FD and give me the amount.

'Sure, son. It was your own money, and you're taking it when you are in need. Not a worry at all.'

On the day of getting the vehicle, my brother and I went to Kollam; then we called Bappa on the phone and told him that he needed to come there. He came to Kollam by bus. He couldn't understand what was going on. We took him to the showroom and gave him the car key. He asked us what it was all about. I told him that once he had wanted to have a bus of his own and that now we were the owners of a car, that the key was the car's.

Tears welled up in Bappa's eyes. He gave the key to the driver. In order to ward off evil eyes, we did the ritual of driving the car over a lemon, and went to my sister's house. From there, we called up Umma and asked her not to sleep early as there was a surprise in store.

It was past sunset when we reached home. Umma had been panicking—what was happening with us? She had felt that we were planning something, that something secret was going on; she had even suspected some trouble. After finishing her evening prayers, she was sitting on the rock under the almond tree across our house, prayer beads in hands. We arrived in the car—in cinematic terms, it's a track shot, of a car pulling in with Bappa sitting at the front; then cut to Umma's face reacting to this incredible sight. We got out and I gave the key to Umma, saying, 'For Umma and Bappa; Anchal Umma's own car!'

'Oh, my dear son!' She hugged me and wept.

That was the most satisfying moment in my life.

I told her, 'Now you need to stop travelling by bus. You are not that fit any more. And you have carried us enough. You have also carried enough coconuts and tapiocas to the market to sell, and raise us all. Now there is no need for any of that. If you feel like going to the hospital or visiting your brother, the driver will take you there.'

It had been Umma's wish to see my second brother, Saif, and Babuka having their own cars. That was the reason why I had given some money to Babuka to buy a car even when I had been facing a difficult time because of the ailment in my leg. Today, my second sister has two cars. Kochumon has bought another. Lots of cars at our home! But it hurts a little that Umma and Bappa are not around to see these things. All I can do is console myself by imagining that the two are watching everything from up there somewhere.

And after the car came, it occupied Bappa full-time—using all his experience and knowledge about automobile maintenance, it was he who decided whether the tyres had to be changed, or whether it was the upholstery, etc. Oh, they were such great times!

That first car is still there with us. Umma's last journey, too, was in that car.

3

MY PARENTS' DEMISE

In 1998 I was working in Udaipur, Rajasthan. The maharaja of Udaipur had a huge collection of the recordings of the renowned court musicians, Moinuddin Daggar and Aminuddin Daggar. These dhrupad vocals were recorded between 1947 and 1967—all on old tapes. And they were discovered accidentally. I got the contract to digitize the tapes for archiving.

I stayed in Udaipur twice for this project. The second time I worked there for a month and a half. Throughout this period, for some reason, I experienced a nagging anxiety about my Bappa. It was like a premonition of some kind of danger or even death heading towards him. One day, early morning, the phone rang in my room. On the first ring itself, I thought something had happened to Bappa. I picked up the phone on the third ring. It was my eldest brother on the line.

He said, 'Bappa had a fall yesterday. He has fractured his hip bone. He is having trouble urinating and all. He is in major pain. We first took him to the Anchal Misssion Hospital. He has now been moved to the Uthradam Thirunal Hospital in Thiruvananthapuram. He requires a hip surgery. He also has urinary block. It's a bit serious.'

I asked, 'But otherwise, is he all right?'

'Yes, he's all right. But the hip surgery has to be done quickly.'

'How much would it cost?'

He gave me the figure.

I said, 'Do one thing, you make sure everything gets done. I will land up as soon as I wind up this work.'

I reported my situation to the maharaja, telling him that I needed to head home immediately. There was still a couple of months' work pending. I promised to finish that in Mumbai. When I finally reached home, Bappa was back there after the surgery.

It was a major surgery. He had been on general anaesthesia. Once anaesthetized, he had started hallucinating. He had even 'seen' Umma inside a fan! He demanded that the fan be turned off in order to save Umma from the dizzying rotation. This had become a major joke at home by the time I reached.

That whole year was pretty critical for Bappa. After the surgery, he couldn't walk for some time. Then he was diagnosed with a urinary tract infection. When he was taken to the hospital, a biopsy was ordered, and some malignancy was detected. It was a prostate growth. That called for another immediate surgery. Umma was not informed about this one. We simply told her that Bappa was being kept in the hospital for further observation. Saif was the man who was running around figuring things out. Even he got scared when he heard of another surgery. When he called, I told him that there was nothing to worry about as they would just be removing whatever needed to be removed. I also told him not to let Bappa know the details and let him stay in the hospital for a few more days. Umma was left wondering, 'Why's this man still staying in the hospital when he can walk? This is going to finish the poor boy's entire savings.' Those days, I used to handle the finances of these kinds of big emergencies although there were other people to help out. You see, I was single, working, and making money, with no other big expenses.

Saif was getting exhausted with all the running around that a hospital case demands. He was also getting quite irritated with how Umma viewed the whole thing. But that was no surprise—he has always had a short fuse. As for Umma, she was suffering from ailments of her own. She generally thought that nobody really cared or had time for her. She was managing her health affairs pretty much by herself.

I called Umma the night Bappa was brought home after the operation. I just felt like calling her. I cheerfully asked, 'What's up, the Umma of Anchal?'

'Nothing, my son, except that I am not feeling too good.'

'Why are you saying that?' I asked.

'Must be the daal I ate. Looks like it's given me gas. I am feeling a bit tired.'

Umma loved moong daal. Every evening, she would eat it boiled with coconut flakes sprinkled on it.

A while into the chat, she asked me how things were with me, and started crying.

I felt terrible hearing her cry. I asked her what was wrong.

'I feel like seeing you, son,' she said.

I said I would come the next day. I immediately called the travel agent. Actually I had a booking in one studio the next day for the Udaipur work. So when I was about to book the flight, I thought I might as well finish that bit and then leave. I was also not sure when I would be able to come back from home. So I pushed the ticket to the day after.

I called home again. I said to Saif, 'Saif, looks like Umma is not feeling too well. Take her to the hospital.' It was around eleven at night. Saif had just driven all the way from Thiruvananthapuram and also had had no real sleep for several nights at the hospital. He said, 'Umma is all right. I will take care of her.' Babukka was also around then, and he gave her some medicine for the gas trouble.

The next morning when I called, they were about to take Umma to hospital. Umma was now no longer being treated at the Mission Hospital in Anchal; she was consulting a diabetologist at the SUT hospital in Thiruvananthapuram. On the way, she vomited a couple of times, but it was nothing serious to worry about.

I was in the middle of a mad rush to finish the work. I kept calling for updates. At noon I was told that Umma had suffered a minor heart attack. But again they told me that there was nothing to worry about and that she was okay. She would be under observation in the ICU for the next seventy-two hours. And she had entered the ICU walking. Then they asked me about my next day's travel plans.

I said I would be coming the next day. I called again in the evening. Umma's state had improved and she was to be taken to an ordinary ward the next day.

I felt immensely relieved. I left the studio and called again around eleven thirty at night. Everything was all right. Around quarter to twelve, a muscle on the left side of my face started twitching. After some time, there was a call from the hospital to make sure that I was coming the next day and to know about the flight number and all. I told them I would be there by noon. I didn't have any serious worries about Umma at that time.

Next day at noon, I landed in Thiruvananthapuram. Usually, it was Saif who came to pick me up at the airport. But this time, Saif was not there; nor were my brothers. Instead, my cousin brother and Sharaf Macha had come.

In the car, I noticed that we were not headed towards the hospital. We were heading towards home. I then asked where Umma was.

They told me Umma was back home. I got suspicious. I asked them to stop the car and demanded to know what had happened to Umma.

The car stopped.

I sensed something and was on the verge of a breakdown.

Macha began, 'Resul. These are inevitable things in life. Umma died at twelve last night. The body has been taken home. We are going home now.'

'Impossible! I spoke to her last night!'

I didn't know where I was after that point. I was in a daze. The car was moving through some vague space. When we arrived at near home, I didn't want to go home. When the car arrived at the bend near our home, I asked them to stop; then I asked them whether they were indeed telling me the truth. I sat in the car and cried for a long time.

'We have to move, everyone's waiting for you,' said Macha.

When we stopped in front of the house, it was like in a Hindi film, a lot of people all over the place. My sisters started howling the moment they saw me. I couldn't take any of it. Umma was lying down—as if she was sleeping. She used to sleep on the mat every day after her prayers, in her white robe. She was sleeping like that, it appeared to me. Umma now had a small bruise on her nose. I touched it. Then I felt like going to the toilet, so I stepped out. Some kids were playing outside. I looked at them and came back to Umma. I asked aloud about how Umma had got the wound on her nose.

Some people came to hold me and sat me down, saying, 'Don't worry, son, it's all right.'

My eldest sister told me that Umma had got that bruise in a fight with Saif's eldest son. He had pinched her nose.

The fact that Umma was dead was just not sinking in. While I sat and stared, the body was taken to be bathed. Bappa was sitting there, all broken. He was not saying a word. After the bath, they brought Umma back and put cotton in her nostrils. Now it was time to carry the body to the grave. It was getting late, people were saying that the body had to be buried before four.

I said nobody should take Umma anywhere. I wanted to keep seeing her. I was hugging her. I kissed her on the forehead. I wasn't quite in a state of mind to know what was going on or who were around or anything of that sort.

I saw her brother who we call Saar Mama standing aside in unbearable grief. He was my Bappa's closest brother-in-law. My Umma's six brothers had held their younger sister the dearest. They couldn't believe that she had left before them.

Bappa completely broke down when the body was lifted. His face had an expression of total despair, clearly saying, 'Ah! Now, what of me!' It had been a fifty-year-old marital life. Umma had been thirteen when Bappa had married her. She had always said she that would die at sixty-three. We used to tease her about that, saying she was Allah's close confidante!

In the occasional argument between them, when Bappa would say something that hurt her, she would always say that he would die only after her—that he would suffer her absence before he died. Once in a while when I felt cross with Shadia, I would remember this and take care not to say things that hurt her heart.

A life partner is about more than being a mere husband or a wife. It's more than about two individuals living together; it's an open sharing of lives, without anything unknown between them. There's no mask in one's relationship with one's life partner. When I was sitting feeling very chuffed after getting the Oscar, Shadia came in and said, 'Hey, go and pay the electricity bill.' Who else other than a wife can say this. Considering the way I am, anything can come out of my mouth, but I always stop myself from saying anything that's seriously hurtful. Umma's words of ultimatum, of her dying before Bappa did, would be used only when Bappa went on to say something particularly hurtful. But Bappa didn't survive for too long after Umma's death.

Umma was buried; I had put a fistful of earth on her without believing that any of this was real. Such a turn of events I had never ever imagined; it all felt as if I was inside a bad dream. All of us performed the ritual prayers for the dead. Only a couple of times in my childhood had I prayed in a mosque; otherwise, I have never really followed any religious rituals.

The whole thing was a rude shock. I had never thought that all these rituals were necessary, that I would one day need religion and the mosque. In our younger days, some of us refuse to see the strong ties that connect our lives to the community and its rituals.

We come back to the house without Umma. A home without Umma? That was something I had never ever imagined. That was why in the days that followed, all things carried an indescribable void at its centre.

Bappa became deeply depressed. He looked like a man who had lost everything. Even the companionship of his children could not fill the deep void of his loss. He became an emotional wreck. In that one year, he aged a decade.

On the eleventh day after Umma's death, a ritual gathering had to be organized. Saif and I ran around inviting all those who had attended the burial. Every household we visited, we felt the special relationship that Umma had with each of them. My place is full of poor people. Umma used to help them all. We have a market in front of our house. Umma used to sell coconuts there. With that money, she would buy fish, meat and tapioca. (And there was a time when we used to sell tapioca by the truckload!)

When we went to one woman's house to invite her, she started crying uncontrollably, expressing her dismay at what Allah had done to my Umma, who was such a caring woman, and who had treated her as if she was her own daughter. Only the previous week, she said, they had met in the market, and

Umma had asked after her well-being. This woman wasn't particularly well off. Umma had given her ten rupees, asking her to buy herself some fish, and had invited her home to give her coconut and rice. Umma had also told her that if she wanted anything, she should come to her. She kept on weeping as she narrated this to us.

A month before she died, when Bappa was in hospital, Umma and I were going to Anchal in a bus. She asked me for a hundred rupees and gave the money to a woman in the bus, saying, 'You are going to the hospital, no? Here, keep this with you.' There were lots people like this who had benefited from Umma's generosity. Nalinichechi in the neighbourhood talked about how Umma would buy her fish and meat during the market days, saying, 'See, you have small kids, feed them something good.' (At the same time, if she got angry, she would also not hesitate to scold Nalinichechi.)

That was Umma—always very compassionate to the poor. It didn't matter whether she was on good or bad terms with the person whom she helped—whenever she saw grief in people's lives, she would respond in ways that she found appropriate. And she was not a rich woman to carry out such charity; it arose from her zeal to always find a space to be compassionate. Such a character trait is fast disappearing from our society as it evolves within new parameters.

Those little trips into people's lives while inviting them for the eleventh-day ceremony were full of loving memories of Umma. They also left me emotionally drained. I haven't experienced such emotional intensity ever again. During that time, I found that I couldn't function properly any more. I started sitting in Umma's room all the time. The room where she prayed remains as it was when she was alive. Even now when I go home, I don't leave it without spending some time in that room talking to her. The most powerful forces that drive me are my thoughts about my Umma and Bappa. I imagine them sitting on my shoulders. Before doing anything important— like 'mixing' a film—I talk to them. In the days when I was working on *Black,* this communication happened every day.

After Umma's death, I stayed back at home for a month and a half. I was not able to leave the place. I still hadn't come to terms with the fact that Umma was gone. I ended up in a state where I couldn't concentrate on anything. I came back to Mumbai, deeply depressed. I couldn't work. I couldn't even bring myself to lift the phone to speak to anyone. Nor did I feel like staying alone. To get me across this state, some close friends from the Institute, Shankar Raman and Vivek Shah, took me to Daman and Diu for a few days. Satheesh was another person who helped me cross this difficult patch.

When I stand next to Umma's grave with my eyes closed, I can visualize her as she was in the old house. She had usually worn a lungi and blouse. When I stand at the head of her grave, I can see her getting up from her siesta mat, throwing a towel across her chest and then calling me, 'Come, son.' That's what her grave means to me. In every particle of that place, I see her face.

I recall how cross Umma had been when she came to know that I had changed my name to Resul Pookutty. I had teased her, saying, 'Okay, shall I call myself Resul Nabeeza Beevi then?' It was only later that I met the director Sanjay Leela

Bhansali who has taken his mother's name—Leela—as his middle name. He would take his mother everywhere. His film, *Black*, has won innumerable awards—and at all those award functions, he had brought his mother. For him, the love for his mother is an intense and deep emotion. I, too, have that kind of love for my mother. I had teased her about the name because of my ignorance. If only I had kept my Umma's name in my name . . . If only I could have taken her with me for the Oscar ceremony . . . These impossible thoughts keep coming to my mind all the time. From somewhere up there, she might be looking at me and consoling me as she had always done when she was alive; she would be forgiving of my ignorance, and would pray for me.

*

Umma's death had a devastating effect on Bappa's health. He grew weaker by the day. Though the surgery had kind of fixed his hip bone, he couldn't walk without the support of a stick any more. Later, he needed a wheelchair, and finally, was totally bedridden. He also suffered from cardiac complaints and cholesterol. Umma's death had essentially destroyed his will to live. In his final stages, he became completely incoherent. No one could understand what he was trying to say. That's how I saw him last. That night is still clear in my mind.

He was in bed in his room. Everyone else had left the room and it was dark. I stood at his bedside and looked at him. He too looked at me and tried to sit up. He couldn't. I bent down and hugged him tightly; he too hugged me. Both of us were crying. He was saying something. There was helplessness in his voice about not being able to communicate anything to me. I heard a cry in his voice. I heard a lament whose origin I couldn't pinpoint—whether it was coming from within me or whether it came from his illegible words. I can never forget that night. In our communication without words was hidden a resounding inquiry, 'Now what?' It was a question we left unasked—overtly. Whenever I was leaving for Mumbai, he used to get into the front seat of the car, to drop me. This time it had become impossible for him to move.

During those last days of Bappa's strife, in September 2001, even my health was going through a bad phase. My leg was giving me problems, and I was supposed to go to Kerala to have it treated. Meanwhile, I had to finish off work for a film that was to be screened at the Venice Festival on 3 September. I was going to the studio to do the mixing for the last reel when I got a call from home saying Bappa was unwell and had been admitted to a hospital. I had a disturbing feeling about it. Baiju Kalluvila was with me that day. I asked him to book a flight for the next night.

In the afternoon, I was at the Fireflys studio. I called home from there and was told that Bappa was in a serious condition and wanted to see me. They asked me to come as soon as possible, the very next morning if possible. I said yes. I could hear Kochumon's voice in the background instructing to confirm the exact time of my arrival. I was seriously disturbed while I went from Fireflys to the Empire Studios where the mixing was happening. It was about six in the evening. I had a feeling that something had happened to Bappa. I called up home, but no one picked up. Finally I got Saif. He said that there was nothing to worry about. He asked whether my next morning's travel time was confirmed and told me he would meet me at the airport.

I had a feeling that they were hiding something from me. We started the mixing process. When I met Rahul Bose, the director, he was in a bad mood. He said, 'As it is, we don't have a full booking, and now you are going. What are we going to do?' I told him my father was in a critical condition and I had to go no matter what, and that I would finish the work before I left. By that time, we were done with the sound design; only mixing was left. That wouldn't be a big problem once the first automation was done. I was trying to do that. The sound of the film had turned out beautifully and everyone was talking about it. By nine at night, Satheesh came there. It wasn't usual for him to land up like that. That was like a premonition. We took a break for dinner. Satheesh asked, 'You're not looking very good, what has happened?' I told him about the situation. Together we called up my home. When the phone was picked up, I could hear the sound of the Koran chanting at the other end. I felt very weak and thought I might fall. I gave the phone to Satheesh and asked him to speak and find out what was happening. Satheesh did the talking and then told me, 'Bappa has passed away, at six in the evening. He has been brought home. Everybody is waiting for you.'

I didn't know what to do. I first went and splashed some water on my face. Then I went to the Rahul and told him my father was no more. 'Still, I will complete this film. I will leave only after that,' I said. He got very shaken; and said, 'No, no. You go home.'

'Go home and do what?' I asked him. I needed to be at the airport only at four in the morning. That meant I could work till then.

I worked on finishing the mixing for the film's last reel, completely aware that my Bappa was lying dead back home. This last reel carried some emotionally important moments. We were dealing with intense emotions. But that was cinema. In real life, I was going through a tsunami of personal sorrow while finishing the work.

I had a similar experience while working on *Ghajini*. That had to do with the death of the sound engineer Sreedhar who had worked for a long time with A.R. Rahman. A few hours before his death, Sreedhar and I were working sitting side by side till three in the morning. Then he went off to catch some sleep. At eight thirty in the morning he called and told me that he was coming to the studio. At ten, I heard he was dead. The next day I was sitting in the same studio, next to an empty chair, doing the song of separation in *Ghajini*, conscious that Sreedhar's body was being laid out at his home at that very time. It was unbearable. But then such is life!

With my Bappa's face filling up my mind, I sat and did the mixing, till three in the morning. Then I got up and told them I was off. I didn't know when I'd be back. There was still some money owed to me by the producers. I had some plans with it. I also needed money for my treatment. I added up all the money I had, wrote cheques for the people I owed money, and left the place.

I was completely overwhelmed and was crying all through the flight. My health was also in a bad shape. I was in pain. My legs were giving me trouble. I had some kind of rashes all over me. I had shaved my head, and was wearing a cap to hide the bald pate. I was on crutches. It was in this strange disguise that I was making my way home.

Someone had brought a car for me to go from the Thiruvananthapuram airport to my home. My mind was completely empty during that ride. A big crowd had gathered in front of the house. The Koran chants sounded like the continuation of what I had heard over the phone the previous evening. I felt the same giddiness sweeping all over me. My eldest brother-in-law came to me and advised me to remove my cap.

I stepped into the house. Bappa was laid on a white cloth. There was a smile hiding on his face. The chanting of Koran verses in suppressed voices and the white of his cloth seemed to spread over the whole place.

When I looked at his face, I remembered our last meeting— the night we wept in each other's arms.

We used to write a lot to each other. We shared a deep emotional bond. After I grew up, we openly discussed anything and everything. Later on, it came to a stage where he could talk only to me about things. He could tell me anything.

He used to go for a walk every day. He had a couple of close friends. He would tell me, 'Listen, you must give something to that Shivaraman Channar—before you leave.' So that became a routine with me—giving Shivaraman something before leaving home. When I would give Bappa money, the first thing he always did was to clear his petty credit at the local tea shop.

Our letter writing to each other went back to many years. Bappa would write about all the domestic affairs in detail, including about the things that emotionally hurt him. But he would never say that he himself was hurt; it was always about how Umma had felt the hurt.

'Ponnumol and her bunch today went for an excursion. No one bothered to tell us. Your Umma felt very bad.' That meant he, too, had felt very bad. I recently found out that I, too, had a similar attitude. Whenever I would not be invited for an event or something, I would say, 'Shadia felt very bad about it.' But I don't divulge these things to my family, only to Baiju Kalluvila. When my son grows up, he might make the same observation about me.

Bappa's letters contained a certain advisory tone. For instance, he would write, 'In summer, you must drink a lot of water. Otherwise, your urine will boil. In case that happens, you must consult a doctor and get medicine for it. Never neglect these things.' He would also describe in detail about temple festivals and Eid celebrations.

When Bappa was being buried, my emotional pain was submerged in my physical pain. When I was doing the last rites where I had to bow down to the body, I couldn't do it standing as I was supposed to, and I had to perform the namaz in the sitting position.

After Bappa's eleventh-day rites, I left for my treatment. I reached there on the evening of 9 September 2001. Two days later, the World Trade Centre came crashing down in New

York. The world reeled under the consequences of this horrific event as the Bush administration launched its War on Terror. But I was immune to these cataclysmic developments— instead, I was going through pain more intense in the mind and the body. I was not even watching television. Nor was I reading any newspapers. My diary bears testimony to my lonely ruminations:

15 September 2001

I dreamt of Bappa last night. Some people were telling me about some phone calls. I have just returned after a trip. Why do I see him again this quickly?

Bappa is standing very close; I can reach out and touch him—his smile, like he had on his lifeless face as we propped him up for the last bath.

I can't forget that smile on his face.

'Our lives are smaller than a death!'

18 September 2001

Bappa came rushing to my mind today. His sleeping face with the smile is not going away from my mind . . .

My first memory of Bappa is of him stepping into the veranda from the dark and the rain. From there on, in the last twenty-five years a series of expressions had gone through that face. The last one in the series was the smile, my last memory of him.

6 October 2001

Today was Bappa's fortieth *Khatam*. Last night, I recited *dhikr* for both Bappa and Umma.

It is now more than forty days that Bappa has left us. 27 August has now become impossible for me to even remember.

Bappa's sleep. The smile on his face. An unerasable smile on his lips. The smile on his sleeping face while he was being bathed. The other day Kochumon was asking me what my last memory of his face was.

The smiling face on his lifeless body. A smiling, lifeless body being given its last bath.

Like Ashish [a friend from Bhopal] wrote: *Our parents leave a part in us when they leave forever.*

I do not know what Bappa has left for me.

*

The next couple of years were a period when I couldn't personally or emotionally get close to anyone. I felt that if I got close, I would end up losing them. I had lost two people I held the most precious. Yes, my brothers and sisters were there for me, but that's different—it was Umma and Bappa with whom I primarily bonded. Even after growing up and leaving home, whenever I got back, I would sleep in the same bed as Umma, throwing one of my legs on her. Umma had a big tummy that folded into three while she sat. As kids, we would play with these folds, calling it the steering wheel of our vehicle. Even after I had grown up, Umma used to call me to help her with her bra hooks. Acknowledging the permanent departure of Umma and Bappa from my life was impossible. I then found out that there was nobody left for me to cry out my worries to. This sudden realization of one's immense loneliness is not something words can communicate.

The void of the absence of my parents is still there, despite the fact that I am now married and blessed with the companionship of a loving and caring wife. My father-in-law and mother-in-law are now like parents to me, but they, too, cannot fill the void left by my Bappa and Umma. That said, the arrival of my kids sometimes makes me feel that it is a re-birth of my parents. Perhaps your children are the closest you can have to your parents, in terms of the quality or nature of the relationship. At times, my little girl's face resembles that of my Umma's. Similar is the case with my boy. Through these two children, I feel that Umma and Bappa have come back to my life. That is how I relate to the phenomenon of progeny.

It was during my attempts to grapple with the void that my parents' death had left me with, that I began thinking about the rites and rituals that society has devised around deaths; I then recognized the validity of these rituals. These rituals help you come to terms with the fact that someone's life is over. A ritual on the third day, another on the eleventh, and on the fortieth day, you place a stone at the burial spot. Till then you are grieving. I started understanding the purpose of these rituals when I went through them. Now I see the validity of some of religion's higher-level functions. Now when I go home, every Friday I visit the mosque. Not so much to pray, but to visit my parents—to go to the place where they are resting, to stand there and talk to them.

4

MEDICAL MISADVENTURES: PAIN AND GAIN

I was very emotionally drained after my parents' demise. But things became much worse when my health also began to suffer. It began soon after Umma's death, while I was working on the film *Everybody Says I'm Fine*. Bappa passed away while I was doing the final sound mixing of this film.

It all started out innocuously enough. I usually get a bit hyper-active during a shoot. That was the first time I was shooting with Pooja Bhatt. She was a big star and at her peak during my student years. So, I was in a state of minor excitement. She was sitting at a glass coffee-table. In order to adjust something, just before a shot, I jumped across this table. In the process, I hit my knee on the corner of the table. It hurt very badly. I put some ice on the spot, and within two days the pain completely healed. The scene had also been shot. This was what I can remember about that injury.

I then decided to do some body-building hoping that it would generally improve the state of my mind and spirit. So I started to do some exercises. I started with a hundred sit-ups. After three or four days of exercise, one day when I got up from my sleep, I felt a pain in my knee.

I thought it must have to do with the strain of the exercise and carried on to the studio. The promo work for the same film was on. The studio was very cold. I got in at nine and by eleven, the pain became unbearable. I then went to Fireflys, Satheesh's studio, removed my pants and checked my knee. There was a swelling the size of a coconut. I informed Satheesh and took an appointment in the nearby hospital for six in the evening.

Satheesh came by three. I was crying out in pain by then. I couldn't even get up. I wanted to have a painkiller, but decided against it and endured the pain since I was going to see a doctor. Satheesh saw my state and immediately took me to the hospital. When the pain became absolutely unbearable, I sat there in the hospital and thought of Umma. Somewhere in that process, I forgot my pain.

The doctor came and checked my knee. He said that I had injured it and that fluid had swelled up inside. It was a condition called 'synovitis'. And 'aspiration' was what was needed to reduce the pain. This meant that the swelling had to be dug out. I was ready for anything to get rid of the pain. The doctor gave me a local anaesthesia and removed the swelling. He asked me to stay in the hospital for a couple of days.

After the removal of the swelling, I fell asleep the moment I hit the bed. I slept away that day and the next. For the last twenty-two days, I had been working like mad, more than twenty hours a day, sleeping only for less than four hours. Such incessant work must have been why my leg gave me trouble and I landed up in a hospital. Neither the producer nor director bothered to come and have a look. Perhaps they might not have wanted to disturb my sleep! That is the cinema industry of Mumbai. After three days, the director called and inquired whether I could resume work. It is cinema that's important, not human relationships. I then remembered what Zanussi had said when he had come to the Institute for a workshop. 'Not cinema, it's life that's important.' I really comprehended the depth of that statement then. It's only when you get a blow in life that you get to see certain truths.

The pain came down. I was discharged on the fourth day. I was asked to come back to the hospital after ten days of medication. That time, I was doing some work for MTV too. One day, during an MTV shoot the swelling and the pain reappeared. I went to the doctor again. He said, 'The swelling is not reducing, I'll give you medicines for another ten days, but don't have it beyond those ten days.'

I called up my cousin brother and asked his opinion. He, too, is a doctor. He asked about the dosage of the medicines. I told him it was for ten days and that the dosage would be reduced as the days passed.

'It's one course, try it out,' he said. Only later did I come to know about the problems with this medicine. It was a steroid. I faced a lot of complications in life later because of this medicine. This steroid increases your appetite like anything. So I started eating more, and became quite fat.

After ten days when the pain was gone, I started attending shoots again. There was an MTV live show, Brian Adams' concert. MTV insisted that the recording be done by either

Satheesh or me. Satheesh called me and said, 'Resul, I can't do this one, I'm out of town. You go. Your leg is also okay now. You just go and sit somewhere. For the rest, I'll send guys.'

I went. But I couldn't 'sit somewhere'. As I didn't trust anyone with the work, I did a lot of running around to make sure that everything was going okay. I also did a multi-track recording and gave them a great mix.

By the time I finished that project, my leg was in a really bad shape. I called my cousin brother. He asked me to get onto the next flight. So I went to Thiruvananthapuram and got admitted in the Uthradam Thirunal Hospital. They diagnosed it as a probable case of bone TB. If that was the case, I needed an open-knee surgery.

The term 'bone TB' brought to my mind an incident that had deeply saddened me. During the Gujarat earthquake, I had worked in Kutchch with the International Rescue Crew (IRC) from London. Our mission was to rescue the people trapped inside buildings. The Rescue Crew's method is to continue with the rescue operations till the point when the dead bodies start to decay. Then they leave—because that's when the epidemics start spreading. So we left the place after five days. There was also a friend of mine who had come to operate the ham radio—Deepa, a woman of incredible dedication. She worked day and night, running around all over the place. But when she left the place, she had already contracted tuberculosis, and later died in a hospital. This incident saddens me terribly. All of us had worked there without worrying about any dangers to our personal safety.

So when I heard that I probably had bone TB, I got scared.

I thought of Deepa. Then I started thinking that I might have got infected during the rescue mission. My cousin came and met the doctor who was treating me. Then he came and told me, 'Nothing to worry, man. You may actually pray that it is only tuberculosis, which is a matter of six months' treatment. Let's hope it's not anything else.' I didn't quite understand what he meant by the last part—*let's hope it's not anything else.* Anyway, we fixed a date for the operation. The day before the surgery, they ran a tuberculosis confirmation test. The result came in during the night. The nurse came and said, 'There's no need for the surgery tomorrow. The confirmation test has come out negative.'

The next day I was discharged. I was given some medicines and asked to take rest for three weeks. If the swelling didn't go down by then, there was one more test to be done. This was the first phase of my woes with my knee.

Then I started getting some sort of rashes all over me. Pimple-sized, they were all over—on my chest, back, shoulders . . . I had no idea what it was. I stayed back at home for twenty-one days. Everybody suggested their own course of treatment—Ayurveda, homeopathy . . . I couldn't decide what to go for. I couldn't figure out what was going on in my body. At home, Bappa was also in a bad shape. To make it worse, he was feeling bad seeing the shape I was in. So I decided it was not worth worrying him and I returned to Mumbai.

In between, I went and met a homeopath, Dr Chandrashekharan from Thiruvananthapuram. In many ways, this doctor played an important role in restoring my confidence in the way I conducted my life. There was another doctor too, Dr Bahuleyan.

Dr Chandrashekharan barred me from climbing steps, and he also gave me several other pieces of advice associated with lifestyle. He told me that if I lived following his instructions, in six months' time I would be fine; if not, I would be back at the hospital within those six months. Then he asked me, 'On which floor do you live?'

'On the fourth floor.'

He told me to shift as soon as I could.

But I found all these restrictions, like the one not to climb steps, rather funny. I quietly chuckled to myself, thinking, what did this doc know, as if it was easy to shift places in Mumbai. I also couldn't think of a life without steps. There are steps all around you. I even thought it could be a good idea for a film! Imagine living in a place like Mumbai without steps!

Sometimes, we think like that—we won't even be interested in believing that there is an alternative solution to a problem. Satheesh and I have given this subject a lot of thought. There are lots of solutions available to us, but we tend to disregard all of them with utter scorn. For example, we eat out for years and eventually damage our system. The simple solution is to employ a cook at home. But such solutions dawn on us only after we become chronically ill. All this stems from our desire, while young, to remain independent. There is a resistance to accept alternative solutions. In fact, what we proudly take to be a glamorous, rebellious attitude is nothing but a mistaken rigid pattern of thinking.

I came back to Mumbai and carried on climbing all the four floors. Sometimes, I used crutches. To cut the story short, eventually, Dr Chandrashekharan's prognosis came true. After twenty days, it showed. This time the pain came on the other leg. I didn't call Dr Chandrashekharan. I called the doctor of the Thirunal hospital where I had been admitted. He said it was arthritis. 'It is getting into your body cycle,' he said. 'This is not a good sign. Hadn't you been told not to do anything that's strenuous on the legs? There was no remedy for this other than taking it easy and resting. And you have to carry on taking all the prescribed medicines.'

I was faced with a panic situation. A lot of changes were taking place in my body. The rashes and pimples were not healing; they were only getting worse.

I called up Dr Chandrashekharan. He prescribed some medicines, but not before shouting at me. 'Didn't I tell you not to climb steps?'

But in 2000, by a stroke of good luck, Baiju Kalluvila came back into my life—as though sent by Allah Himself, like Umma would have described it. Baiju! My dear childhood friend and current manager of my affairs, the very original Baiju Kalluvila; my karate guru! During every crisis in my life, he has been present. And I had been present for his crises too. (Let me now digress a bit. I had informed Satheesh about my wedding only after I decided everything. Satheesh couldn't believe I was capable of such a thing. As for Baiju's wedding, he too told me about it only after everything was finalized. So what I did to Satheesh, I got back. The rewards and punishments of this life are not awarded in the afterlife. The judgement takes place right here in this life. You'll carry on getting exactly what you have been giving. So if you can make out why you are getting what you are getting, life becomes meaningful.)

At that time, Kalluvila had been working in a construction company in Bangalore, after returning from the Gulf. He had been earning good money. But when he heard I was ill, he chucked his job and came to attend to me. This is what human love and caring is all about. The earth is a sphere. It's constantly turning. There are some human beings on it. They make this life and this sphere go around by loving and helping each other. That's what Basheer said about life. And this has been a practical truth in my life. While the sphere rolled, my dear friend dropped out of nowhere to appear in front of me. Kalluvila then took over my life: cooking food, giving me medicines on time, taking me to the studio for work . . . Even from my own family, there was nobody to do all these for me. I am not saying that my family didn't support me; of course they did.

It was during this time when I was feeling empowered and emboldened by the help of Kalluvila and a walking stick, that the post-production work for the film, *Everybody Says I'm Fine*, came up. So I thought I might as well do the work. I would also be getting some money. Anyway, I was in no condition to work in outdoor locations—post-production work was the way for me. Satheesh was doing a film called *Agnivarsha* at that time. That, too, I agreed to do, working on dubbing and other such things. When I calculated my financial situation, I found out that there would be enough money coming in for the next five or six months.

When the swelling appeared on my other knee, the director of this film had suggested an orthopaedic. He was the same doctor who had spotted a fracture in Sachin Tendulker's leg. He asked me to do a blood test and meet him with the test report.

He couldn't find any sign of arthritis. He also said that my age ruled out such a condition. All tests to detect arthritis turned out to be negative. There was still the probability of a special condition called 'seronegative arthropathy'. So he suggested that I consult a rheumatologist, and referred me to one.

I was very depressed when I got back to my house that day. The next day I met the rheumatologist. He checked me and said that rheumatology is a vast science; there were a hundred kinds of arthritis; so to analyse my condition any more, we had to wait for another attack; for the time being, I should carry on with the present medication. I showed him the pimples and rashes that I had all over me. He immediately referred me to a skin specialist. Now just look at the situation I was in—I was getting passed around by many specialists, with nobody having anything comprehensive to say about my condition. I had no idea what was going on inside my body. I grew very tense.

That's when a friend of mine told me about Kottakkal Aryavaidyashala in Kerala. He told me that a lot of people went there with the kind of knee pain that I had, and he had seen them returning home happily after being able to walk following the treatment.

Immediately, I wrote to this place with all the details. They wrote back saying I should get there as soon as possible and not to delay any further. I made a booking for 10 September, thinking that I could finish the film that I was working on by then. Then I went to consult the skin specialist.

My work on the film was also carrying on amidst all this. And then Bappa died. By that time I was in such a state that I couldn't even move without a walking stick. I reached Kottakkal Aryavaidyashala on the evening of 9 September after attending my Bappa's eleventh-day rites.

At Kottakkal, they immediately started treating me for arthritis which didn't yield any results. The next week Dr P.K. Warrier came to check me. He scolded the other doctors. 'Just because the allopaths say it's arthritis, does it become arthritis? Don't we know the symptoms? Shouldn't you be considering those things before you decide on the treatment?'

He changed the course of my treatment. By the second week, I didn't need the crutches. I stayed there for a month—and I returned from there walking. That gave me an amazing boost of confidence. In fact, all my troubles had originated from my knee injury. I also came to know that the rashes and pimples on my skin were the side-effects of the steroids that I had to take.

While I was at Kottakkal, I read *Ashtanagahrudayam*. Also *Ashtangasamgraham*. But that I couldn't understand much. I can't understand if you tell me the composition of a medicine. Still, I figured out a lot of things by interacting with the doctors. By the second time I went there, I started understanding the process of Ayurveda much better. That's what got me into thinking more about illness and health.

I was never interested in the vernacular or folk medicines. I used to think that modern diagnosis was the ultimate thing. But my experience at Kottakkal dealt a big blow to that kind of thinking. It slowly dawned on me that there was a lot of wisdom in Ayurveda saying that man and nature are inter-related and that there should be an integration between the two. No more did I find it ridiculous that a remedy may lie in plucking a leaf and eating it. Dr P.K. Warrier enlightened me that there were no medicines for illnesses! All our illnesses, he said, emerged from eating the wrong things and not eating the right things. He also blamed our changed lifestyle for bringing about such a situation. What I was taking as medicines, he told me, were in fact only some stuff that my body required to regain its balance. The only effective remedy was to change the way we live, he added.

That was a huge realization for me. I returned to Mumbai riding on the kind of confidence that such wisdom had given me. Baiju was also there with me. When I reached Mumbai, I discovered that I had been practically written off: Resul's legs are gone; now he won't be able to do sync sound; he can't walk; he's finished! I wasn't there for some time, and so the industry decided I was finished.

But again, when life seemed bleak, good fortune intervened. That's when Kaizad Gustad called me and asked me to work on his film, *Boom*. I had seen him for the first time when I was in London to mix the film *Snip*. He had come to the studio many times to meet the film's director, Sunil Sippy. That's how I got contracted to do *Boom*—my first assignment with Amitabh Bachchan, and the first sync sound film I did after a long gap.

My attitude before going to Kottakkal Aryavaidyashala had been that my life was shattered, finished, and that I wouldn't be able to shoot any more. Yes, I had gone and done mixing in London and all that, but they had all become just memories. I had thought that I would have to lead a retired life, surviving on medication and diet. I had even thought of taking up a teaching job at the Institute. But the film *Boom* heralded a grand return and I was freed from all such regressive thoughts.

All through that difficult period, Satheesh, too, had been of great help, in giving me internal strength. When I would be stuck and penniless, he always found me some work. He would call me every day. We would almost always be together. I would accompany him for his shoot; even otherwise I would be around. When he drove, I would be the navigator. That's how I learned of Mumbai's roads and signals.

Satheesh would say, 'But Resul, for that right turn, you should be telling me when that signal comes, not now. What kind of a navigator are you!'

And I would reply, 'But Satheesh, how would I know of all this? I didn't even know there was any difference between yellow and red, remember? Did I ever even look at any signals?'

'Oh, yeah! That's right. Actually, there's no point blaming you!'

Oh, how many such things! Satheesh is such an integral part of my life.

*

Boom was my toughest film. The second schedule of the film was to be carried out in Dubai. That time, I was following a strict, uncompromising diet and a medication regime. So when it came to leaving for Dubai for the shoot, I was really worried about how I could take all those herbs, oils and concoctions to Dubai. If the airport authorities didn't like the herbs, I would be behind bars! The only valid document justifying me carrying the herbs was a prescription from Kottakkal. I would also have to carry another Ayurvedic medicine called *thikthamrutham* (bitter nectar). This nectar is incredibly bitter; I had to take it to reverse the effects on my auto-immune system which had gone crazy with all the steroids I had been consuming. I sent this substance to a lab in Bangalore and got a certificate saying that it contains such and such things. Then I proceeded gingerly towards Dubai. Luckily, nothing happened; nobody caught me. So I could continue with my medicinal oil bath at least once in a week as per the doctor's instructions, throughout the shooting schedule.

By the time I was going to London for a 'mix' after the Dubai shoot, I had recovered almost completely. While travelling in the London underground train, I thought about how a year ago, I could never have imagined that I would ever be able to walk without support, or travel abroad for work. That is life—that bouncing back is life! Being depressed is not going to take anyone anywhere. To be able to return to the full swing of life, like I did, gives one ultimate joy.

I never had to look back ever again. Now I know my body—I have learned about my body. I have developed a communication channel with my body. That is the biggest

secret of health. When something happens inside you, your
body will tell you about it. Don't ever turn a deaf ear to that.
It's like how we relate to nature. You should know this thing:
you are one thing; your body something else; but there's
communication between the two. Like there's a link between
you and nature. However, knowledge about such things is
not common. The fundamental principle of health is that
one should begin to understand one's body. With such a
realization, I started studying the human body. I also started
studying about all alternative medicines—from magnetic
therapy to acupuncture.

That said, I still make it a point to go and meet
Dr Chandrashekharan Nair, my homeopath from
Thiruvananthapuram. During each of my health crises, he
made it a point to explain to me what was what and how
something had happened.

I usually work till three or three-thirty in the morning and
sleep for four and a half hours. I enjoy this kind of a schedule.
For me, holidays or relaxation are not really enjoyable; work
is the ultimate enjoyment.

I started thinking a lot about medical science once I myself
was subjected to the phenomenon of pain. When you are
writhing in pain and get to a hospital, you see another guy
who has just survived a more intense pain. It puts you in a
meditative frame of mind. We can even overcome our pain by
observing our immediate surroundings.

After a lot of thought, I arrived at this important conclusion
about medical science: there can't be medicine without wisdom.
That was also precisely my problem with allopathic medicine.

The allopathic system may be great at diagnosis. It's very specific—it is capable of specifically pin-pointing the problem area. But the same excellence is absent in finding the right solution to the problem. Depending on who is doing the diagnosing, the remedy could change. Allopathy is a field where information and expertise combine, but that has got nothing to do with wisdom. During the days of my suffering, I felt that there was something wrong with modern medicine. I am sure that if I had started my Ayurvedic treatment six months earlier, my health wouldn't have deteriorated that much. I didn't do it then because of my blind dependence on modern medicine—for me, Ayurveda then was the jasmines in my front yard which had no smell.

As I started thinking deeper about medicine and health, I even contemplated whether I should formally learn some stream of alternative medicine. At one point, I almost did so. I thought it held a greater cause than doing sound for cinema. The medicinal field is ultimately about helping to heal the suffering. And when you are suffering pain, entertainment would be the last thing in your mind. That was how I looked at it. But then, I haven't been able to make time for such a study—I still think that I should take up this study so that I can have a practice once I retire from the cinema field.

*

You and your body are two different things. I had to scale many steps before I reached that state of enlightenment. But in the high of film-making, I would often forget to look at my body as a separate entity. Like we delay the paying back of the money borrowed from a close friend, we postpone the needs of our bodies. And I think that this syndrome prevails in our culture excessively. At the same time, dealing with these inter-relations and inherent paradoxes is the path to realizing such truths at a personal level. This kind of knowledge is not necessarily attained by reading or meditating in a closed room.

All I had to do while working on *Everybody Says I'm Fine* was to take some bed rest. If you are suffering from inflammation, it sustains as long as your body doesn't get enough time to recuperate. I was experiencing the continuous weakening of a joint. And I carried on dealing with it through some quick fixes.

And though proper treatment and rest have healed my knee, its joint remains weak. As a precaution, I still wear knee support while working. But once the work begins, I get hyper and the work becomes a physical activity for me. In a film shoot, if someone says he has nothing to do and it's boring, I would say he is not really working on that film. Because any shoot will require you to do so many things; you'll have no time to relax. During a shoot, my brain gets as active as my body. And my weak knee swells up at the slightest provocation of a strain. The frequency of such instances has been coming down steadily, though not my knee is fully healed.

I hadn't completely recovered when I was doing *Black*. In fact, it wasn't wise of me to do that film although it's the most magnificent piece of work that I have done in my entire career. You see, most of the film was shot in a two-storeyed house. So I had to constantly climb up and down. I handled

the whole shoot on heavy painkillers. It was a compromise
I made with my body. I have no theories to justify this
compromise. But it's these compromises that have brought
me to where I am in my life today. Maybe my Third World
cultural subconsciousness has played a role in helping me deal
with such compromises. That too has its value—sometimes
even more than that of Ayurveda!

Before *Black,* I had done a film called *Amu.* It was physically
a very exhausting shoot. Once we had to shoot a train
sequence in Delhi which lasted till two in the morning. The
train was stationed outside the platform areas. The crew had
placed a piece of stone for people to climb up and down the
train. When I was getting down, the stone flipped and I fell,
bruising my knee. Although I applied some medication, it
swelled up the next day. (I was a mobile Ayurvedic pharmacy
at that time, carrying with me all possible concoctions, oils
and ointments.) It was a weekend and there was no shoot
slated for the next two days. But the swelling didn't subside in
those two days; and it hurt very badly.

The pain was unimaginably intense. Indeed, after a point, I
couldn't register the climbing pain except with a constant stream
of tears. But as Umma would have it, Allah then sent somebody.

I called my then assistant Amla Poppuri and told her that
I was unable to move. She came and saw my knee and said,
'God, it's a huge swelling! My dad knows magnetic therapy. It
works for this kind of problem.'

I said, please call him.

The next day, Amla's parents arrived with some magnets.
They were staying in Delhi at that time–an hour and a half's

drive from our location. Her father touched my knee and fixed some magnetic pellets on it, telling me that it wasn't so bad and to let the magnet be there for a week. I had only heard of magnetic therapy till then and had no idea what the whole thing was about. The next day, I went to the shoot on crutches with a bandage over these magnets. With the crutches, the feet don't touch the ground and there won't be any strain on the knee and hence no inflammation. I always carry a pair of crutches for my shoots.

That day, I was shooting the toughest bit of the film. We were doing some clandestine shooting on a street outside Delhi's Jama Masjid. Though the film was fictional, we were shooting it in documentary style. I was in a severe state of pain—I couldn't walk or even stand. The street was extremely crowded. I set up my equipment inside a bangle shop and sat on a chair with my leg held ramrod straight. There was no way one could do any kind of crowd control there; a huge number of people were in a state of constant motion. We were taking a chance; there was no guarantee that we were going to get anything worthwhile.

That time my boom operator was a woman from Australia. After a few days of dealing with our schedules and our way of functioning, she couldn't handle it any more. She would come in the morning, pick up the call sheet, read through the scenes of the day and start crying—almost every day. While she wept, she would say this was not going to get over in ten hours; and she couldn't work for more than ten hours. It was unthinkable for her.

But for us, we could manage chaos, not order. We always

know that nothing is going to get finished according to the timetable. Ten hours would often become fifteen hours. We are also used to working eighteen–twenty hours non-stop. We have the mental strength to manage this.

So we were shooting in that narrow street. This was the scene which had the most critical dialogues of the film. The moment the shot was ready, I would jump into the street with my mike and recorder. Like guerrilla warriors, we would appear out of nowhere, take the shot, record the sound and disappear. Still, we couldn't control the overwhelming crowd from getting into the frame. Our attempts to block the crowd by forming a human chain also didn't work. People flowed through, breaking all barriers. The Australian boom lady started crying. Had it been an Indian in her place, he or she would have enjoyed the chaos and continued with the work. Although this lady was very sensible and excellent at her boom work, situations like this broke her down.

After the day's shoot was over, by evening there was considerable improvement in my leg's mobility. I was very surprised—how come? I checked my knee in the room. The swelling was gone–in one day! I couldn't believe it. Allopathy would have taken at least a week to get things to this shape. I was very fascinated.

The next week, the moment I got a break, I took off to meet Amla's father. He was a retired professor from Delhi University and a serious student of magnetic therapy. He was also treating people and treating himself for diabetes. It was very exciting visiting him at home. There was a magnetic bed at his home. He gave me some books and some advice on diet control. From then on, I started learning about this therapy. He told me that I had developed this condition because of excessive uric acid in my body and that I should get it checked. I hadn't known much about uric acid. The next time when the pain occurred, it reminded me of the uric acid levels in my blood. That was one more connection I discovered about my pain. In short, we ourselves have to figure our body out through many ways—who else would have the time for that? Now for minor pains, I do my own treatment.

There's another genre of alternative therapy that I have come to know about. I have a friend called Priya. One day she was looking stunningly beautiful. She was sparkling.

I asked her, 'Priya, what has happened to you? Are you in love?'

'Love is there at one side,' she replied.

It turned out that she was getting married in two weeks' time. Then I asked, 'But the wedding is yet to happen. Then how come you're glowing like this already?'

Then she revealed the secret. She was doing acupuncture. Cosmetic acupuncture!

She was preparing for her wedding.

I exclaimed, 'Ah! Is that so?'

As I still had rashes on my face after the allopathic treatment, I wanted to meet Priya's acupuncturist and get my face fixed.

So I went to meet Dr Jasmine. I narrated my entire medical history beginning with my birth. The knee still had some friction here and there. She administered an overall treatment regime for me, for a month. At the end of it, there was major improvement. Even the lost strength in my legs returned. After that, I haven't done any special treatment in this regard.

Acupuncture does something to the meridians of the body. Magnetic therapy, too, does a similar thing—it's on the same spots where they put the magnets that they stick the acupuncture needles. So both systems are aware of the relationship between health and the meridians. Nowadays, it's only acupuncture for me, for any ailment. When I spend one whole month working twenty hours a day, I usually go to this place and tell them that I hadn't slept for twenty-five days and that I need a shot. They would put in some needles and I would sleep there for a couple of hours. When I got up, I would feel such freshness, as if I had slept for a whole week.

5

TYING THE KNOT

One of my biggest joys has been finding a woman like Shadia. She came into my life at a time when I needed a companion the most. And to think that we came so close to not getting married!

But this story of how I met my wife begins long before I even met Shadia. Let me explain . . .

For a long time in Mumbai, I was not in love. Meanwhile, Satheesh was secretly trying to hook me up with an honest girl. Let's call her 'Sathyavati' for the time being. (Yes, that's all you need to know!) Sathyavati was a film enthusiast. The rest of the time she dreamt of America. For most young men and women who had moved to Bandra, America was the big dream. The thing between us never developed into a full-blown romance. The jottings in my diary, detailing how she didn't get the things I said, were all that came of it. But she became a very good friend.

I then became infatuated with a beautiful Brahmin girl whom I saw by chance during a film shoot. The very sight of her destroyed my sleep; I was lovestruck and my life became miserable. I discussed the matter with Satheesh. I didn't have Satheesh's sophistication in dealing with not only Brahmin girls, but girls of any caste or creed. I was straightforward and not interested in hanging around pretending to be in love. 'Can I marry you?' was the only relevant question with me.

One fine morning I was going for an MTV shoot. As I sat in the taxi looking at the Haji Ali mosque which always seems to move away from you as you get closer to it, I made a call to this Brahmin girl. I told her that I was seriously in love with her and asked her whether it was possible for me to marry her. At the end of a long pause, she said she would call me back later. That call never came.

Later, I called my scientific advisor, Satheesh, and reported the experience: 'The Brahmin girl has been sorted out.' I was feeling very light. After airing the whole news, I settled down like a deflated balloon. Peace once again prevailed in my life. It was no longer relevant whether she was interested in me or whether she would marry me. Getting myself to ground level was the most important thing for me.

Life flowed forward smoothly and uneventfully—until Umma's sudden demise. Within a year, Bappa too passed away. That was also the time when my leg was giving me serious problems. The foundations of my life had become shaky. The deaths of my parents proved to be a bigger shock than I could bear. I went into some sort of an unresponsive state. It took me a month and a half to get back to work. Then work became a hiding place from everything else. I developed an escapist attitude and decided never to get close to anyone, because I wouldn't be able to handle losing them. Eventually, all my family members started raising their concerns about me—that I was alone in Mumbai, didn't I need a companion? I maintained that I didn't need anybody else other than my brothers and sisters; it was for the betterment of their lives that I was living. I didn't have much money or anything—I was the sort who would spend all that one earned. I had looked after my parents as best as I could, and had taken care of their treatment. And before Bappa's death, I had even bought a property that Umma had liked very much. After doing all that, all I wanted was to continue in the same vein.

But my family would not give up on the subject of my marriage; the pressure kept mounting—get married, get married. You need company. To put an end to their constant nagging, one day I simply told them, 'Okay, go look for someone.' Immediately, my name was registered into a marriage bureau. Within a month, some letters and phone numbers arrived.

I was there when the letters came. They came into my hands. I didn't show them to anyone. Then a temptation crept in: I should check this out. It was some kind of curiosity to find out who had responded to me. It was for fun's sake.

I dialled the first number posing as my eldest brother. It was a girl from Thiruvananthapuram, studying for MBBS. The father picked up the phone. I said it was for my younger brother who was a sound engineer. He said, 'Oh, my son is also an engineer, you please speak with him. I have no clue what this sound engineering and all is.'

The son came on the line. He, too, had no clue about

sound engineering. I went eloquent and the boy got super impressed. They wanted to come and meet me. I realized the danger in this. So, like an elder brother, I managed to get things under control by saying, 'Let me discuss this with the boy and get back to you.'

I moved on to the next number. It was to Hyderabad. Once again, it was the girl's dad who picked up the phone. I was again posing as my eldest brother. As the conversation progressed, a question came from him: 'Sunni or Shia?'

Oh, there were such things too, I realized. I was caught off guard, so I went on to say, 'Shia.'

'Oh, Shia? Then we are not interested.' He put the phone down.

I put the phone down and wondered, I don't even know whether I am Sunni or Shia. Then why am I even thinking of marriage?

After a couple of such fun incidents, I disappeared from home. I didn't tell anybody about those phone calls. In Mumbai, Baiju Kalluvila would read aloud from the Grooms Wanted section of the matrimonial columns every day, looking at me pointedly all the while. I would usually ignore him, and continue brushing my teeth or combing my hair.

Baiju too, was calling up a few places posing as my brother. One day he made a call to a house in Trombay, a Mumbai suburb. The girl was studying for MBBS, and her mother was a relative of a distant relative of Mammooty, the Malayalam movie superstar.

I thought, very well, I have no job or any regular income, might as well marry the MBBS; at least I will get free medicine in my old age. Kalluvila, posing as my eldest brother, poured eloquent praises about me. He thought that if these people were relatives of Mammooty, they wouldn't mind marrying off the daughter to somebody from the film industry. Actually, two proposals had earlier been rejected after the girl's family found out that I worked in the film industry. One of them had said that even if the boy was a clerk, they wouldn't mind as long as it was a government job, but no way did they want a cinema guy. I had narrated this incident to Baiju, telling him that the chances were slim for a cinema guy to find a girl to marry; that we needed to be careful about how we described my job. Now I hope that after my Oscar victory, things may change dramatically for sound engineers. In fact, a sound engineer colleague who was unmarried recently called and told me that he would benefit from my Oscar as it won't be difficult any more to find a girl to marry.

Anyway, with this Mammooty relative, Kalluvila's calculations were that my film background would not be a liability. He held talks with the girl's mother. She was also very excited. He then agreed to present me in person. I asked him, 'You are totally off your head or what? Let's first check the girl out.'

He didn't listen. He fixed a day to produce me in front of them and even organized a car to take me there. Then a phone call came. It was the girl's dad. I happened to pick up the call. We talked about many things. I told him in detail about the sound library I had released. I explained my future research plans.

Then he said, 'See, this girl is studying for MBBS. We are actually more interested in a marriage into a doctor family.'

I said, 'Ah! Yes, okay.'

Kalluvila couldn't believe what had happened. He called the girl's mom the next morning. She told him, 'Even if this wedding doesn't happen, we should remain good friends.'

Secretly, I had hoped that the wedding wouldn't happen. I now also had an excuse: see, I tried; now nothing is going to happen; leave me alone.

Back I went to my carefree life.

*

One day a call came from my second brother-in-law: 'Son, we are in a house in Thiruvananthapuram, regarding a proposal. The girl's dad has spoken to Babukka. He came home too. He is interested in our situation. We have come to meet them. The father is a doctor, and Umma an advocate. The girl has finished her MBA and is working in the Techno Park. She has a younger sister . . .'

Apparently, in the course of the conversation, the girl's parents mentioned that they were distantly related to the famous Malayalam director, Fazil. Then my brother-in-law told them that if they needed to know anything more about me, they just had to ask Mammooty.

Now, yes, I had met Mammooty once. This was when I had sworn to make a film based on Anand's *Govardhan's Travels*, which I had absolutely loved. I had once even met both Anand and Mammooty to discuss the possibility of a film. But that was it. In fact, I felt that Mammooty might not even remember the meeting.

Either way, the girl's family was suitably impressed. I was told that I had to go and see the girl as soon as possible since her father, who worked elsewhere and had returned home for a short while, needed to go back to his workplace soon. But I was busy with work then, spending my time between Rajasthan and Hyderabad. So the girl's dad went back. However, I started getting incessant calls from home to please come and see the girl. So I landed up home completely unaware of the seriousness of the situation. I had gone there to just put an end to the nuisance of the daily phone calls. I hadn't even discussed the matter with Satheesh. Otherwise, these kinds of things were always discussed with Satheesh. At home, I was in a totally relaxed mode. But soon I realized that things were getting messy.

I went to Thiruvananthapuram and straight to the house of Chandramohanan Nair, the professor who had taught us acting. I told him that things were getting messy and that I had been dragged there. I explained that I had come to his place to have a bath in peace.

He said, 'Sure, go have a bath.'

When I met him after I had my bath, he told me, 'Of course, it is needed; marriage is a necessity.' After giving that precious pearl of wisdom, he presented his calculations: 'See, Resul, you said the girl's mom is an advocate, right? That makes her at least about fifty years, which means she has been practised law for at least twenty-five years. Imagine around thirty to thirty-two years ago, a girl from a Muslim family going and studying law! Hers must be a very evolved family. You know what I mean, no? These are things which we should really think about. I don't think there's any problem in getting involved with this family. And the dad is a doctor, you said. Ah! So whichever way you look at it, you are getting into a family that's not bad at all. Even you are pretty educated and all, aren't you? Then what's the problem? Marriage is something we have to do at some point or the other; very essential, really. Come, let's have a cup of coffee.'

He thoroughly brainwashed me. I got very confused. As I was listening to him, I had some intensely filmy expressions on me, but they were of not much help. I went home and asked Kochumon, 'Hey, what are you guys planning?'

He said, 'Come, let's go and have a look.'

So, the next day we organized a car and went to 'have a look' at the girl. I was accompanied by Kochumon, Saif and my second brother-in-law.

This girl's family had suffered a tragedy just a week before. One of her cousins, a young boy, was killed in a bike accident. So when we reached their house, the atmosphere was restrained. There was none of the cheer and festivity usually associated with the occasion of the first meeting of a prospective couple. We walked into a big house with almost nobody around. I felt very strange. I never thought I'd be in a situation like this, ever. I sat very quietly. Kochumon was all eyes and ears, checking out all the possible details.

The girl was called in soon. That was the first time I saw Shadia. Suddenly I felt terrible about the circumstances under which we were meeting—four or five guys sitting and calling a girl out from her room, and then proceeding to stare at her from top to bottom! I lost all respect for myself. Am I really this kind of a person? Up until that moment, I had been regarding the whole thing as some kind of entertainment. That moment I grasped the seriousness of the situation, and felt myself shrinking to the size of a worm. I had always maintained sublime notions about humanity and women. But look at me; here I had made a girl present herself to four strangers for examination. This, I felt, was very demeaning for a woman. This was the yes or no binary situation in a girl's life. If I say yes, this wedding will happen; otherwise no. I had that power; but on what right, on what basis? And I had brought myself to this state of being. I couldn't feel worse.

Then the people announced that we could talk to each other if we felt like it. That also bothered me. What am I going to tell her? I hadn't even seen this girl before; she hadn't seen me either. What kind of a conversation can we have; that too, when all these guys around are keeping an eye on us from different corners?

Despite my discomfort, I somehow managed to ask a couple of questions. But I knew I had to get out of there as quickly as possible. I got inside the car. The guys must have noticed my expression; nobody said anything to me till we reached home. At home too, nobody said anything. The question came the next morning. I said I had no opinions.

I had decided by the time I left her house that I had lost my moral right to say yes or no to her because I had dragged her into a situation like that. The fact that I had gone there showed my willingness to marry her. That was my responsibility. But by being an accomplice in dragging her into that situation, I had lost all voice to express my opinion. The right to say yes or no belonged to her alone. I took the serious decision that it was going to be her choice. Now I needed to know whether she liked me or not.

I dialled her home number. Her mother picked up the phone. I said I wanted to have a word with Shadia. I was told Shadia was not at home. After I put down the phone, the mother called back. It was my sister who picked up the phone. She asked my sister to tell me not to ring Shadia up like that. All that could be done only after an engagement, she said. I got very pissed off. I needed to talk to her even to decide whether there should be any engagement. I was really enraged.

Five days after I reached Mumbai, I got an email from Shadia's father. He had come to know that I had tried calling Shadia and what her mom had told my sister. He wrote that he didn't have any problem with me calling or talking to Shadia (their apprehensions had arisen from the fact that I was a cinema guy). But I shouldn't be giving Shadia false hope by those phone calls. That line, 'don't give my daughter false hope', touched something deep in my heart.

He was entirely justified in saying so. This was a father's way of expressing his concern for his daughter. I felt really bad about the way I had been reacting. Probably, I had overreacted.

Still the decision had to come from Shadia. With her mother, I couldn't have any communication. I sent a friend to Shadia's office. He told her, 'I have come with a request from Resul; he wants to talk to you personally. You have not been reachable through the home phone. So would you give your mobile number?' He got the number from her.

But like an idiot, Shadia went and reported everything to her mother, who immediately called my sister and complained about me—how I was sending my friends as messengers and how it was not proper to do so; she told my sister to please tell me not to do such things.

Whattheheck! Theseguysweregettingitallcompletelywrong. I was doing something which I thought to be the right thing. Anyway, whatever might happen, I needed to talk to Shadia.

So I called and spoke to her. I tried to tell her about the kind of guy I was, what I did for a living, what my views on life were, and how cinema was more important than life. Would she be interested in living with a guy like this? I wanted an answer from her. I don't remember her reaction. However, I think I got the feeling that cinema was not the most important thing for her. But over the next six or seven months, we were in touch via emails and telephone.

In the meantime, Shadia's father had sent me a couple of emails. Everyone was getting concerned about my decision. I wasn't saying anything to anyone. One day, my eldest brother-in-law and Saif called me up. They asked me, 'So what's the plan? All of us would like to see this wedding happening soon, what do you say?'

'I'll let you all know when it's time.'

'What are you saying! It's already been almost a year. How long can it go on like this?'

I said, 'Haven't arrived at any decision yet.'

'You or she?'

'We will talk about it later, okay?'

'No, no. Tell us, what seems to be the problem?'

I made a request to them to not please push me into anything, and that I would tell them when I was ready.

'Okay, then shall we go and look at some other girls?'

'No, no, no! Don't look at any more girls. Just sit and relax.'

Shortly after, I went to do a film called *Matrubhoomi: A Nation without Women*. Just before that, Shadia had asked me what my plans were and how I viewed the whole situation. I told her that I was going for this shoot, and would talk about the matter once I was back. When I returned to Thiruvananthapuram after the shoot, we planned a secret date. So we met and talked. Afterwards, I proceeded to the Ayurvedic hospital for my treatment. Babukka accompanied me. After we reached, and when Babukka was about to leave for the journey home, he said to me very pointedly, 'See, Kochi is on my way.'

'Yes, sure it is! Or has the city changed its position recently?'

'It's not a joke. The girl's uncle lives in Kochi. I had told them I would find out about your plans and meet them on my way back.'

'Why the hell do you take up such responsibilities without consulting me?'

'No, no. You see, we should have a clear opinion, right?'

'You don't worry about all that. Opinion and all I will let everyone know when it's time. Please don't take up any useless errands like this again.'

Since I was planning a film script based on *Govardhan's Travels*, along with Mahesh, I thought it would be a good idea to send Shadia a copy of the novel. I asked her to read it and let me know what she thought of it. She tried really hard for almost a whole week and managed to go through some twelve pages. She then called me and asked me not to give such hard tests; there was no way she was going to finish the whole book; and please forget about the marriage if her reading and completing the book was any criterion.

Even I felt that it was a bit too hard; that I shouldn't get too stubborn on this; I should have a bit of humaneness and compassion in life. Still, I wanted the decision about marriage to come from her side. But in the end, one day out of the blue, I called her up and asked whether she was interested in marrying me.

'Yes,' she said.

'I hope you know my situation and nature of work completely. After all that I have been trying to tell you over the last one year, you still want to come with me? Whatever happens, I want this marriage to be with your full consent. Because I have nothing to say any more, I want your decision.'

'My interest and consent is full and final,' she said.

I called up home and told them that the marriage was okay with me.

A volley of phone calls ensued. My second brother-in-law called Shadia's father and informed him. The engagement was set in two weeks.

I issued special instructions for everyone in my family: no one should say a word or anything about dowry or any kind of money transactions; they would give their girl what she needed, and no one should interfere. But somehow, my instructions didn't reach my uncles. They were out to cut a deal for me, saying that I was the most educated guy in the family, the nicest guy around, that this would be the last wedding involving the siblings in the family, and that I had lost both my parents.

'So standing in his parents' position, I am telling you, the boy should be rewarded appropriately.' This bomb was dropped by one of my uncles. My uncles are loose cannons, completely capable of blowing up anything.

Saif consoled me, 'Whatever he said has been said, we can't do a thing about it. Our uncles have no sense.' Luckily, things didn't develop any further in those directions.

The wedding or nikah took place on 18 August 2003. The nikah is an agreement that the boy makes with the father of the girl. This is followed by the tying of *thali*, the traditional pendant of matrimony, and then an exchange of floral garlands. These last two things are part of general Kerala traditions and not particularly Islamic. While the nikah happened at home, the rest of the ceremony took place at a public auditorium. We had called a lot of people since this was the last wedding in my family. There were a lot of people from Mumbai, including Satheesh.

We went home after the wedding, then immediately moved to the girl's house and stayed put for seven days, just as the custom dictated. Guys like me usually run off after three days.

Those days I was strictly following the diet prescribed by my Ayurvedic treatment. Nothing fried or grilled; nothing sour or spicy; just fruits for breakfast. I had become a pure vegetarian! Not even eggs, and only the water of milk. Also, no listening to loud sounds, or looking at brightly coloured silk cloth. I was practising a radically extreme sort of vegetarianism!

But in Shadia's house, nobody ate vegetarian food. So much so that I should say even for seasoning, instead of mustard seeds, they might be using some kind of tiny fish! The dinner spread on my first night there was as follows: mutton, beef, eggs, chicken, pomfret, prawns, salmon, kingfish, mackerel, dry prawn chutney, dry fish soup . . . A sumptuous non-vegetarian fare. After a hi-resolution scanning, I located a plate of chapattis. I announced, in a rather loud voice, without taking my eyes off the chapattis: 'I must get vegetarian food; that too, freshly made.' I had clear instructions from the doctor not to eat anything that was not cooked freshly. Even the sambar from the lunch wouldn't do.

Shadia immediately got up and said she would prepare something herself, quickly. I was completely unaware that she couldn't even boil water to save her life.

She asked me, 'What will you have?'

I said, 'Do something with some onions and tomatoes. Don't put red chillies, use black pepper instead.'

She disappeared into the innards of the house and reappeared after ten minutes with a dish in hand, in my favourite colour, sparkling black. I lovingly tore a piece of chapatti and softly dipped it in the curry and put it in my smiling mouth. In a split second, the secret of the black colour was revealed. It was ungarbled pepper that had been added only for the colour. Besides, the concoction was a super-saturated solution of salt. I didn't say anything. I didn't want to have the reputation of a fussy groom on the very first night at the in-laws' house. All I could do was to resign myself to my fate and behave like a gentleman.

I lived there happily for another three days feeding on salt, ginger, curry leaves and pepper. The third day we set off to Vilakkupara, in our new car. Apart from the newlyweds, the car carried lots of small kids, a sister-in-law and Saif, who was doing the driving. As an experienced driver and as someone who drove around in big vehicles, my small car must have felt like a toy to him. At around eleven in the night, we stopped for fuel and then continued. I was sleeping. Suddenly, I was jolted out of my sleep by a sound—the car had crashed into a farm wall, knocked down a post, and somehow stopped a few inches short of crashing into a tree. Though it was a pretty serious accident, because of the car's strong build, nobody was seriously injured. But Shadia's legs got jammed as the driver's seat got pushed into the back seat. She was crying in pain. I was thinking how, after all the confusions before the marriage, it had to now lead to a car crash. Shadia's mom went hysterical when she heard about the accident. She wanted to see her daughter immediately. We went back to Thiruvananthapuram the next day, got her legs X-rayed, and rested for another week.

The car had been bought precisely for the big occasion of the wedding. So when the accident happened, the car's insurance period had not matured. The travails of getting the insurance money would read like a thriller story. The ensuing events were exemplary proof as to why no one should insure their vehicle in this country. If something happens to you or your vehicle in an accident, repairing the damage may involve a couple of lakh rupees as expenditure. But you have to first make this money yourself and do the payment and then submit the bill to the insurance guys. They will look at the bills and cut out all the expenses they think were unnecessary and give you a reduced amount. That's how insurance works in this country. It was a long legal battle. Just the air fare to send Shadia from Mumbai for the insurance case came to a huge amount.

After three weeks of wedded life, my savings dried up. I came straight back to Mumbai, accompanied by my wife. Shadia's first night in Mumbai turned out to be quite something.

Upon reaching Mumbai at around ten thirty in the night, I immediately got a call. The censor board had asked for some changes in the film *Boom*. I *had* to be there. I told Shadia that I would be back soon and left. I could only come back the next evening at six. There had been no drinking water at home. As for food, there had been some rava and one tomato. The next morning I had not been able to get through to Shadia because the phone was dead. I had sent home some bread, eggs, milk and water through someone. When I came in the evening, she told me that someone had come and knocked a lot on the door and windows, but she had not opened the door. This was the guy I sent. So, she had spent a whole day without even a drop of water—but she didn't complain. Later she would say, 'Resul then realized there would be no problem if he were to leave me alone at home.' Since then, I should say that this lady has donated to me, without any protestations, an infinite amount of her time.

Our house in Mumbai was as big as the servant's quarter of Shadia's house, if not smaller. There weren't even any vessels in the kitchen. Luckily, the poor thing didn't know how to cook.

All she had to do in her earlier life was to utter words like tea, omelette or dosa and they would all come flying to her. There were three or four servants at her home. Then imagine her plight in Mumbai living in such circumstances.

It was I who taught her how to make tea. And that, too, with the full theory of it. She still hasn't understood the theory part!

This is how I explained to her the theory: if you need to make two cups of tea, you have to take one and a half cup of water and add two teaspoons of sugar to it. Then I asked her why the water had to be boiled with the sugar in it and not without.

'How do I know?'

I explained the whole science of it: 'When we add milk to water, it becomes thin milk. The boiling point also changes. It will then become the boiling point of watery milk, somewhere between water and milk. So that's not the way to go about it. Instead, boil the water with sugar in it. The sugar increases the boiling point. That much more germs will perish. Then add half a cup of milk into it. Then it will boil over once more. Stir the potion and add two teaspoons of tea. Watch it for a few seconds. The tea will rise, then put a lid on the whole thing and turn off the fire. Keep it like that for a minute. That way the essence of the tea is retained. Then open the lid, stir it once again and pour it into cups through a clean strainer, and drink while it's hot.'

But despite such a lecture and even a demonstration, I haven't yet got a cup of tea from Shadia that was made on these lines.

These things were happening much the same way that Vaikom Muhammad Basheer had once mentioned. He had put it quite succinctly: you can't make women do something according to the way you had instructed or explained; submit to what they do and go along with it; don't even ever hope that some day they would do things as you desire; a woman is a 'Hunthrappy Bussota'; don't even try to understand them.

That's true in my experience. I have never got a cup of tea in line with my theory. Still, every morning after giving me tea, she would ask, 'How is it?'

My opinion would be unutterable.

But this woman, who once didn't even know how to make a cup of tea, is now a first-rate expert cook. But that had cost me a lot of money in telephone bills. She would put water on the stove and call her mother, 'Umma, how do you make fish curry?' If the mother's instruction was to wait till the dish cooled off before covering it with a lid, the phone would be disconnected only after the lid had been laid on the sufficiently cooled dish. That was a time when long-distance phone calls were expensive. With that money, I could have easily ordered food home from some five-star restaurant.

But now the situation is that friends call to find out when Shadia is making the next biryani, and whether they can come. Today her biryani and some other dishes are quite famous. But the tea is still far from perfect, the one thing I had taught her! Here let me share with you a pearl of marital wisdom: don't ever try to teach your wife anything.

*

After my Oscar victory, newspaper guys would call and ask me to give my opinions on anything and everything. One magazine wanted to find out why I love women and my notions about women. I was asked to submit my views in writing!

As far as I was concerned, if a man doesn't love a woman, who would he love? It's a natural thing. At the same time, it's not that simple either. There are a million sub-clauses. I had to write something. So I decided to write about femininity. 'Yielding water is a feminine character. All concave surfaces—the valley, the pit and the dunes are all feminine in nature.' I shot some lines like that and added that femininity is what writer Kamala Das was about, it's what Mehak—the character of my film *Papu Can't Dance Sala*—is about, and it's what Neeta of *Meghe Dhaka Tara* is about. I also quoted from Basheer, saying that a woman is a 'Hunthrappy Bussota'.

I read this out to my wife.

'Oh! So it's Kamala Das, not me!' And she walked off in a huff. I called out after her, 'Hunthrappy Bussota!'

She came back casually and asked, 'Hunthrappy Bussota? What's that? Why don't you go and pay the electricity bill?'

My salutes to the great Basheer. A woman is indeed an unpredictable wonder. She changes colour just like that. So does her personality. Shadia is not the same person after marriage. She had changed almost instantly. After motherhood, things are even more different. The husband doesn't feature in her scheme of things any more—I should consider myself lucky if I am acknowledged at all. Shadia now says that Resul is her third child.

I, too, try to tell her the same thing, except that she wouldn't listen. We have a fourteen-month-old daughter. She falls while trying to walk. Then Shadia would shout at her, 'Didn't I just tell you to sit there quietly?' She doesn't get the irony of it all. There is not much difference between fourteen-month-old Mia and her mother than in physical size.

And I know it wouldn't end here either. After, say, another five years, I would have to be the arbitrator in the fights between these two. I am sure Shadia would come to me and say, 'See what she told me when I told her to do that. This is what she did when I told her to do that . . .'

Rest assured, there would be big fights between them in the future. But between Monu and Mia, I don't expect any major fights. But in order to broker peace in the war that would break out between these two women in my life, I may need to take semi-retirement in five years' time. That's one thing I have firmly figured out the way my married life has been going.

*

After my stint at Kottakkal, my body recovered, and I began living healthily. And once my wife and kids came into the picture, my health improved even more. At the same time, there was a psychological reorientation that helped.

Now in my life, yes, there's a bit of tension—about my kids. Shadia is with them full-time. She doesn't get unnecessarily worried when they trip and fall; but usually I get only an hour to spend with them, and I get very worried when they fall down even once. So you could say that having a wife and kids somehow brings in the fear element—I am always wondering and worrying about my kids. So, whenever some major work comes up for me, Shadia and the kids proceed on a vacation. Then I feel no tension. I just have to look after my work. But I am getting such time for my work entirely because Shadia has been very gracefully giving it to me. That's something fantastic. You need to be blessed to get someone like that as a life partner. Ultimately, the real secret behind good health is a combination of your own knowledge about your body and the presence of someone who knows you really well.

6

WORKING WITH AMITABH BACHCHAN: FROM *BOOM* TO *BLACK*

My sweetest memories of Hindi cinema are about Amitabh Bachchan—Bollywood's biggest living legend.

It was for the film *Boom* that I first worked with Amitabh Bachchan. The shoot was happening at a place called Raz al-Khaimah in Dubai. It was the first time I was going to use the microphone on him. He gave me a look, a full-body scan.

'What, yaar?'

'Need to do the mike,' I said.

'I am Amitabh Bachchan. Why do you need to mike me?'

Amitabh Bachchan knows too well that he is a major phenomenon. And he always has some fun with that idea. He has fun watching people's reactions to his presence. Once, during another shoot, he had come to the set. A kid, the son of a production assistant, had come there to see Amitabh Bachchan, but for some reason, the kid had started crying when Amitabh Bachchan walked in.

'Who is this kid, yaar?

People rushed to the scene to make the kid disappear instantly.

'See! It's Bachchan! See the star power!'

This is how he deals with such situations. In fact, he's a tender-hearted man. He will play these games with you and arrive at an impression about you on the basis of how you react.

So, there he was, running a full scan on me. As if asking, who's this dude, recording ambience and stuff?

The shoot was taking place in a closed room. So if you switched off the air conditioner there, it would be boiling hot. But the AC's noise was going to be problematic for sync sound. However, it was a sure thing that Bachchan would be pissed off if we switched off the AC.

I told the director that there was no other way but to shut off the AC. He said I should tell Bachchan that. No one had the guts to break the news to him.

I didn't say anything to anyone. We started shooting without the AC. In a few moments:

'Hey! It's too hot; what is happening! Isn't the AC working?'

'Sir, the AC has been switched off.'

'What? Why has it been switched off?'

'The sound guys said the AC has to be switched off.'

'Who?'

The ball had now fallen into my court. I should do the explaining. That is his game. If the director had first explained to him that the AC would be switched off for sound recording, the problem would have ended there. But the director had not been very enthusiastic about that role; he had been very reluctant to take that responsibility. Then I marched up to the front and declared: 'Running the AC during sync sound recording is out of question.'

'No problem, I will dub,' said Bachchan.

I said, 'Whether to dub or not and all are later considerations. It is not a good practice to decide right at the shoot itself that the scene was going to be dubbed later. There's no way we can have the AC on.'

The whole unit was suspended in pin-drop silence. Bachchan ran another full-body scan on me: an undersized human being with a beard. I then said that we would switch off the AC only during the actual take.'

'It's too hot! It won't work, my friend, it won't!'

I called out: 'Production, bring a cooler here.'

I had the solution ready: a cooler at hand to be switched off only during the take. That way, he wouldn't feel too uncomfortable with the heat. He gave me one more scan. Then he turned to his make-up man and said, 'Hey, note this fellow's address, telephone, fax number, everything.'

It meant he liked me. He realized I was serious and that I would be able to come up with a solution if a problem cropped up. He was also having his fun. But I didn't know that. I went straight to the make-up man and gave him my phone number (022-2673 . . .) and my complete address. I had no fax with me. And Bachchan was laughing big time all the while. That was my first encounter with the phenomenon called Amitabh Bachchan.

Another encounter happened on the same day. Bachchan has this habit of practising on his own. He would learn his lines while sitting or walking. My method is to have a rehearsal before the actual recording. So I asked him whether he would give me a rehearsal. He did. I listened to everything closely and recorded it. Then I listened to the recording. That's my recording method. I listen to something naturally, then check how it sounds through the mike and then do the final mike configuration based on that comparison. He was watching all this. But when it came to the take, his performance was different. I said this take was not good. He asked me why.

I told him that his performance in the take was not the same as what he had given me during the rehearsal. And that I was recording according to what I had heard in the rehearsal. My process is to analyse the internal balance of a scene against what happens to it when comes through the system, see if the changes are justified and then record accordingly. I told him all this. 'If I don't understand your performance,' I said, 'I won't be able to do justice to it. In other words, it would mean you are not allowing me to do my work.'

He was stunned. Maybe it was the first time a technician was talking to him like that. I explained to him my problem. I told the same thing to the director. He said, 'Man, all that stuff is your look-out; it's not nice to drag me into all these things.' Bachchan heard me out. He realized what I was dealing with. After that, till date, he has always given me proper rehearsals, and after a take, would check with me whether it was okay.

Bachchan always comes very well prepared and rehearsed. His lines for tomorrow's shoot have to be given to him tonight. If you change the lines after that, there will be a problem. He is also very careful about anything in those lines that doesn't suit his image. He won't say anything that's not politically correct. (Nowadays, even I can understand these things a bit. With my sudden prominence in the wake of my Oscar win, many harmless things that I have said have been taken with undue sensitivity by many people.)

If there would be any change in dialogue, Bachchan would give another kind of performance. Sometimes he would say, 'Hey, I won't say it if the dialogue is changed. First go and ask the bearded guy. If he says so, I will say it.'

That would bring the director to me, asking me to ask him. All of this was a game for him. It created lot of fun and excitement for me too. I don't think there is anybody else I enjoyed working with, more than Mr Bachchan. Despite his intimidation games, there is still nobody who loved you so intensely and had such respect for your work, even if you were young and new.

*

When Bachchan heard that *Black* was going to be in sync sound, he told me, '*Arrey yaar,* I just finished one film in this so-called sync sound. I speak from here, but the final voice will be heard as if it's coming from some ditch. Shouldn't we reconsider?' The sound in that particular film he was talking about was done by someone else. Now it is true that, when using sync sound, there are instances when the dialogue wouldn't be clear or audible. That had to do with improper post-production arrangements; if the post-production part is not done properly, sync sound can turn very bad.

One of Bachchan's prime concerns is that all that he does should reach the audience. He insists that every nuance of his voice should reach the audience. He suggested that maybe it would be better to dub *Black*. His performance in *Black* was phenomenal. At the preview, when the film got over, he began weeping uncontrollably in his seat. (If you talk about Bachchan's persona, you have to say that it has the innocence of a small baby. A politically correct baby, though!) No one knew what to tell him. I was standing slightly away in one corner. I was the junior-most member of the team. He came running to me, lifted me off the ground, hugged me and said, 'What brilliant work you have done! Everything can be heard, even the sound of my breath! What a great work!'

I have never felt happier. And no work has given me more satisfaction.

He was overwhelmed with joy and had no clue about what to do with himself. 'Come on, let's have coffee,' he said. It was two in the morning. He brought us all from the Film City to a star hotel in Juhu. When we walked in, the hotel guys informed us that the coffee shop was shut.

'What do you mean, shut! Call the chef. Amitabh Bachchan has come! What are you talking about, man! Call everyone.'

We were quite a group; apart from Bachchan and myself, there were Jayaji, Bhansali, Ravi K. Chandran, actors Rani Mukherji and Sonam Kapur, Bachchan's friend Sunil Doshi and his wife. Before the coffee came, a crowd started assembling around. Then he said we should move from there. 'Let's go home. We can sit and talk in peace.'

We got out from there. His home was nearby in Juhu. He suggested that we all walk. Amitabh Bachchan walked in front, with all of us behind in one neat line. He turned around and said, '*Arrey*! Walk with me, folks! Can Bachchan ever walk alone?'

At home, the security guys were all in deep sleep. They hadn't heard any car coming. He walked in and woke everyone up. 'Get up, everyone! Come here. Make some food!' Jayaji intervened and tried to get the situation under control. 'Relax, relax,' she said. 'Everybody's sleeping, let them sleep.'

'Okay, yaar,' came the prompt agreement from Bachchan, quickly switching to the role of the husband at home.

By then, it would have been half past three in the morning. Abhishek also arrived. Lots of chatting took place. By seven in the morning, breakfast came. When it became time to go, Bachchan woke up his driver and asked him to drop me home. But I didn't feel very confident about getting into his car, so I got into Ravi K. Chandran's car. That morning, the morning walkers of Juhu saw the entire Bachchan family on the road; and Amitabh Bachchan seeing off a small man to a car.

That breakfast was an unforgettable experience. An event to wipe clean all the many distasteful experiences I have had in this industry.

That night when I was walking with Bachchan in Juhu, we talked about many things about cinema. I explained to him that several of the powerful scenes of *Black* were not done with music, but with sound design. I still can see his face vividly in my mind, carefully listening to me while walking along. In fact, he is someone who likes sync sound very much. He comes from that era of film-making. He knows precisely what to do in sync sound—where and how to modulate his voice, and so on.

When I was working on *Black*, he presented me a book. A volume published on the occasion of his sixtieth birthday. He wrote on it: *It's a privilege to work with you.* I was incredibly touched. I said, 'Sir, you are giving me an honour by saying you consider it as a privilege to work with me! It touches me deeply.'

He replied, 'It's not like that. I am not looking at how young you are or anything. I learn many things from you. I get to learn many new things by working with younger people. That's what I meant by privilege.'

*

Amitabh Bachchan has a very clear understanding of the scope and limitations of cinema as a medium. So he is relentlessly learning and thinking about how to go about his profession. Often, young newcomers don't understand the value of such an exercise. Hindi cinema is a gathering of untrained actors. Moreover, here, the kind of training that takes place does not have much to do with the technical knowledge of the actor's craft. Here, what the youngsters who undergo training to be actors learn is—to do stunts, drive, ride horses, dance, etc. And most important of all—body-building. I can tell you one reason why Dev Patel was selected for *Slumdog Millionaire*. When the director Danny Doyle was hunting around for an Indian actor, he found out that most of our known young actors were body-builders—so muscular that their arms looked like legs; only biceps and triceps, nobody really normal.

It is also because of this kind of a situation that I say that we all need to learn from Amitabh Bachchan. He comes to the sets and prepares thoroughly. He goes through the focus marks—you see, when a character enters a shot, he or she will have an entry point; in cinema, people move through pre-determined paths for the camera. These are technical details. Bachchan understands and follow these technicalities—that marks him out as a really trained actor.

'Okay, this is my mark? Is this all right?' he would ask, taking two steps backwards. Then he would transfer all this into his mental map. By the time the shot is ready, he will be there at the correct point, at ease and all natural. These are simple things. But they come from training. Bachchan has translated his entire experience into training. He never shows off; nor does he intimidate anyone in the set with his formidable experience bank. I think that's the secret of his youthfulness. This flamboyance is also something that exudes from the inside. That's also part of one's spirit which shows up on the face. Even in an out and out commercial movie, it's a pleasure to watch Mr Bachchan. The film may be a complete disaster, but we will never get bored watching him. We get our money's worth. That's the secret of his stardom.

And this stardom is not only apparent in the movies, but also on the sets. When we were shooting for *Black*. His shift would begin at nine. He would be there on time; that meant we all had to be there on time as well. Bachchan doesn't sleep much. Much before sunrise, he would have finished his routine of exercise and newspaper. Then it seems he wouldn't know what to do with the time that was left before the shooting began. One day he drove by himself to the studio. He was under the impression that for the nine o'clock shoot, the rest of us would have reached by eight. The moment he reached the set, we all started getting panic calls.

'Bachchan has arrived at the location, come quickly!'

'But isn't it a nine o' clock shift?'

'Whether the shift is at nine or seven, I have no clue. But Bachchan Sir has come. Come quickly!'

So when he landed up, there was no one at the location.

'No one's around?' he would call out. Then he got inside his vanity van.

There was some controversy around something that he had said in his blog about *Slumdog*. Later when the film received Oscar nominations, he called a press meeting in Jaipur and announced that as far as he was concerned, the biggest thing about it all was the nomination for Resul and that he felt very happy about it.

By chance, I was watching this on television. I was stunned. I contacted him immediately. I knew his valet Praveen Bhai very well. Amitabh Bachchan called me back in five minutes.

'Resul . . . this is Amitabh Bachchan. I am so happy for you, man. I wish you all the best. I am sure you will get it.'

I told him I had already got it.

'How?'

'There are millions of people in this country waiting for a call from you. As far as I am concerned, this call from you is my Oscar.'

He laughed loudly, 'Ha ha ha ha ha . . .'

When I actually got the Oscar, he sent me a magnificent bouquet along with a note:

Dear Resul,

CONGRATULATIONS!!!
You continue to make us proud. But then again we always knew how brilliant you are. Now the world knows!
All the best.

Amitabh, Jaya, Aishwarya and Abhishek

PART 4

SOUND CONVICTIONS

1

THE ART OF CRAFTING SOUND

As I said, all I know is sound. I am very sure of what sounds correct and what doesn't. I work based on these sureties of mine. Backed by such an instinctive conviction, decisions are almost always made based on instinct rather than intellect, and it turns out to be correct more often than not.

There is a path that leads to this marksmanship. If I skip that part, the whole thing will appear to you as overly simplistic. This surety and conviction is a tick-mark made by the ink of all my past experiences; it is a reflection of the knowledge that I have accepted or rejected. Now don't mistake this tick-mark to be something that's just about the tip of a pen; I shall explain it further.

When I came to the Institute, I had no idea about sound and its possibilities. By the second year, I started concentrating more on these aspects. Let me say I got more enthusiastic about these things. Still, I didn't know anything deeply enough about it. I was at a level wherein hearing a good track made me analyse the technicalities of its recording.

It took me years, well into my professional days, to realize that, what is more important is to understand *why* something was recorded in a particular manner than *how* it was recorded. That realization was a significant step in my growth as a technician and as an artist.

In the days of my childhood, the only source of entertainment was the radio. There was a routine to listening to your favourite programmes. Seven fifty-five in the evening on Sundays was about a news programme, then there was a play, then you had dinner and then you went to sleep. Your sense of time was so in tune with the radio. Film songs at one thirty in the afternoon and news at twelve thirty. Though you never really looked at radio as a medium of sound, you did experience all of its effectiveness—you could hear a car door shutting or a car leaving in the radio plays. Radio was surely my first experience of sound as a medium apart from the real-life sounds. But though these memories might have been influential, they didn't constitute a codified knowledge bank.

The whole of the first year at the Institute was dedicated to the study of cinema as a medium; this gave you a solid foundation. It was a beautifully designed curriculum. The study of sound became more serious in the second year, starting with recording equipment like the Nagra mixing console and their workings and designs. Sometimes I wondered why I was going into the circuitry of an equipment to design sound. Sound in cinema is an artistic blend of technology and aesthetics. So it's important to develop a solid base about the technology of sound. After the first two years, we were left to pursue our individual quests in the field. What we acquired in the first two years was put into practice and applied to make a product in the third year—this was the basic philosophy of the Institute's curriculum.

Till the second year, we learnt things inside a cocoon, as it were. We mainly figured out equipment and learned the basics of music recording. The professor would come and ask us to identify the instruments used in the music piece he had made us listen to. We needed to understand what frequency range each instrument produced. Then we started the recording exercises. This was particularly useful. Essentially, this is what constitutes the work of a sound man: creative interaction with sounds of varying frequencies—the layering and mixing of these frequencies is what finally goes on to create the aesthetic experience.

This is but one aspect of film sound. There are many more: recording dialogues; recording effects for both the location and for dubbing; and recording Foley, music, songs, etc. Blending all these sound components in an artistic manner is the final mixing. This final mixing is what I enjoyed the most and I wanted to specialize in this. But it's studio-bound work and I didn't want to spend all my life inside a dark studio; so I decided not to opt for this. Now I have become someone who does all these.

By the third year, I was dealing with my ideas and confusions about cinema and figuring ways out to discover my individual approach to cinema. It was also a period of a minor disillusionment: I would often be plagued by notions that I was not a film-maker but just a technician who does sound for someone else's film. I reasoned that I couldn't even call it *my* sound. What gave me solace was the prospect of doing my diploma film exactly the way I wanted it done. The diploma film is a group project: the direction student writes and directs; the camera student shoots; the sound student does sound; and the editing student edits. So I had a critical role in the process.

While doing all this, there was still an anxiety lurking at the back of my mind that once I started working professionally, I would be just another guy who did what the director asked him to do. It would only be a technical job and I wouldn't be making any creative contribution to the film.

I started wondering why I was studying sound. There was a nagging thought inside me that my final calling might not be this; I was having this anxiety about my place as an artist in the ecosystem of cinema. The third year was also a time of more fundamental confusions where I wrestled with coming-of-age questions: Who am I? Where am I? What am I?

I tried to change the script of the diploma film to make it *my* film. Finally, it turned out that together we hadn't made *one* diploma film. The director wrote a script and made *his* film. The cameraman interpreted it to make it *his* film. The editor did his own editing. I brought in *my own* sound. Four completely different streams of thought and the film eventually turned out to be a spoilt dish made by many cooks. Many diploma films suffer from this multiple-cook syndrome.

It was only after I got out of the Institute that I realized that this was not how film-making works. In the case of the diploma film, nobody had a vision about the final product.

All we had was our individual obstinacies. If any of us had any overall vision, everything could have been integrated. I was aware of the importance of having a personal holistic vision while I was still at the institute. All thanks to the opportunities I had to work with people like P.M. Satheesh and Vikram Jogelaker during those years. When Jogelaker did a documentary on classical music maestro Mallikarjun Mansur, I had the good fortune to sit with him through the entire mixing session. With Satheesh, I had the chance to be at location for the shooting of the film, *Limited Manuski*. These were experiences that helped me put together my notions about how films were really made and about the professional conduct of the technicians in real situations. Though there were many doubts about a lot of things, I started an inquiry into myself about my kind of cinema and about what I was all about.

Now I can say that there are three important phases: as a student you have to learn the art; as a professional, you have to give form to what you have learnt; and then you have to turn the whole thing into a working professional model.

Today I know that what is important is how you conduct yourself in all these three phases—here it's immaterial whether you are talented, capable or aesthetically precise. Moreover, these are qualities that any student who passes out of the Institute would possess—on these counts, you can trust these students with your eyes shut.

But in their ability to conduct themselves professionally, I have my doubts. They may have all the talent and capability, but the core issue is about how they conduct themselves and evolve into craftsmen in a professional industry. Therein lies the key to success. There is not much point in declaring one's passion or behaving as if you are in the throes of passion— the passion needs to be channelized to take it to its logical conclusion—then you'll be successful. This is an area the Institute should provide counselling services in.

The Institute has a beautifully planned curriculum otherwise. Actually, many of the things that I am talking about here are not in-built into the Institute's learning structure. I am able to point these things out only because I have reached a certain level after doing my own thinking and working very hard. That might not be the case with everyone.

All doctors are not experts. A very popular doctor could have performed poorly in academics. After a stage, academics stops being the core strength of a professional repertoire. We will all come to learn that ourselves. But the individual's conduct is of critical importance.

When I look at myself, I realize that one of my strengths is my memory power. Once I have heard something, something good, I never forget it. If I hear a nice sound while recording, it will stay with me. Certain visuals evoke certain sounds from my memory. Then the rest of the work is about searching for those sounds. I am always sure that those sounds will work with the audience.

In cinema, audio too, is a visual concept. My visual concept is something that has been distilled out of my aesthetic opinions formed in the three years at the Institute, the films I have seen and my interest in and loyalty to those works. Imagine a glass breaking. In recording that sound, you don't have to come up with the best glass-breaking sound in the world; what is most important for the film is to record the best glass-breaking sound that suits that particular visual. The accuracy of reality might not be what we have to capture every time.

A sound artist or a naturally gifted sound person differs from a film sound person in that respect. The ideas in film sounds are driven by the visuals. The sound of rain needn't be created by getting into the rain; an image can evoke the acoustics of rain. This is very interesting indeed. We hear and quantify the auditory sensations as a part of the visual scene. Hearing becomes seeing. So the concern of the sound artist is to visualize sound. When you reach a stage where you can actually *see* sound, your convictions take over and become critical. Then you proceed to execute your decisions based on the logic of the single correct solution for a given situation. That is something that comes from your inner vision—how you saw the sound in your mind.

Most of this is intuitive. I cannot explain many aspects of this process in an analytical manner. Often others have analysed and pointed out interesting connections in my work. That's when I, too, think about it and realize, oh yes, that's true. That's why I would rather put these things more as matters of the heart than the brain. What I bring into sound is not something that I arrive at out of pure reasoning. And it always works. There is some sort of truth in it. This faith is what I call my convictions about sound.

While judging sound, along with such abstract convictions, your common sense also plays an important role, on another parallel track. Suppose I need to give sound to a particular brand of car. This is a very specific thing. You need to keep in mind that in the audience there would be people who know about cars. So I have to go and find the exact brand of car. But how to use its sound and in what way are decisions that are completely under my discretionary powers. My concern should be whether the sound I have suits the visual in question. I should be concerned about whether the track helps in the drama of the scene; I should be constantly judging whether the sound track enriches the narrative and the cinematic aspects or not. That is what finally helps me decide whether the sound level of the car should be high, low or whether it should be played in the ambience track.

So I design a loudness graph much like how you have a narrative graph in literature. This graph is based on a few components like dialogue, actors' behaviour, and the atmosphere and the effects that create the mood of the movie. In mainstream films, there would be one more element—that of music which pushes the emotional quotient of the scene. It is the interactions of all these elements that work as the emotional quotient that advances the experience of a sequence.

I resolve and design these components separately. But when I do it this way, the total emotional control over the film may not stay in my hands. However, each small fragment is done anticipating the overall emotional intensity of the film. I would have a sound script of the film; it's by using this script that I make decisions—such as on the degree of intensity that I should impart to the sound of footsteps in a particular scene; the actor might not have moved with the kind of intensity that my sound captures, but then I would have arrived at my decision after hearing and judging all the other elements of the scene.

Now suppose the script says, 'He storms out.' The image it evokes in me is of a person walking out forcefully, making a lot of sound. If he goes out through a door, he would slam the door behind him. By this time, I would start hearing a lot more sounds in this. Then, what I try to do is to enhance the vision of the director, using my intuitions that come from my understanding of cinema and art and their history. By then, my involvement in the whole thing goes beyond being just an insignificant technician executing a job. I am involved in it with the entire weight of my understanding, aesthetics and vision. That will take the film to a higher level. Here, from a technician, I transform into an artist. This is how I sustain my convictions about sound.

*

The sense of reality that sound creates in cinema is a manufactured one. When working with Foley artists— technicians who specialize in reproducing everyday sounds for films—they would often say, 'You just run the picture.' Meaning, I shouldn't argue, instead I should just sit back and listen to the sounds they were making for the visuals. When they work with such conviction, I follow their lead. Then I wouldn't worry about how they had made that particular sound. If it matches the visual, that's good enough for me. For instance, they would create the sound of a horse running by knocking an upturned coconut shell on different surfaces. If you look at the process, it would never sound appropriate. The associations won't match. It will work only if you are looking at the visual on the screen and hear the sound.

In cinema, the visual provides the clue for the sound—the sound you hear is based on what's happening on the screen. The visual hitches you to a certain sense of reality, and once you are hitched to that film reality, the sound man can take you through many avenues. Then the possibilities of sound become huge. This is the opportunity to lead the audience to another level or to another image track. People like Tarkovsky are known to be masters at it.

This process enables the sound man to take cinema to a level where music becomes unnecessary. In the early days of sound, the whole film was made on the shooting floor. Sound effects were not added later, like how we do today. If you needed a bird's sound, a man mimicked it during the shooting process. The entire ambience was created by people mimicking various sound effects.

I was thinking about it of late. In films, a lot of sounds that you think are real are not—like how the sound of a horse running is made with coconut shells. I decided to record at least ten such sound effects.

Let's take the sound of rain as an example. You can mimic the rain sound by making sugar fall on a piece of plain paper; but if you just hear the record of such a sound, it might not sound like rain. Only along with the visual footage of the rain can you feel that it's raining. Kabir Mohanty and I prepared a list of ten such sound effects and recorded them.

What we heard was absolutely amazing; much more powerful than we had expected. These sounds could trigger fantastic imagery. I was discovering the possibilities of sound as an art. Like how you use colours in painting, in sound art, you are creating an effect by the inventive use of sounds. Sound art is becoming trendy and is being explored all over the world. My friends Rajivan (Rajivan Ayyappan) and Kabir are some of the people who are seriously working in this field. In sound art, the microphone becomes the main instrument. We hear the sound close or distant depending on how far we position the microphone from the sound source. Like a musician playing the tabla, harmonium or violin, as a sound man I use the mike. I can hear the same sound in many ways with a microphone.

I, as a technician, wield my microphones in an intelligent, creative and artistic manner in order to pick out particular sounds. The sounds I distil out of this process can be made into an original composition. This insight I acquired after thinking about the whole process and that's how I made my way into the world of sound art. I then discovered that this is a much evolved art form abroad. My newer works touch these levels of sound art.

Once I did sound for a project that had only still pictures. They were the photographs of the Mumbai riots shot by a journalist. There were thousands of photos, published and unpublished. He had selected some forty pictures and arranged them in a particular way and shot it with a video camera.

A still photograph has a fixed moment of time frozen in it. Compared to it, a movie has real time. Because of its continuity, we could say that a movie's temporal element is alive. A photograph's frozen moment from the past becomes alive when it is captured on video—here the frozen time of a still photo is transformed into cinematic real time. It was all about experimenting with a medium after understanding it thoroughly. It was also a very individualistic expression.

I saw this video in order to do the sound. What I saw was a cinematic experience being shaped out of a series of still images. I felt that the frozen time of the images was flowing out. What he had done was amazing!

Before starting on the sound, I gave it a lot of thought. The story of a time period was in front of me as a piece of cinema, but entirely made up of frozen time and its images. So, what would be the nature of the time element of this work? An image has a visual space, it's two dimensional and in a way horizontal. Sound is spherical. Here, the sound had to get the audience inside the horizontal visual space. The question in front of me was what kind of a temporal element I should attribute to this piece of work.

I decided it didn't have a temporal element. Or its temporal element was that of the viewer in relation with his auditory environment. Other than that, this cinema didn't have a sound of its own. The sound I designed for this work was based on this decision.

Suppose the viewer is seeing this work without its sound. He would be looking at it while surrounded by the ambient sounds—the whirring of a fan, the hum of an AC, traffic on the road, kids playing or crying, etc. This sound ambience and the accompanying visuals would form a relationship subconsciously in the viewer. He might shift his weight from one leg to the other or move in his chair. Those movements are triggered by some things that affect him from the overall experience. The interactions of these three elements—sight, ambience and the viewer's movements—was the sound idea I arrived at for this project.

All that was left was to create it. For that I took this film to my studio and played it in the monitor. I put a couple of guys to watch it and recorded all the sounds of them watching. I repeated this process in many locations. Then I separated some aspects of these sounds. Then those aspects were reconstructed as the temporal elements for this film. It now had a form and rhythm. That was how I designed the sound track for the film.

In one of the recordings, I got the sounds of carpenters hammering upstairs. When reconstructed later, it sounded like a train. It developed a close relation to the train in the photograph. This could be looked at as a sensation that the viewer feels. The viewer, when I was recording it, must have felt the same sensation. That's what I had captured. This is beyond technique. There is communication at special levels here—something that transcends the obvious. This has connections with Indian philosophy. In Siddhavaidyam of Ayurveda, the fireplace for boiling medicines is dug inside the earth. The medicine pot is underground. The ingredients inside the pot will change colours with the change in temperature, and you need to add more ingredients at the right sequence and time. The medicine man can see all these. You may ask, how can you see the things happening inside an opaque pot dug in the ground? You can and you must. That's the quality of a real medicine man or *vaidya*. You see these processes with the eyes of knowledge. That is how he concocts his medicines, says Sage Agastya's medical science.

This is the Indian ethos. Like the medicine man, I 'saw' the movements going on in the inside while doing the kind of work I mentioned here. These works are pure explorations of art. There is no technique in them. I used the mike as an instrument; when I tweaked the microphone's behaviour to make it a musical instrument, the above-mentioned sensation of the viewer was captured. What's important in this kind of work is the fact that I used my convictions about sound creatively at a higher level.

2

THE CHALLENGE OF VISUALIZING SOUND

I had mentioned earlier while talking about Rashid Saar, my teacher from MSM College in Kayamkulam, that there comes a particular stage of learning when you feel you have learned everything that your teacher knows. Now both the teacher and the disciple need to explore new territories of knowledge. But for that, you may not need a teacher any more—you can do it all by yourself. During the final mixing stage of *Private Detective—Two Plus Two Plus One,* I felt something similar. I wondered whether Paddy completely understood the film while doing the final mixing. He was not being able to execute many tracks the way I had intended them to be executed. I felt terrible. I would even cry without anybody noticing. This was not the cinema I had in mind. After that mixing, I strongly felt that people were doing things just for the sake of the director. There were no discussions. My ideas were not getting across effectively.

I then decided that I should make the audience hear the sound exactly how I had visualized it! Or at least, I should be able to make the director listen to how I imagined the whole thing. That's something I would insist upon. Whether it gets rejected or accepted would not be of major concern. Then a need arose of getting a space where I could freely execute the sound that I had in mind.

All the sync sound films that I have done afterwards were not just films with live sound, but also a struggle to take cinema sound to its absolute logical conclusion; they were a demonstration that the sound designer's work doesn't conclude till the sound is done exactly the way he had visualized it; and that the whole process reaches fruition only when the audience in the theatre hears it the way he wanted them to hear it. The conditions in the studios of those days were not ideal for such a scenario. I realized that I needed my own set-up to try my ideas out.

Satheesh and I thought and discussed this thoroughly. Satheesh was prepared to invest and he set up a workspace at his house. Later, he bought a studio space and shifted the whole set-up there. That's how Fireflys Post Sound came into being—from the intense necessity we felt for doing sound the way we wanted it done. *Snip*, my third film, was the first one I did in Fireflys. I didn't look back for the next five or six years. I would call the directors and make them hear the sound—many a time, I have made them hear two or three versions of it! We were exploring the infinite possibilities of digital technology.

But digital technology had its limitations at that time. Film sound was possible only up to 16-bit recording in the beginning. The same sound would have more depth if recorded in 24-bit. It was a time when digital technology was still evolving in these areas. In a manner of speaking, the growth of Fireflys and the films we did there were all part of the evolution of sound technology in India. Protools has evolved and has been upgraded many times since then. Our sound libraries have grown by many folds. There are a lot of new people in the field now. From the first film to now, we have come a long way—in supersonic speed!

I have cried copiously while working. It's got something to do with the emotional loyalty I feel towards the film I am doing. The tears have had nothing to do with self-pity or a feeling of loneliness that arises from 'ah-no-one-understands-me' sort of mindset. I am not one for such sentimental isolation. What makes me feel emotional is my own intensity in work.

There is a phase in every sound editor's career where they get possessive about what they have done. I don't feel such an attachment to my work. Once I have made the director listen to the sound I have done, I become detached from it. Then my focus is on whether the whole film is evolving in the right direction. What I am concerned about is the cinematic experience that will be conveyed through the integration of the many aspects that go into the making of a film: my work, what the director and the cameraman have done, and what the music director has composed. At that juncture, in the

overall scheme of cinematic experience, some parts of my own
work can become redundant. I have no issues with trashing
those bits. Many times, my own assistants have protested
about this. They would say that if I had insisted, some of
the things which we had painstakingly done could have been
there in the final film. But it doesn't matter to me at all as long
as the film works. At the same time, of course, I do fight for
the details which I think are important for the film.

What makes me really cry is when the one who does the
final mixing doesn't at all hear what I had so clearly envisioned;
worse, he goes on about his work and makes some kind of
khichdi stuff. I have a serious problem when something I
have visualized is overlooked, missed or overruled for some
inferior alternative. Here, there is also an element of power
play. The guy might have done mixing for several successful
mainstream films, and he has the trust of the producer and
the director that he knows what the audience wants; so I get
overruled in the process. That creates a problem.

This is how I look at it: the guy who does the final mixing
gets to know the film for only ten days, or the days it takes
for the mix; whereas I have been living with the film for one
whole year. And I don't think such a long association with
the material dulls my objectivity towards it. Yes, when we
see something over and over again, it might soften the edge
of our instinctive reactions. That is the only reason why I sit
with a new guy for the mix—for a sharper, fresher sensitivity.
I would have prepared all the tracks based on my personal
instincts. It has a certain sharpness which should remain and
be carried into the final film. The final mixing is also the last

chance to get any more reactions and make alterations. A new guy is called in to maximize the scope of that, not because he is a guru with deep knowledge in sound and the nature of the cosmos. We go to a new person to do the final mixing to get a fresh perspective on the whole thing. In reality, this new perspective often turns out to be disastrous. Most of these guys rely heavily on standard techniques, whether it is about film aesthetics or sound laying. They don't know how to humanize the technique. This humanization is what elicits the appropriate emotional reactions from the audience, thereby helping the film to transcend technique and technology.

Great technique just by itself doesn't guarantee anything. Why do you think a lot of Hollywood films look and feel like popcorn? Batman and all are doing amazing feats, but in the end you feel it is hollow. It's not humanized, not just the super heroes, but the whole film itself.

So, how do you overcome this situation? Squat like a true satyagrahi and protest, that's the only way. Squat and don't move till you get things done by everyone in exactly the way you want it to be done. But that's a hard path to tread as you become the conductor of an orchestra with many rebels as musicians!

All the way through shooting, editing and designing sound for the film *Black*, I was under the impression that the film was not targeted at the mainstream audience. Later, we pitched it for the mainstream market. That changed everything: the nature of the mix, the pace, the use of music, all of it. It became important to make the film accessible to a wider audience. While making a film, you have in mind the intended audience; you become a spokesman for them during the filming process. That is what makes this otherwise laborious task a pleasant experience, deep within. You need to explore newer terrains in each work; it's like rediscovering the artist in you every time.

Popular film has its idiocies. But what makes it worth your while is the hope you feel in addressing a large populace as an artist and being their advocate by understanding them. That's valuable, artistically and politically.

Black is a good example of such a thing. What I did in *Black* was to push the envelope a little more while still staying within the boundaries of mainstream sensibilities. I created different soundscapes and played with sound rather than music. I consciously did many things with natural sounds. Naturalness earns you the audience's trust, and once you have their trust and they start believing that everything they are hearing is natural, then you go a step further and build your fiction from there. That's exactly what I did in *Black* in many sequences. It was dramatically effective and we had the audience in our hands as we never denied their existence. The director, Sanjay Leela Bhansali, was the one who made me understand this process.

I had fights with him during the mixing phase. I even staged a walkout. I said this was not the film we had shot, edited or did sound for. I told him he had gone completely wrong with the whole thing. His reply was, 'I know my audience. I am making mainstream Hindi cinema.' I thought about it and realized that he was talking about something which I didn't know anything about. I didn't know this audience he was talking about. He had done three films. The last one was a huge hit. So when he says with such conviction that he knew his audience, then my role is to follow the man's vision. I said I would go with it if he was so convinced about it. 'Still, I need to do one more mix—my mix. You should hear that.' He said okay.

So I did two mixes for the film. One was in a European sensibility with subtle movements and minimal music—only where it was absolutely necessary. That's not the version that the mainstream Indian audience finally saw. This taught me a valuable lesson about balance and where to pitch a film.

In the film, *Gandhi, My Father*, the situation was just the opposite. Feroz wanted the film to be subtle. I said the film was already very subtle; we needed to make louder. After all, this was to stand out against other Bollywood films. This entailed amplifying the world of the film through strategic deployment of sound. Arguments ensued, fights happened. But he agreed in the end.

We were working in Los Angeles with people who worked with James Cameron, the director of *Titanic*. The white guys couldn't figure out what was going on—a sound recordist fighting with the director! That's not how it happens there. Nobody questions the director! His word is final and that's that. And here was this guy arguing that the director was wrong. They were stunned.

Where do you pitch a film? That's what I pay attention to, as a sound designer. I carefully listen to all the sounds that've been done. I prepare sketches. Then I tell my assistant, I want this sound in this scene. He may say, 'But the rustle of leaves is outside the window glass, how will you be able to hear that?'

But it doesn't matter to me whether the leaves are outside or inside. All I want to hear is the sound of the leaves rustling in this scene. In such instances what I follow is gaze—the gaze of the audience. After a shot comes on screen, the audience starts looking for the next. In my sketches, I would have marked that out already. I have to make them hear what they are looking for. My focus is on pre-empting their gaze. That is what leads the audience on and then the drama unfolds. This is how patterns and compositions emerge.

Many a time what I demanded would be illogical. I have had fights with sound designers Shajith (Shajith Koyeri) and Amrit (Amrit Pritam) several times on these issues. They would say that what I am asking for is absurd. I would say, yes, maybe, but that's what I want, that's how my sketch is. It could be a murder mystery or a gangster film, but that's the way I do things. Sometimes, I do a whole film only to carry out a scene in a particular way; yes, I have taken up films just to do a single scene differently!

When I get a film project, I look at it in terms of what it offers me. Once I find that out, I take it a step further. That is the only way I can exist and sustain the way I work.

Otherwise, your goal will be reduced to only making money. You will easily slip into that comfortable circle of fame and money. Like some cardiologists back home, 'Oh you have medical insurance, then let's do a bypass surgery.' There is no need for that; the patient can carry on with the same heart for another five or six years. But the doctor's wisdom is that since the patient has a medical insurance and in three years after retirement he won't be entitled to any medical reimbursement, let's do it right away. You mustn't let yourself fall into this trap of logic. We have to constantly reinvent ourselves.

*

For the film *Zinda*, I went to Bangkok to record the effects. It was unheard of in Hindi cinema, to go to the original location to record the effects sound of a commercial film.

Actually, sound was the only thing that could be done as something original in this film. The whole film is a frame-by-frame copy of a Korean one. I told them: 'Just don't say no to only one thing—the effects sound has to be recorded at the real location. Then we can take the film to another level.' They agreed.

Zinda became the first Indian film to have effects created with surround-sound recorded on location. It's also the first film to have multi-track effects recorded on location in the 24-bit digital medium.

There was no 'surround microphone' with us then. Instead, I used two MS stereo microphones. This involves a physically cumbersome technique of arranging a 'mid mike' and a 'side mike' in a particular way so as to create spatial effects. And I had to perform this task from a high-speed boat—one wrong step and I would be history.

One scene was at a place called Pattaya. There was a wooden bridge at this place jutting out into the sea for about three hundred metres. The film has scenes of the protagonist standing there and reminiscing about his past. Later, when I went there again to record the ambience, most of this bridge had been destroyed in the tsunami. I was standing on this damaged bridge and recording. I didn't know how strong the bridge was. But my visual memory from last time told me that it was strong enough for people to walk on it. It never occurred to me to think about what the tsunami would have done to its structural strength. All my attention was focused on what I was hearing and recording. Suddenly, a part of the bridge gave way and I fell into the sea. The equipment hanging from my shoulder was a Portadrive recorder. Nobody had this thing in India then. That, too, fell into the water!

The production manager lifted me up. Salt water had gone inside the recorder. I washed it with tap water. I knew this machine inside out, right from its design and development stage. Satheesh and I had gone to London and discussed every bit of this machine with the engineers who had designed it. There was no component that could get damaged easily. I was given this equipment for field testing while doing the film *Amu*. I had also used it in *Black*.

I washed and dried the machine. Then I undressed the mikes and washed them too. I waited for two hours, meanwhile undressing myself and having a bath. I gave it a little more time and switched it on after a while. It started working as if nothing had happened. I played the recording and everything was intact. It even had the sound of it falling in the water! I recorded the next day too and I came back to Mumbai after a few more days of recording.

Satheesh used to tell me to never ever take chances, especially with recording. But this was something I had disregarded here. I hadn't taken a back-up of the data from the recorder. I hadn't bothered about it as it was only a four–five days' affair. I also had great trust in this machine—nothing could go wrong. I came back to Mumbai and switched on the machine. It was dead. The hard disc inside had all the data. If I could retrieve it, I might survive. I tried recovering the data for two sleepless days. I knew everything about this equipment. But nothing worked. In those two days, I tried all the possible processes and softwares. I sat and studied in detail the intricacies of how the data was recorded on the hard disc and finally somehow managed to retrieve everything. But the stereo-sound data had a problem. Stereo sound has a phase correlation. Even a minor error in the stereo data's phase correlation will ruin everything. The retrieved data was usable only if it was absolutely intact. And it wasn't!

Now I needed to break the news to the producer, who had let me do something no one had ever done in the history of Hindi cinema. But I had messed up everything. How was I to tell the producer this?

I had two options in front of me. The first one was to send the hard disc to the manufacturers in London and ask them to retrieve the raw data. That might just work but we were already running out of time with the release date. The second option was to go again to Bangkok and record again! I took that -went and told the director and the producer about what had happened. I apologized and told them that it was completely my fault. I also told them that I intended to go back and do the recording again and that my travel expenses and the equipment rentals would entirely be borne by me.

Sanjay Gupta was the director. He said, 'Don't worry, buddy! Suppose the camera jammed while I was shooting, we will reshoot it, right? This is just another situation like that. You go ahead and record it.' He stood by me. I will never forget the faith he had in me. I will do any of his films without a second thought. He knew that I was trying to do something which would improve the quality of his product. I consider it my great fortune to have worked with people like him. It's indeed a source of great inspiration when people put their faith in you having recognized the fact that what you are trying to do for them nobody else would.

That evening I told Satheesh I was going back to Bangkok. They got me my ticket by the same evening. Satheesh then sent me a message: 'This is a revolution in our film industry, nobody has ever done anything like this before!'

I went back and retraced every place that I had recorded earlier. I worked hard and recorded everything exactly like the first time. While doing that, I fought the twin feelings of exhaustion and boredom—you see, I was doing the same thing all over again, at the same location, and for hours together; moreover, I had been physically and mentally drained by the travel and the stress of having lost my material. In the end, however, I managed to get better material than the first time.

Those were also the days I desperately wanted to be with my son. It was his circumcision ceremony. I had to cancel the ticket that I had booked to Kerala. I told Shadia that I had no option but to do this work. I still remember the messages that I sent her: 'Some day, my son will come to realize what his Bappa has achieved.' I even tried to find out if it was possible to postpone the ceremony. In another message, I wrote to Shadia asking her to tell him some day—when he's grown up—that his Bappa tried but couldn't make it for the ceremony. I was very emotional during that particular time.

I finished my work in Bangkok, came back to Mumbai, transferred the data and handed over everything to Amrit Pritam for editing. Then I caught the next flight home to Kerala. On my way, I called home asking them to wait for me as I would reach in two hours. I just wanted to see my boy once before his *sunhat*. But the doctor had a busy schedule. He didn't wait for me.

*

My art is largely influenced by my personal experiences. There is a childhood memory of a rotating fan that I've used as a motif in some films. This image dates back to the time I had jaundice in my village. I was a delicate child and suffered from many ailments. I had polio when I was two. My entire right side had got paralysed. I was treated and cured at the Uthradam Thirunal Hospital, I am told, but I don't really remember. A cousin of mine who also had polio around that time is still confined to a wheelchair.

The time I had jaundice was a more dramatic affair, though my memory of the actual illness is rather dim. I was in fifth standard then. The home test for jaundice was usually to soak rice in the suspected patient's urine and see if the colour changed. The test tube was a coconut shell and was left outside the house. But the crows upturned the test many times. A couple of days went like that. Then I was taken to the ESI hospital in Anchal. That was the main hospital for us then. There, because of Bappa's work, my treatment was free. I was detected with jaundice.

From the hospital, I was brought to Umma's house as it was closer. Herbal medicines were the remedy. I remember being fed such concoctions. Then I was brought back to our house. Bappa had come that day. I was sitting on his lap and playing. Umma was reciting something from the Koran. She was also preparing to cook for dinner. I remember only till then.

The next thing I remember was waking up somewhere. I saw a fan spinning. It made a distinct sound: *kwooong* . . . *kwooong*. We had fans only at Umma's house. But this wasn't that house. I asked where I was and demanded to see Kunji, my eldest sister. I was later briefed about the drama that unfolded after I lost consciousness. I had broken into violent fits, and even bit Bappa. Then I went limp. When I was eventually brought to the Mission Hospital and given a morphine shot to calm me down, the doctors announced, 'The boy is going to die. There's nothing we can do. You may call your near and dear ones!'

I was brought to Umma's house and my body was laid out for the last rites. At this point, Umma rushed to a jeweller's shop in Eroor. It's an interesting story. We always teased her about this part. Bappa, of course, married Umma only once, but the local goldsmiths would say she had married many times, because she altered and remade her mangalsutra many times over. That was not because she followed the latest fashion, but because she was very calculative. When she would sell the year's tapioca harvest, she would take the money and the mangalsutra to the goldsmith, add some more gold to it and remake it. The soil was fertile then and we used to have loads of tapioca. Umma had rushed off to the Eroor jeweller because her chain and money was there and with the money she could take me to a better hospital.

My fourth uncle's wife, Nabiza mami, was also there at Umma's house. All my mamis were very caring, especially Nabiza mami. Her husband was also very close to us. He is not alive now. Nabiza mami was the one who prepared and fed me the herbs. As the last rite, she put some drops of milk on my lips. My lips moved and I drank the milk. She cried out loud, saying, 'My boy is alive, my boy is alive, please save him.'

My Umma's second brother, whom we call Saarmama, took a car and rushed me to the medical college. I underwent a complete blood transfusion there. The first bottle of blood which went into my veins was of this uncle. The next bottle was of Babukka. Babukka was a popular SFI (Students Federation of India) leader at that time. Lots of his student supporters came forward with more blood. I woke up after eight or nine days. And the first thing my eyes focused on was the rotating fan. I remember that very clearly.

If you notice a whirling fan's sound in any of the films I have done, it has a connection to this episode in my life. I have used this in the film, *Mixed Doubles*.

Amrit Pritam was assisting me when I was editing that film's sound. He tried many kinds of fan sounds. I rejected every one of them saying that was not it. He didn't know what I was trying to get at. Our entire sound collection didn't have the sound that I wanted. I went around recording fan sounds for a while so as to get the right sound. Nothing worked. Finally, I found a recording that Satheesh had done of an old fan whirring with a distinct *kwoooong . . . kwoooong*. I used it as a recurring motif in *Mixed Doubles*. This film has many moments of stillness. While the scenes and the film have nothing to with my near-death experience, the sound of the whirring fan comes from those memories.

I have seen and heard many fans in my life, lying on my back. In Mumbai, in the days of no work, all I had was a fan above me. In lean periods, I have spent months lying down on my back, looking at a fan.

I used to compare my situation with that of the fire force guys. They, too, would be lying down on their back looking up at a fan till a call comes of an emergency or fire. Then they would quickly gather their gear and rush out. Freelance work is like that. The only difference in my case and the firemen's is, if there is no work, I don't get paid. But lying on your back and looking at a whirring fan stirs a lot of things in your mind. It can inspire many creative ideas.

*

When I watch a film before doing its sound, my mind grabs certain things from it; its visuals make me hear a corresponding sound inside me. This is a sort of awareness that comes from knowledge. This knowledge shines in my head as working information and it forms the core of what I need to do for the film. If you follow the sound images that form inside your head and apply them in the film, then you are working without any doubt or uncertainty. And after the film was done, somebody would call me from some corner of the world and tell me that the sound in the film was very good. So, as far as I am concerned, creating a plausible soundscape is my way of attempting to converse with that someone located somewhere else in the world.

During the course of the making of a film, my search is for the sounds that suit the images in the film. This search is the beginning of a conversation I intend to have with someone somewhere in the world.

Take the film *Saawariya* as an example. I feel sad that the film didn't do very well commercially. But that's not the point. I have created four nights in the film, four different kinds of night. The varying soundscape of a dreaming man's four nights: a night after rains; a night when the rains are approaching; a night laden with expectations; and a night of falling snow.

A night of approaching rain. I have heard plenty of such a night's sounds in my childhood. Such nights in Kerala have the full orchestra of frogs, but not in Mumbai. I have waited many nights, sometimes till three in the morning, knee-deep in mud, in the wet areas of the Film City, to capture this sound.

The Film City is a dangerous place to be in during late nights. People don't hang around there late into the night. There are leopards there that come out from the bordering national park. The guys who come to assist me wouldn't step out of the car, or they would cook up some excuse and leave early.

But I am in search of the sound that I have in mind. During the course of such relentless recording, I might get just a piece of what I am looking for. The final sound would often be created from these bits and pieces recorded over many times over many nights and edited over many layers.

At the time of recording a particular sound, I would know where it would fit in the entire scheme of things. I record new material for all my films, because every film has its own sound texture. You can't use the library stock beyond a certain point.

While I am recording, whether it's in a crowded street or in a deserted place, my mind is empty. Only my ears work. Then I get the feeling that life on earth has a great order. Sometimes, in a lake, a fish would unexpectedly jump out with a 'pluk' sound. In *Saawariya*, I have used many such effects from the still nights that I had recorded in the Film City.

While I am in that state, no leopards walk into my mind. Even if a leopard happens to drop by, I know he would stand aside. When you have a purpose, nothing can deter you from carrying it out. It's like if someone has resolved to kill you, then you have no other alternative but to die at the hand of that person. I start off with that kind of a resolve.It's also a spiritual experience. In that state, the tapes rolling, the mikes bringing in countless sounds, you get into a rare communion with nature.

Nature has ordained every creature its place. Through sound, you can enter into this amazing system of order. You can hear the entire planet at once. The soft breath of a breeze; two drops of rain; the tinkling of running water; a bunch of cicadas here and another somewhere else; frogs near the running water . . . The sound frequencies of cicadas and frogs are different. They have their own layers. And once in a while, these layers come together and merge. It's a huge spectrum. And the rain makes this spectrum of co-existence even more intense. What I capture are these co-existences on each layer and the conversations amongst them. While capturing this infinite dance of vibrations, a sense of the dynamics of the cosmos fills your consciousness. You feel a profound oneness with the beings that you are capturing; you feel nothing else.

While doing a piece, I am also attempting to conduct a conversation. People who have seen *Saawariya* have called me from New York and Los Angeles. One of them specially commented on one particular night in the film. That means I have been able to communicate something to someone living in some other corner of the world—that I have been able to complete a conversation. I have had a fulfilling experience with the film.

This may not happen with every film. But it did happen with *Saawariya*. It happened with *Gandhi, My Father* too. It also happened with *Black*, but at a completely different and ecstatic level.

This conversation is one of the major things that takes place through sound. In my student days, I had heard of Robert Bresson saying that all of this is possible in cinema. He is someone who has worked with the idea of grace in cinema. In Christianity, grace is deliverance. Bresson says you can attain grace through cinema as well. All Bresson films are about that. As a student I went through these theories as serious, personal academic exercises. However, the truth of all these I experienced only later.

The gist of the matter is—only through cinema can one evoke society, staying in a particular time and space, experiencing a different time and space. You can even communicate smells through cinema. This has been worked out in *Slumdog Millionaire*. In it, through the use of the sounds of Mumbai, the smell of the city gets evoked; you can get this smell even if you don't know about Mumbai—it's a subconscious feeling.

I have felt that about South America when I saw *City of God*. Sound can provide many anthropological insights. It can also trigger memories. The sounds of Rahman's music have that quality. When you hear his music, you feel that you have heard its sound somewhere before. It could be the sound of a tabla or a base guitar, or an instrument that we have never heard before, or it could even be sounds from an unknown civilization—but when Rahman uses them, you get a déjà vu auditory experience. We are intensely attracted. There is an infectious lilt to his work. That's a connection, a conversation and an evoking of memories. He does this intuitively. He is a genius.

I have cherished lots of sounds from the films I have seen. Bresson's film *Mouchette* has some unforgettable footstep sounds. Then in his *L'argent*, there's this sound of a slap. A woman gets slapped; then the scene cuts to coffee spilling from the mug she is holding. I have not seen a more powerful slap in world cinema. Similarly, there's the sound of the protagonist biting a stone in the rice he is eating in Adoor Gopalakrishanan *Elippathayam*—unforgettable! It's also a remarkable cultural statement—*biting a stone in your rice* is a phrase in Malayalam for an unpleasant personal experience. This single sound effect says volumes about a family which has reached a stage of stagnation and crises—unpleasant and private, much like biting into a stone in the ball of soft rice you put in your mouth.

There are examples of extremely sophisticated sound design as well. Like the sound of Francis Coppola's *Apocalypse Now* which was done by Walter Murch. The movie is about the Vietnam War. War is spectacularly filmed and highly romanticized in this movie. When we watch the deaths and killings, we don't feel the violence of it all. Then it strikes us. It's the use of sound that makes us experience the whole thing in that way.

In recent times, there's Spielberg's *Munich* for which Ben Burt had done the sound. Really a great film. It's a period film about the Munich Olympics massacre and the events around it. The tension is built with effects like just the sound of a car passing—without any accompanying music. Yes, you get a feel of the time period through the settings and costumes, but it's through the sound that the actual ambience of the time comes alive.

I have done such things in *Gandhi, My Father.* There the big challenge was to capture the time period through sounds and create a dramatic effect. I compressed some sounds to make it sound like news footage. I used the recorded sound of the present to create the sounds of that past era. Using these sounds, I was trying to create a texture—that was the aesthetics behind it. Then the drama had to be built employing these elements—there art came in. I was playing multiple roles, switching quickly from one to another. It's essential for a sound man to have this ability to switch roles. That's when he is able to complete his 'conversations'.

3

THE UNSUNG HEROES OF INDIAN CINEMA

I will tell you about some other sound types. Not about bass, baritone or tenor but about 'sound personalities'. They are not only very sound as personalities but also extremely versatile in the way they can create sounds. They are called Foley artists. You name the sound, they will make it. Foley sound effects are sounds that synchronize on screen. Footsteps, hand movements, movement of objects, the rustling of cloth, they are all foley. Also fights, gunfire, sword fencing, horse races are all foley, and are separately recorded in the studio.

The Foley artists are fantastic characters, especially the group I work with: Chowdhuri, Gupta and Karnail Singh. Everyone calls Karnail Sigh, Paaji. Chowdhuri is physically spherical. I call him *Saand*, Hindi for water buffalo. He is a stainless Muslim who is also a ferocious eater of pure non-vegetarian food. Gupta is a stout six-footer from Uttar Pradesh. He is an engineer (that's a secret).

All these three giants appear to be perfectly normal

humans, till you see them in action. Chowdhuri has this habit of transforming himself into one of the characters of the film he is working on. During the recording for the Amitabh Bachchan starrer *Shahenshah,* he used to walk around in the studio like Shahenshah, wearing the Shahenshah coat and mouthing his dialogues. During *Snip,* he wore Saurav Shukla's wig and would imitate him. When they get a film, the three of them would watch it together and divide their work.

The history of independent Hindi cinema is also the history of these characters. They have done many films without charging any fees. They have worked on Mani Kaul's and Kumar Shahni's films without taking a single paisa. They knew that these directors were doing films based on some major thoughts. But if you ask them, they would say: '*Behnchod, hum ko toh kuchch samaj mein nahin aa raha hai hum kya kar raha hain.'* (I couldn't figure out a thing about what the fuck I was doing.)

They know of the entire Hindi film industry. They can take one look at a film and tell you whether it will work or not; they will tell you whether it's going to be a hit or not. They also sometimes offer edit suggestions. And they are okay if you don't want to listen to these suggestions.

Mani Kaul found Chowdhuri's behaviour interesting and gave him a role in his film.

I asked Chowdhuri, 'Oh, you have acted in Mani Kaul's film and all? You must be a major guy.'

'What the fuck! I didn't understand a thing. They took me from here to there. The shot was going on and on. Then Mani says, Chowdhuri, now go, you go inside. I will walk inside, do something and come back. Twenty-five days I drank and enjoyed myself; didn't do any acting.'

Actually, this guy needn't act at all. Just being himself is enough of a spectacle. The man is a complete clown. Mani used him as the *sutradhar* in his film *Idiot*. Chowdhuri didn't know that he was being the *sutradhar*. Mani would just let him get inside a frame and Chowdhuri would go ahead and do whatever he wanted to do!

Sometimes we get films that need to be finished in one schedule. We might have only three or four days at hand to finish the work. The trio would come and create a complete mess in such situations. Order and organization are not their core strengths. They don't know or care about the intellectual things about sound. You just can't let them loose in your work. Making them work is like riding a cart hitched to three rowdy horses.

But if you get the knack of working with them, you can do wonders with these amazing talents. They are gifted with intuition and completely involved in what they do. Gupta can look at a frame and tell me all the sounds that can go in it. If I wanted to go a step further, he would say, 'I know the sound you are talking about. But it's damn tough to make that.'

I am very specific about my sound. Sometimes I would recreate inside the sound studio the floor that the actors walked on in a particular scene. They don't like all that, but they wouldn't protest. They would somehow know that I was doing it in the correct way. For *Black*, I had recreated a scene's floor in the studio. For *Zinda*, I had reconstructed an entire set inside the studio.

The foley guys focus only on sound and the possibilities for their craft. They may detect some things like the movement of a character which I might have missed. With their contribution, the possibilities of detailing increase many folds. These guys are amazingly spontaneous.

Abroad, there are awards in the field of foley, given out by the Motion Picture Sound Editors' organization. In India, these artists mostly go unrecognized. People here are not even aware of the fact that there is a bunch of guys doing this sort of work. They are important artists in sound and it's essential that the public acknowledge their contributions. The audience don't realize that some of the most wonderful sounds they hear in the theatre were created by these people.

Protools was in use by the time I was doing *Mixed Doubles*. With this software, you can have separate sound layers in many tracks. But I decided that this film shouldn't have such levels of details; that I should do it like old times. That would bring in the spontaneity that old-time works have. In the pre-digital era, there would be only three or four tracks for foley. Two tracks for footsteps and another two or so for all the other incidental sounds. So, in *Mixed Doubles*, I decided to take all the props of the set and record their sound effects in one go. I thought this would be the best way to explore these foley guys' spontaneity.

So I took them back to the old times and began doing each scene in one go. If a mistake happened, I would have to start from the beginning of the scene. They were not very happy with this set-up and abused me before we started out. But I was sure that I needed an undivided focus for each scene.

Once it was done, it had a fantastic quality to it. For me, the best part of the film is its foley work.

There's a point in the film where the narrative graph peaks, dips and heads to the climax. It's a kitchen scene. The characters in it are a young couple going through a misunderstanding. They are sorting out the vessels and things in the kitchen. You can see some wine glasses too. For the tingling sound of the wine glasses, I had specially ordered fine glasses. There was something special about the way my foley guys were handling the glasses. There was a special audible reverberation, other than the tingling. That was a sound you didn't hear normally. It wasn't natural. But the naturalness it created inside the fiction was awesome. That sound affected me emotionally. They also did the sound for a card-game scene in the film. They did it in one go. It went in complete sync with the scene. They would ask:

'Why do you have to do it like this? What if something goes wrong?'

I would reply, 'Nothing will go wrong. You just do it! Please do it, my friend!'

I would insist and make them work. Then Chowdhuri would use his last trump to embarrass me. If asked to bend down and pick up something, he would take off his shorts. The Foley guys wore minimal clothes such as a vest and shorts to avoid the rustling sound of clothes.

The next day, I brought in a girl to assist me in the recording, as a deterrent to Chowdhuri's exhibitionistic tactics. The girl posed a problem for them. In the evening, they came and pleaded, 'Brother, please don't bring the girl here, please.'

Foley is completely a man's world.

Paaji is the best for doing the footsteps of women. He walks around in women's footwear. He has the smallest feet of them all. He loves women and is a lover at heart. Only he can imitate a woman's movements flawlessly.

Water effects are created by Chowdhuri. Hits, punches, strikes and car explosions are also his domain. He carries a lot of junk, including a car bonnet, as props. Sometimes, he would just drop a suitcase and create unimaginable sound effects. The skidding sound of a car would be made with a punching mask. These Foley guys use their props like musical instruments. Their whole body, too, becomes an instrument. A lot of sounds are completely invented. Chowdhuri is also a master at horse sounds. When you hear his range of horse sounds from neighing to its violent hiss to its 'whurrr . . .' way of crying, you will never be able to figure out that they were made by a man and not a horse. It is quite something to hear when he does the horse-hoof sounds—they sound different on different surfaces. The entire horse-sound effects in the Malayalam film *Pazhassi Raja* is Chowdhuri's.

They also did very inventive stuff for *Black*. The challenge was to enhance the sensations of touch through sound. Touch was a medium of communication in the film. We needed and created the softest of sounds.

Many things I did myself and showed them. They would join in and ask me to show them again. Remember, I have a mimicry past. They treat me as a friend more than as their recordist.

In *Saawariya*, I showed them certain tricks; not that they

can't do those things by themselves. It's just that some kind of resistance and laziness come in the way. They have done these things a million times and tend to get bored. Then you need to work on them and get them excited. They can't be blamed—Foley recording is as tiring as dubbing. You need to be focused and should be able to take lots of decisions on the run. Sound has this capacity to immerse the viewer— it carries you into the scene. Here, Foley plays a crucial supporting role. It enhances the performances on screen. We give a lot of credit to the actors for their performance. The actors themselves think that the impact comes purely out of their performance. However, there are a lot of unknown people—their lives and work—behind all this. That's another thing that makes sound a vast field—the number of people involved in it and the extremes they are willing to go to get the right sound.

When I was doing *Agnivarsha* with Satheesh, we needed to simulate the punching sound for a scene in which a bunch of soldiers were beating up the bare-bodied protagonist. We tried many times for that effect but were still not getting it right. Finally, I told Chowdhuri to take off his clothes. I stuck microphones on him. And then I hit him. The sound was perfect. But I felt really bad about it later. Like most film-makers generally do, I too behave cruelly sometimes.

If you have to shoot in a house in some location, you end up taking over the place completely. Your intention is purely selfish—you want to get the shot or the sound exactly the way you want it and you don't care about anything else. That comes from an ambition. Then you become inhuman and

insensitive to the environment and people around you. I have
behaved like this while doing *Zinda* too. My reference for the
film was the Hollywood thriller, *Fight Club.* It has the best
sounds of body punches. I analysed the film fully and wanted
to make better sounds.

Zinda had some fencing scenes. But with real swords, I
was not getting the sounds I wanted. So I went with Karnail
Singh to a gurudwara in Santacruz and brought a few bronze
swords from there and recorded the metallic clashes. The
sound had a machine-like edge to it which went very well
with the cinematic reality of the scenes. I had consciously
stressed on the cinematic-reality part than on getting the
real sounds of real swords. To capture this reality, I had even
dismantled the film sets and reassembled them in my studio.
The Foley artists then performed in this studio setting to
simulate the sounds that the actors and objects had made at
the shooting site. To get the best sounds of body punches, I
knocked Chowdhuri down, striking and hitting him many
times. That was because Gupta and Karnail Singh were not
hitting their friend properly. My motive was devoid of all such
humane concerns. All I wanted was the best sound possible.
That made me selfish. I hit him very hard. And when I went
about attacking him, I wasn't aware of an important thing—
Chowdhuri was on a fast that day. It was the Ramzan season.
Yes, I too am a Muslim, but I wasn't fasting. But Chowdhuri
was and he hadn't eaten a thing.

But then, you tend to forget the dos and don'ts in the
excitement of cinema. All you can do is to apologize later.

My first Foley work for cinema was with these guys.

Chowdhuri had told me then: 'Coat *silaake rakhna . . .*' Meaning, get yourself a suit stitched. But I never went on to win a national award for any of my works. However, whenever we were doing a film together, my foley guys would keep telling me that I would win one for this one. When the Oscar nominations were out, I told them that the time had come to stitch the suit. 'Didn't we tell you then itself?' was the reply. They are such great guys. I still haven't managed to go and meet them with the Oscar statuette. One of my most satisfying moments would be when I see my Oscar in their hands.

*

'I was under the impression . . . that I possess . . . one of the loveliest names in Kerala. But Resul Pookutty has corrected my misplaced notions. He is the owner of the most beautiful name. Resul means the Messenger of God. And Pookutty . . . means something that shines . . . like a flower sparkler in the fireworks. In front of the man who owns such an appropriate and beautiful name, what chances does the name Sukumaran (meaning, handsome) have? I also thought I was a great orator! But Mr Pookutty has snatched away even that title from me . . . with precious few words!'

That was how the noted orator Sukumar Azhikode began his speech at a function in Kerala which was held to felicitate my Oscar victory. I remember his posture and the delicate gesticulations with which he created spaces and pauses. Wow! What a performance! What spontaneity! He is the king of oratory. If Gulam Sheikh was present there, he would have swayed gracefully in matching rhythm to the words, even without knowing the Malayalam language that Azhikode was speaking. Gulam, too, is a king in his field. He is my boom man.

Boom men are the least recognized people among the location sound crew. They share this fate with the focus pullers in the camera department. No one really knows about these guys. But without them, you can't make a film. Nobody would have anything to tell them if they did their work well; but if they faltered a fraction in their work, there would be instant and loud abuse in their direction. Thanks is not a word they are used to.

Gulam Sheikh, is one of the best boom men in the world. He has terrific observation powers. He has the ability to sense the drama in the scene that is being shot. Depending on the camera's lens, its image size and field of vision, he has the sense to make out the kind of sound and projection that would be needed. He is like a good doctor who can take one look at a patient and prescribe what he needs. He can estimate everything just by looking at the camera from afar. Indeed, a good boom man has a thorough understanding of all aspects of filming, including lighting.

I will tell you what a boom man does so that you get an idea about his importance. When you are shooting, there is a space that you see through the camera frame. That's your field of vision. This space contains the things you need to see. The characters and actions are all in this space. Just outside this frame, there is a mess of people and machines; the audience is not supposed to see this mess—that's one of the fundamentals of fiction film-making. That's how you as a viewer can be pulled into the flow of the story. In the case of documentary film-making, you don't really have to follow this dictum.

While shooting, there is a mike hanging just outside of the frame that the audience sees; this mike is always moving, almost touching the boundary lines of the frame. If it is a shot of a man running, and the camera is running along with him, there is also another man running along, with a microphone, keeping it barely outside the frame. He is the all-important boom man.

In sync sound, the thumb rule is to get the mike as close to the character as possible. At the same time, the mike must never be seen by the audience. The boom man should also be someone with a capacity to balance his action physically and technically, moving along without touching the camera, cameramen, focus puller, director, lights and characters. He is the key man, who with his own aesthetic sense, helps the sound recordist capture the dialogue and performance as well as other sounds of the film.

Abroad, he or she is called a boom swinger, because they would always be swinging the boom to match its position with the action. The boom pole is a telescopic rod that can be extended up to eighteen feet and is made of carbon fibre. The mike is attached to one end. Holding an eighteen-feet-long rod with a two-kilo mike at its end, for five minutes is as good as lifting a fifty-kilo sack. If there is wind, it gets even more difficult. But in Gulam's case, it's always a case of flawless work, even in situations like getting on top of a train so as to help me accurately record the track that you hear in *Slumdog Millionaire*.

I met Gulam for the first time when he came with Satheesh
to work on the film *Limited Manuski.* I was studying at that
time. Two years later while working on the film, *Split Wide
Open,* I called Gulam to work with me—that was our first
project together.

Gulam's Bappa, too, had been a boom man. In the Hindi
film industry, ninety percent of the boom-man community is
Muslim. This has always amazed me. I don't know the historic
reasons, but a lot of people connected with the recording field
were Muslims. Most of them have their origins spreading
from the Mehboob Studio of Mumbai.In the olden days,
cinema sound was recorded along with the performance. The
boom man was an important figure then. When shootings
shifted out of the studios, live recording lost its critical role
and became a two-mike pilot-track affair just for reference
for dubbing. Now that sync sound is in vogue, pilot-track
recording has become an elaborate activity—different kinds
of mikes for different situations; headphones for the boom
man so that he can listen both to the sound he's recording
as well as to the instructions from the recordist . . . This has
made possible a creative, live interaction between the recordist
and the boom man.

Till recently, the boom men were daily-wage workers. I do
try my best to bring them to the forefront, but the industry's
psyche is still reluctant to recognize them. In many films I
have imported foreigners as boom persons. Foreigners always
get respect here. It's a vestige of our colonial past.

When we are shooting, sometimes the microphone,
when it's held overhead, casts its shadow on the frame that's

being captured. This shadow may fall on the characters, on the props or on the walls of the set. Boom people take very quick decisions and assume incredible postures to avoid these shadows. I think it's high time an award is instituted to accord recognition to talented boom men—as also to proficient focus pullers.

Saawariya was shot inside a studio. Eighty special lights were imported from abroad for this shoot. These were overhead halogen lights with special attachments. The light would hang just above the field of vision. It's a soft light. So, in a situation where the lighting is from the top and the mike is held above the characters, it's inevitable that the mike's shadow is cast on something or the other inside the space that's to be filmed. And soft lights create soft shadows with fuzzy edges—these shadows are extremely difficult to cut out; they can't be corrected with lighting either. So for *Saawariya* when large areas were lit up for the shoot, the biggest challenge lay in tackling the shadow problem. It was a more demanding problem than recording the sound perfectly. But when you watch the film, things appear simple: two characters interacting in a space. What you don't get to see or experience are the myriad other things: the lights; the boom mikes; umpteen technical and aesthetic decisions about camera movements and sound recording; the challenges that certain situations threw up; etc. Many a time, Gulam and I had done experiments with three or four boom poles in different configurations.

It is impossible to do location sound without boom mikes. A boom mike gives the most natural sound pick-up. As you would know, in the case of the camera, you get different magnifications when you shoot with different lenses; for example, while with an 80-mm lens you can show a face closely, with a 20-mm one you can make a wide angle as when you want to show an entire room. So while you shoot this space, the boom mike gives you a perspective to the sound that would be appropriate for this space. And when multiple characters move around in this space, there would be an internal rhythm to their interactions; and depending on the nature of the actors and the lens used in the camera, this rhythm could vary. This variability is connected to the perspective of the scene. The boom mike then captures sounds that give us a clear sense of the perspective of a certain 'lensing'.

You will get a clearer picture of this concept if you think of the difference between stage and cinema. In cinema, you can go closer or farther to a character as you wish, but in theatre, that is not possible. In cinema, while you take the characters closer to or farther from the audience, their positions in terms of sound can get accurately recorded using a boom mike. The interplay of the characters is communicated to us through this sound captured by the boom mike. Sound direction in films is nearly impossible without the boom mike. So the boom man has to be a thorough technician with a great sense of sound—only then can the desired results be achieved.

A few more things about sound recording on location. There are many kinds of mikes available to us, with differing pick-up patterns. Each mike hears the sound differently. Technically speaking, there are four types of microphones, based on their pick-up pattern: 'omni-directional', 'cardioid', 'hyper cardioid' and 'bi-directional'.

There are many companies making all these mikes—such as Sennheiser, Neumann, Schoeps, Brüel & Kjær. Each of these companies have developed their own circuits and diaphragm technologies. So, each company's mikes have a different timbre to the sound they capture—they differ in their frequency responses. For example, Sennheiser gives a rounded sound, while Schoeps gives off another quality.

As a sound man, you have to exercise your judgement skills to decide which mike will be best for a given situation. You have to know what make of mike can capture a sound quality in the best possible manner; it's your call as to whether Sennheiser or Neumann is to be used in a romantic scene— your decision would be based both on the nature of the sound in the scene as well as on the quality of the actor's voice. For example, Amitabh Bachchan and Shah Rukh Khan have different and special timbres to their voices; so, you have to choose the mike that can capture this timbre most naturally. Then there's the matter of controlling the sound and acoustics in a particular scene—for this, you should again choose the right mike. These are among the countless aesthetic decisions that a sound man has to take for every sequence of a film.

However, what is unfortunate is that even some of our biggest directors don't know much about these aspects. No institute teaches these things as a discipline. Film schools have hair-splitting discussions on what kind of an image you are likely to get when you shoot with a 100-mm lens; but then, even a director with no formal film education would know what would happen to his narrative space when the lenses are changed.

The qualitative differences you get in the sound of an image with a Schoeps' 'modular' microphone and with a Sennheiser's 'gun' microphone are as important. But the directors don't seem to be aware of such things. So, in a set, I become the only guy who knows about such things. Then it becomes my concern or choice alone. In my entire career, I have never come across a director saying he wanted a particular mike in a shot. Except perhaps for Mani Kaul, there is not a single director capable of that in India. (You get a lot of such directors in French cinema.) Here, the film sound field is all about personal, individualistic pursuits. So our breed of sync-sound recordists has become powerful individuals. Dear directors—we have already decided upon the sound for your image—thanks to your ignorance!

Let me now share with you a piece of knowledge. Why do we feel like singing in the bathroom? The reason is 'psycho acoustics'. In the small space of a bathroom, sound waves reflect back and forth.

Normally, when you open your mouth and utter something, you hear three kinds of sounds—the sound from the mouth, its reflection from the surroundings, and the sound conducted through your body, or bone conduction. And we comprehend sound through two kinds of hearing. The first two kinds of sound you hear with your ears and the third kind through the whole of your body. That's why when we hear our voice on a tape, we find it a bit unfamiliar. The tape can't record the sound that you hear through the bone conduction within your body.

We don't find our recorded voice on the tape very appealing.

In the bathroom, your voice gets a bit enhanced because of the reflection and a bit of delay and reverberation. Your voice gets a little prettier. When you hum a tune, it gets sustained. Then you might even be able to hit the lower notes of the legendary singer Yesudas!

The cadence of an actor's voice changes in different acoustic environments—like in a hall, a corridor, a room, etc. But they don't seem to realize this factor. I have seen only one actor who is intelligent enough to know this and modulate accordingly—Amitabh Bachchan.

While recording for films, I noticed that he was paying careful attention to these things. Once we were dubbing for a scene shot in a hall. The hall had a bit of a reverb, so his dialogues used to 'hang' there for a little while. But when he came to the studio for dubbing, there was no reverb there. You see, a sound studio is a 'dead room'—while dubbing, an artiste can hear his voice only through the headphones. Bachchan demanded that he should be able to hear the reverb in the hall where the shooting had taken place. He knew that this was the only way he could match his original performance on location. That's intelligence. That's what makes him a true great of Indian cinema. When he performs he believes in whatever he is doing, however mindless the requirements of our popular cinema are. He also brings into these exaggerated, over-the-top pop idioms of Hindi cinema, his own superlative craft.

As I mentioned, in different environments, the rhythm of an actor's performance changes. It's the sound recordist's responsibility to detect the changes and capture them accordingly. You need to do total justice to the actor's performance. So, it's critical that I choose the right mike for a particular acoustic environment. It's a decision as important as the selection of lens, for a director to get involved in. Instead, I handle these things like a dictator. The directors are completely unaware of this part.

The boom man is the one who helps me to do justice to all this stuff that I am talking about. His actions are dictated by the different mikes that I give him. For example, the 'long-gun' microphone's angle of coverage is different—when you use this mike, you need to swing the boom differently to catch the dialogues. The angle of coverage is a characteristic that changes with different mikes. While wielding the mike, the boom man also has to handle complex issues like cutting out extraneous sounds, and maintaining the mike's focus while being on the move. Gulam Sheikh is someone who handles the boom with a thorough knowledge of all these subtleties.

*

Now a word about focus pullers. Let's say that you are filming a scene wherein the character is walking towards the camera; then you will have one guy continuously adjusting or 'pulling' the camera lens's focal length according to the reducing distance between the character and the camera. The man who is doing this 'pulling' is the focus puller; he has to do a lot of mental calculations in his job (and remember, things like video monitors came into the filming process only recently—

earlier, it all depended on the judgement skills of the focus puller). Actually, I consider the focus puller a more skilful worker than the cameraman. Similar is the case with the boom man. When you see on screen someone moving at a hundred-kilometre speed, you have to understand that there is also a camera moving at the same speed as well as a man adjusting its focus at the same speed, throughout. Simultaneously, there's also a guy running with the microphone. Cinema is an art form where maximum human skills are used to generate human happiness. And in this art form, sound is always handled by hidden hands. If by any chance the hands become visible and the boom appears in the frame, that shot becomes useless. Likewise, if one of the frames goes out of focus just for half a metre, the shot becomes useless. If it's all done well, nobody says anything; but a fraction of a fault will trigger a volley of abuse! That's Indian cinema. We have no respect for our technicians.

Compared to their ilk elsewhere in world cinema, none of these guys are highly paid. Only after I started objecting loudly did my boom man's wages get into the thousands; five years ago, it was in the hundreds. Post-Oscar, for the reception organized for me at the Institute, I had also brought along Gulam and my entire team. I called them all on stage and introduced them. There's no sound without them, you see.

We still see only the actors and actresses getting credit for the success of a film. I did not want my success to be seen as something that had been achieved by a single individual; behind this success is the hard work of several people. If they had gone unnoticed, there wouldn't be any difference between me and the regular film stars. However, in the general panic of my Oscar speech, I had forgotten to mention their names. That was a mistake on my part. I had finished that speech in thirty-eight seconds. You see, the Oscar ceremony is a big television show timed to the tune of seconds. After your name is announced, you have only sixty seconds to get up from the seat, go up to the stage, receive the statuette, deliver the speech and come back. If you take longer than that, they will cut your mike, and you will have to leave the stage. They had sent the instructions and videos well in advance so as to give me guidance about my conduct during the ceremony. These are all part of the West's impeccable pre-planning regime. Moreover, that was also my first time—I had never been to, or seen an Oscar show. Gripped by stage-fright, I missed many things I had wanted to say and ended up saying things which came to me at that time. I was not able to take the individual names of my crew members—all I could do was to give them a general credit: *everybody who contributed to this film.* I really consider this as a mistake on my part. There is nothing I can do other than to apologize to all of them through this book. I also swear that I will do whatever I can so that this invisible community gets the recognition it so richly deserves.

4

ORGANIZED CHAOS: THE DYNAMICS OF THE INDIAN FILM INDUSTRY

Hindi cinema has many streams. To get into the popular mainstream cinema and to work and reach a respectable position in it is a tough task. It involves a lot of games. Someone like Satheesh is not fascinated by the mainstream. His pattern is to do the kind of projects he wants to do and do them differently from the run-of-the-mill sort. He considers the comfort and satisfaction he derives from this as a matter of great importance in life.

I am a bit different. What drives me is a powerful inner desire to communicate with more people. This attitude has support in many of my other character traits. I don't get completely disheartened by monetary losses or when cheated by others. I might have an immediate emotional reaction in such situations, but eventually, there is some kind of God's grace that helps me ignore profits and losses, and leads me on to my next project. I still have kept with me all the bounced cheques worth lakhs of rupees. It doesn't worry me much.

I came to the Institute having seen only mainstream films. Those are the films that excited me and got me ambitious. Yes, later when I studied cinema, its possibilities had excited me in another way. But mainstream was always my true calling.

Only by staying with the mainstream can we make people aware of the changes that we bring into cinema. Indeed, our mainstream can definitely do with some changes. There are people outside the mainstream who know cinema better. They and their works are undeniably very important. Unfortunately, they don't have the money to make the films they want to. And even if they have the resources, their cinema might eventually not reach the public at large. So if I hang around in the non-mainstream space, my work becomes a narrow, subjective trip. What has always propelled me has been popular culture. I think the youth of today tries to identify with the popular media. So if you want to talk to them, popular cinema is the platform. I want to be as close to that generation as possible. When kids call me to their colleges, I happily go. Those are places where you get a sense of tomorrow. My best friends are the kids of my brothers and sisters. My interactions with them have given me invaluable insights into the current trends. That's the mindset I came with, to work in mainstream popular cinema. But the field is full of nasty games that people play. If I start talking about that, I might sound as if I am contradicting myself. But what I am talking about is the spirit with which I approach the whole thing. I try to find a balance between this spirit and the realities of the industry of popular cinema. It's tough. Maybe some day, someone might do some research and find out the artistic merits of this tough task.

Let's look at Bollywood. They start by making a package, an empty box. It's a hollow, empty matchbox. On the outside, they put some live, burning matchsticks. Amitabh Bachchan, Shah Rukh Khan, Katrina Kaif or Kareena Kapoor could be these hot numbers. This is the show that brings in the money.

Among producers, there are guys who make films without ever spending even a rupee from their own pocket. The money comes from somewhere else. This is the most popular modus operandi. A lot of them have been doing it for generations. And this is the only operation they know. Their technique is to pay only those people who are in the front of the show. They specialize in finding ways not to pay the rest of the crew. There are people who have been respectfully doing this for many years.

Wittingly or unwittingly, this was the scene I jumped into—in order to do sound. I am the kind of person who takes people at their face value. I trust people easily; I am not the calculative type. When I see a good project, I get all excited and emotional and jump into it. If there is an opportunity to do good work, I am willing to make some compromises. But often this compromise is limited only to my payment. There have been occasions when I have had to sacrifice my payment in order to release the work I had completed from the studio premises—by diverting my payment into it. At a business level, I can say I also do the executive producer's job, free of cost!

Post-production plays a major part in cinema's sound. Music directors get paid because they are known names. When I started off, I didn't even have money for basic survival. When doing the film *Boom*, in London, I lived on the ten pounds a day that the producers gave me. And I had to spend money from my pocket to finish that work and return.

But it was that film that helped me make my way into the popular stream. Amitabh Bachchan, Jackie Shroff and Gulshan Grover were the lead actors. Madhu Sapre and Padmalakshmi too. It was also Katrina Kaif's first film. It was good fun working with all these people. I really enjoyed the work. As an artist, I came to understand Seema Biswas through this film. I become friends with Padmalakshmi. Katrina was then a naïve, young girl from London who didn't know anything about the Mumbai film Industry. I also got my chance to closely interact with an actor like Amitabh Bachchan. It was a cheerful, youthful world.

When I do these films in Satheesh's studio, I end up becoming the guarantor for payments and eventually pay from my pocket. In films that are known to be done artistically too, I have been through similar situations.

That is one aspect. Yet on the other hand, there was a passion to get into those 'artistic' movies and do a different kind of work in order to earn a name.

But Mumbai has another side to it, which fascinates me. Mumbai never abandons anyone. If you have faith in that city, it will hold you. Step out and take a round. There will always be good-hearted friends to help you out. Mumbai always had that in her.

I have employed many agents and managers to collect the money owed to me. I had one friend, Gita, who used to work in an NGO. In the course of a conversation I happened to mention to her about the kind of money that people owed me. She got excited.

'I will get the money for you. I'm your manager, right?'

'Okay. You will get ten per cent commission.'

'How much is owed to you?'

'Lakhs.'

She quickly calculated and found out that she would make a huge amount. She had some experience fund-raising for the NGO. She also knew that she was pretty good at it.

But around five months passed without any news from her. Then I called her and asked how it was going.

'My God, Resul! I have to bow down to you, man! The guys you are dealing with are so shameless. I can't do it. If you need it, I can give you some money from my NGO fund—if you have no money to survive.'

When Baiju Kalluvila came to Mumbai in 2000 to become my manager, he energetically took up the issue of collecting the money that was owed to me. He would take a daily taxi fare from me and go about collecting these monies. Eventually, he too realized that it was just a waste of both time and money.

Then we started telling the defaulters heart-rending stories of poverty and hospital expenses. But the answers would invariably be: 'How can that be, Resul? You are doing so well!'

Yes, I was doing very well—except that no one was paying me.

*

Generally, people think that everything that's connected to cinema is entertaining. But it is far from the truth; in fact, things can turn quite dangerous during certain shooting assignments.

In my case, once a shoot starts, I forget everything else. In one instance, while recording the sound of a train, I was standing very close to the tracks and got caught in between two trains going in the opposite directions. I thought my story was about to end. When a train passes, it creates an air suction. I was caught and pulled into this suction. Luckily, the suction of the train coming from the opposite direction pulled me out of the other train's suction. In that split second, I somehow lay flat on the ground. When the trains had gone, I thought if I continued in this fashion, I would very soon be reaching the end of my own track!

I have escaped major accidents by the proverbial breadth of a hair. Once I was recording the sound of a helicopter. In my attempt to capture the whining sound from up close, I walked dangerously close to the fast-spinning rotor blades. You see, when I am recording, I don't see, I only hear. Luckily, people came running and pulled me out. I had reached inches away from the blades.

Another instance was when I had gone to Tamil Nadu to shoot a documentary. It was about a tribe of people who catch snakes, eat rats—that kind of stuff. They are an amazing people. While on a casual walk with them, sometimes a guy would put his hand inside the grass and come up with a snake. I would get shocked because he had actually picked up the snake from right under my feet! The day we started, they had caught a massive cobra, a magnificent eight-footer with a huge hood!

We were filming it, feeling a bit nervous. The cameraman had told me to give him instructions live, because he couldn't really make out the real distances while looking through the camera. He didn't want to get too close unwittingly and get bitten. And I could see everything, only my ears were occupied.

We were taking the shot of the cobra aiming its strike at the camera. I was only a foot away from the snake. My feet were well within the snake's striking radius. There were a few Russell vipers, next to it in an earthen pot. A viper started making a whistling sound. I pushed the mike towards the viper, without taking my eyes off the cobra. I moved the mike slowly and rested it on the pot. I thought it would be great to have the viper's whistle sound to accompany the shot of the cobra striking. So I was busy capturing the ideal sound for the visual. And my attention wavered because I was trying to focus on two separate things at the same time—something strictly against the basic safety rules of filming. Here the danger was from snakes. Elsewhere it could be from something else. But that's the thing about cinema—you get uncontrollably excited about the things you do. Therein lies the pleasure as well as the peril of the profession.

On the one hand, I was to control the cameraman's proximity to the cobra. On the other, I was moving my mike slowly to the viper's pot. This multi-tasking made the mike move slightly. You know what happens when a snake comes close to a moving thing. The viper suddenly struck the mike. I was hearing everything through the headphones. When the viper struck the mike, I felt it had struck me on my forehead. It was a momentary illusion. I was convinced that the viper had bitten me on my face. I threw the mike away and screamed! In a second, I came back to my senses and figured out that the viper had struck the mike, and not me. I looked at the mike. Snake poison was dripping from it.

In cinema especially, you must not do anything carelessly. Now I will come to the other story. It's a story told to me by cinematographer Ravi K. Chandran. It happened when they were shooting the film *Virasat*. One boy used to come to director Priyadarshan's house, daily. He wanted to assist Priyadarshan. The boy was one crazy film buff.

Finally, just to get rid of this daily nuisance, Priyadarshan asked the boy to come to the set the next day. The next day, the boy was promptly present at the set. The location was close to a waterfall. Priyan told his associates to put the boy as an assistant in some department. They gave him the job of a clapper boy, the first step to direction. The boy was really excited. He stepped into the waterfall to give the clap. In his excitement he slipped, fell down and drowned.

He was only five minutes into his first day at his first job! Nobody knew who he was or where he was from or anything. That's one big problem with our industry. Anybody can come from anywhere without any address or experience and join the industry; they don't even have to mention their name.

The death became a big issue. Priyan too didn't know anything about the boy. They found a phone bill in his pocket. They called the number; it was a girl who picked up the phone. They told her that there had been a minor accident. She told them how happy he was when he had last called. He had told her Priyadarshan had finally let him work on his film and had asked him to come to the shoot the next day. She was his girlfriend. That's how they located the boy's house.

That day's shoot was cancelled. Ravi was narrating this story in the middle of an interview with a television channel when the interviewer had asked him if he had any message for the youth. Then Ravi went on to add that this was not an isolated incident and that such things happen when one gets too excited about cinema, forgetting oneself in the process. And that this excitement might affect the safety of one's own and others' lives. He stated that youngsters should enter the film industry realizing that it's a profession like any other.

The interviewer then told Ravi, 'Thank you, sir, for giving such a great message. The boy who died that day was my brother.'

Ravi was left speechless.

I always remember this story. Anybody who works in the film industry should know about this story and keep it in mind. Especially, considering the situation in the Indian film industry—here, anybody can work without any experience or training. In fact, these are the people who get exploited the most.

*

The Indian film industry is a strange creature. A lot in this place occurs without any planning. It is a space where chance rules the possibilities. One could say that this industry runs on the fuel of desires. Those desires could be of a scriptwriter, director or producer.

In Kerala, at one time, it was usual for people to head to the Gulf countries if they couldn't do anything at home. And some of these guys went on to make some good money. Then, at the age of forty or forty-five, these guys would develop a burning ambition to produce a film. They would say that they are ready to invest a couple of crores in making a movie. When I went to Kerala after receiving the Oscar, many such wannabe producers had come up with interesting requests. One guy was willing to invest up to five crores, and even said that he wouldn't mind it if he didn't get any of it back—all he wanted was to make a name internationally. I now have become a channel for fulfilling such ambitions.

At the same time, one can't dismiss the aspect of ambitions. In Indian cinema, most of the actors are the products of this kind of burning ambition. A lot of great artistes, including people like Shah Rukh Khan, have made their inroads into the industry completely driven by their madly intense ambition. What propels them is this intensity and the strength of their aspiration.

I tell my juniors sometimes: 'What is important is not the sophistication of our methods, but the strength of our idea. The execution of the idea could be good or bad, great or moderate; but the idea itself has to be strong. It's the same with ambition. And if we possess the right combination of idea and ambition, the result will be explosively powerful. You can clearly see this pattern behind all the great successes of Indian cinema. Generally speaking, it's not an industry driven by planning and design.'

The aspect of planning is even less in Malayalam films. But Malayalam cinema differs significantly from its Hindi counterpart because of its obsession with literature. Malayalam cinema is closely linked to reading and writing. In its early days especially, it was driven by people with a solid foundation in literature. The current bunch is only a shadow of those stalwarts. That's why Malayalam cinema has now become spurious and soulless. Moreover, even the good storytellers' talent to tell their stories has been amputated by the changed nature of marketing strategies. The people behind Malayalam cinema are now driven more by marketing ambitions than by a desire to make a great film.

Perhaps there's no other industry in the world that is as much driven by the phenomenon of ambition like the Hindi film industry. And, curiously enough, intertwined with this surging ambition is our wish to hang on to the past. We are a deeply nostalgic people. The epics, the Ramayana and the Mahabharata, became such huge television successes not because of anything else. The storytelling, the craft and the general execution may be of appalling mediocrity, but the association with the story content is so strong in the minds of our people. It is a subject for deep thought as to why we are so interested in staying stuck to the past. One reason could be that in our society, social securities are not built by the state, but by human bonds. Ours is not an individual-centric society. Indeed, our society may be far better than individual-centric societies. That is one of the reasons behind the success of *Slumdog Millionaire,* I believe.

In *Slumdog's* final sequence, when dealing with the last quiz question, the hero is not motivated by the prize money. He continues playing even when he doesn't know the answer to the question. If he loses he loses all the money, and if he wins, he gets all of it. That's left to fate. And his fate is such that he gets his sweetheart back. The message of the movie—that profits and losses are not the be-all and end-all of life—became especially relevant as the movie was playing at a time when the Western world was going through a severe economic depression.

Even now, the individual Indian life is not governed by profits and losses. It is this Indian characteristic of life that excited the audience abroad and made them take to this film with such passion. It created a connection and caused an awakening. *Slumdog* generated entirely different reactions as well. Most of that came from the Indians living in the US. For them, the film posed an image issue—they have this amplified notion that Indians are no less than anyone in the world. So they got a bit bewildered when their homeland's slums and urban low life suddenly came into the limelight.

Staying on the topic of ambition, I have to say that it is this trait that has helped the top-notch artistes of Indian cinema become magnificent folk artistes. Shah Rukh Khan is totally folk. So is Amitabh Bachchan. The stalwarts among the popular heroes of Indian cinema function at that level. One aspect of folk artistes is that they have no inhibitions. In the middle of a crowd, they give full play to their celebratory instincts—they beat their drums, sing their songs and dance out their narratives which have been part of the community for generations. So on that count, Amitabh and Shah Rukh are towering folk artistes of our time. And popular cinema is the ultimate folk art of our time. As was the case with the folk performances of olden times, people now throng to the popular movies—to see, to hear, and perhaps at times to even participate.

I entered into this scene with a background of formal training. That gave me a tremendous positioning. From the very beginning, I understood and was aware of the difference between mainstream and niche—popular and art-house. I understand each type has its own sensibilities, its own visual and aural symbols, and its own logic, as it were. I consider myself lucky in that respect—as one who is conscious of how these two streams of cinema operate. However, this understanding was enriched and consolidated in the years after I passed out of the Institute. Working in the field gives you a different insight altogether. You realize that what you've already learnt might need to be improvised and modified anew. This understanding was a good thing, but can also be dangerous. That's because once you understand something, you need to have the conviction to continue. And once you have that conviction, you might have to actually modify your work. There are aspects of your craft that you have learned formally and which you use judiciously—you need to overcome such practices emotionally. Then you have to make it work in a new framework with conviction.

I had figured this out in my third year at the Institute. In the last eight months of my final year there, I was engrossed in a struggle to fit into that framework of popular cinema. You see, I had come to study cinema when I was emotionally on fire. When I look back at life in the Institute, it now appears to be a separate island—but a robust one at that. I reached there at the peak of my madness. But once I actually reached there, I realized that madness was not the reality there. When I look at the fifteen years that have passed since the Institute, I see that my sensibilities have moved on from what I had learned there. Yet, I can't ever discard what I learned there, because that is my foundation.

The works of Ritwik Ghatak made me realize the need for emotional conviction—as opposed to intellectual conviction—in one's work. It's only with such conviction that can you translate your insights into the simplicity of folk expressions. The core of Ghatak's cinema is melodrama—feature-length Indian melodrama.

What we need to consider here is not whether Ghatak's films were commercial successes or not. What's important is his stand. In the case of Malayalam theatre, there are a few plays of the KPAC (Kerala People's Arts Club) without much political overtones. Or plays like *Kattu Kuthira* 'Wild Horse'. These plays were once part of the Malayali's collective conscience. One common element in all these plays is the helpless situation—a situation that every Malayali can identify with. These plays were all huge successes. But even if they hadn't become big hits, their merit would not have suffered. Ghatak's films belong to this category. That's how I view his work.

During our feverish student days, cinema meant everything to us. Then Ghatak came in and said some things that had the effect of a hammer strike on our heads: 'I have chosen cinema because I couldn't reach that many people through theatre. Tomorrow if a new medium appears, which can reach more people than cinema, I will shift to that.'

He is no longer alive. And if he was alive, I am sure he would be doing television now. His aim was to reach the maximum number of people. Currently our TV is totally crap. TV is far superior abroad. I have wondered how Ghatak would have positioned himself in TV. And I have found answers for it—mainly that he would have done things with emotional conviction. Those things might not have had a lot for the brain, but would have had enough for the heart. Ghatak's films have helped me to direct my aims towards reaching more people through a language of the heart.

For many people with formal training, it's a knotty issue as to how to position themselves in the emotionally vibrant and throbbing world of this modern folklore. There are many among my batchmates who have not been very successful. But then, it is not about professional success or failure. It is about the emotional intensity one needs to have in order to feel the pulse of the crowd. I think it's an important quality.

The films of David Dhawan have this ability to sway the crowd. He is the most successful director the Institute has produced. He has an identity. Everyone says he makes crap

films. But what he makes are comedies. In combination
with the actor Govinda, he has given us terrific comedies
which have also been great hits. The films they have made
are absolutely idiotic stuff, but done with great conviction.
That's because of his faith in the project. I would equate
David Dhawan's films with those of Bunuel's, although the
latter's are completely surrealistic and on the other end of the
cinematic spectrum. Mani Kaul's works, too, are at the other
end. Both these ends work—what doesn't work is the middle-
of-the-road stuff.

Rajat Kapoor's early films belong to that middle-of-the-
road category. They didn't work. But they were part of Rajat's
search to find his own ways of film-making. My beginning
was with him. I have done all his films. So I am a witness to
his growth.

One problem that I have found with his films is that he
doesn't commit to anything. A bit like Eric Rohmer. I worked
on Rajat's first film, *Private Detective*, thinking that it would
be a great film. I later realized that it didn't become a great
movie because he had gone the middle-of-the-road way. Yet
that film is a terrific study on the part of Rajat of the thriller
genre. If you know this genre academically well, you will be
able to enjoy *Private Detective*.

In this film, while staying within the thriller format, Rajat
has done a lot of things that are actually outside of that genre.
For example, in a thriller the good detective knows everything;
in the end, the detective is the one who reveals the plot to the
audience. But in this film, the audience gets to know many

things that the detective doesn't. The audience becomes the detective. The movie is fantastic—at the script level. It's not explicitly Brechtian, but can work like one.

Cinema has been intellectualized a lot. I am not saying it's a bad thing. But it doesn't make it accessible to everyone. Cinema should be accessible to everyone. That's what gives me joy. Otherwise, it turns into an elite indulgence. If a film is not accessible to most people, then the kind of hardship that went in behind it becomes merely a cinematic exercise. Yes, you can indulge in such an exercise if you have a lot of money. But then, at the end of the day, all you can say is, okay, good exercise!

Ritwik Ghatak becomes relevant here. He was extremely intelligent. But he never indulged in any kind of intellectualism in his movies. He was constantly striving to be a better communicator. He was a master of the mis-en-scène, the elements that go into the construction of a cinematic or theatre scene—visuals, compositions, lighting, movement, acting, sound, cut . . . everything.

It's the French who theorize about all this. They have deconstructed films like James Ford's *Stage Coach*. That was an intellectual exercise they had done in the publication *Cahiers du Cinéma*. When you read it, *Stage Coach* comes across as a great film. The French have deconstructed Alfred Hitchcock too. I don't know whether Hitchcock himself ever meant it to be that way—the kind of things that have been attributed to his films. He is a master craftsman of the thriller genre. But nobody had considered him as a master in the beginning, around the time of the French New Wave Cinema. It was Jean-Luc Godard and his likes who were considered the masters. But now in world cinema, Hitchcock is the most popular director.

Once you read up about the mis-en-scène concept and then watch Ghatak, it would seem that he has done things with extreme ease. One scene in *Meghe Dhaka Tara* is a good example. It involves the central woman character. She has a job, and a lover. Her younger sister gets very close to this lover. The girls' mother is interested in the younger daughter marrying the man as she doesn't want the daughter with a job to get married and leave the house. When the younger sister and the man are talking, the mother asks the elder sister to serve them tea. This is a pivotal scene. There is a shot of her bringing a cup of tea. It's a frontal shot, taken with amazing ease at a slightly low angle. The girl's face is blocked by the tea cup—we can't see her face. In the foreground, her lover and her sister are talking. The serving of that cup of tea signifies the elder sister's exit from the life of her lover. This is classic mis-en-scene. It's an intensely emotional scene, all soaked up in the Indian ethos. The specialty of Ghatak's genius is that he never made a frame that the audience couldn't identify with. Here, too, with this depiction of an Indian domestic situation, he doesn't step out of the realm of the familiar and the identifiable.

But the cinema that falls in the intellectual category steps out of this structure. It will take you to spaces that are alien and unidentifiable. Ghatak's material is straight from the heart. Indian cinema hasn't had a more intense film-maker than Ghatak. The Malayalam film-maker John Abraham was a potential Ghatakian. Today in Indian cinema, I can point to no film-maker and say that he or she is on fire like Ghatak was.

India has the biggest film industry of the world. But if you take mainstream Hindi cinema, you will find only one film that works at all levels—story, acting, music, camera, sound—and that film is *Sholay*. Till date, here has not been a single mainstream Hindi film that can stake a claim to taking *Sholay*'s place.

In the case of Malayalam cinema, that place goes to *Padayottam* which hit the theatres in 1982. It was the first purely Indian 70-mm film. *Padayottam*, too, excels in all aspects—technical and cinematic—and was a big success.

These two films are larger-than-life spectacles. Even pure fantasy. Still, they carry a slice of real life that we can identify with.

On seeing *Sholay*, you might even think that the kind of friendship that Jay and Veeru share, is an exclusively Indian phenomenon. The relationship between Baiju Kalluvila and me is like that. We are even ready to die for each other. That is the Indian ethos. I don't think you can find a parallel to it in the West. Hollywood doesn't have a story without a gun. They might come up with ever more sophisticated gadgets—but essentially, they are all guns in one way or the other. Eventually what Hollywood talks about is of fear. Even in Hindi cinema, these days there are a lot of films that amplify the fears of Mumbai—these movies look at Mumbai as if it's a different country altogether. This trend has to do with the fact that the scriptwriters are now prone to reacting instantly to real-life stories rather than coming up with stories from their imagination which needs gestation time.

In this respect, the early films of Amitabh Bachchan stand apart. *Sholay* has the Indian ethos at its core. The success of Amitabh Bachchan as an actor lies in his portrayal of a character who is doing the right thing but at a wrong time. That's mainstream cinema's take on the Mahabharata's character, Karna. You see, we are a people who live submerged in our ethos. Legends and sacred texts are big things for us.

The story is no different with south Indian films. In Telugu films, N.T. Rama Rao only portrayed gods and righteous heroes. Similar was the case with MGR (M.G. Ramachandran) in Tamil films. In Tamil cinema, now there's Rajnikant in his various avatars—of autodriver, bus conductor, and because of technology being very much part of our lives, even as a software wizard. The common factor in all these heroes is that they are the right guys at the wrong places.

A parallel thought prompts me to say that the entire Indian democracy is in the wrong place. In India, everyone has accepted corruption as a norm. This has to do with the decay that has crept into our management system over the last sixty years or so. Our only hope lies in the judicial system. But there too, corruption must have infiltrated. I know a friend of mine's friend, a judge who says, 'I am not an honest man, but I am not corrupt.' This sort of mindset is reflected in the actions of our cinema heroes as well.

But the situation is not that bleak—there are still some good people around. There are some exceptionally first-rate bureaucrats in our country. They may not have the sophistication, but they have the goodness of truth in them. All said, as a whole, we are a collective of people who desire overall goodness. It is this collective conscience that reflects in our cinema.

Our people want to embrace progress. The man who runs a tea shop is educating his kids so that they can doctors. Our society as a whole is driven by hope. We have no room for gloominess.

The West is not like that. It's gloomy. People there function in a straight line. They can't handle chaos—for instance, there's no chaos while getting into a bus or crossing the road. However, emotionally, there is chaos in their lives. But in order to collectively maintain the straight line, they manage their internal chaos with psychiatric therapy.

We look at psychiatry very differently. If we go by Western standards and look at our society, more than half of our people need psychiatric help. But we don't opt for that. We go ahead and function full steam. We are powered by our beliefs, an ethos we have had for generations. But at the same time, we are a monstrously complex society. Even so, our strength lies in the concept of unity that everyone shares—this unity is very much a reality although we are a divided lot religiously and although at times some political games are played by the various religious dispensations. I am sure all Indians accept one thing—that we are all part of a collective whole, that we are collectively one. And that there is a truth that exists somewhere in the middle of all this mess.

This is what sustains and strengthens us as a society even in the absence of sophistication. It's amazing how we manage our chaos. We are forever trying to find order in it, whereas the western society is managing an organized environment. It can't deal with anything that is not organized.

During the shoot of *Slumdog Millionaire*, Danny was often not sure whether it will all happen at all. For example, a shot has to be taken at ten, and you need about five hundred people for it. But at ten, not everyone would be ready. That is something the Westerners can't accept. But by eleven, before leaving from that location, the shot would have been taken. It would have been accomplished in an incredibly chaotic and noisy manner. But once done, the shot would have amazing spontaneity. You can work in India only if you can accept the chaos. As Danny put it from his Indian experience: 'Don't expect to change anything here. You will not be able to change anything. You have to go there, be there, be one among them, and accept that you have to work within this.'

For me, Danny Boyle is someone who has completely understood Indian life.

If a film-maker comes here, checks the call sheet and asks why we are not taking the shot at nine twenty, we will say, get lost! We are only bothered about one question: have we done today's stuff?

Done.

Okay, good.

That's it.

PART 5

HOLLYWOOD CALLING

1

DANNY BOYLE AND THE SLUMDOG EXPERIENCE

In 2007 I had to go to Haridwar to do a commercial. That was three months before I met Danny Boyle for the first time. The commercial was produced by a company based in Bangalore. They hadn't sent me the script or any other details. So I decided to carry all my equipment in order to handle any eventuality. I had a dozen bags full of stuff. I had told the producers that I preferred travelling by road from Delhi to Haridwar; but in case it was to be by train, they should book a whole coupé for me and the equipment.

When I reached Delhi, there was no vehicle or coupé. They had just booked two seats in the train. I just lost my cool. I called up the line producers—two strangers, Pravesh Sahani and Sanjay Chawla. I was shaking with rage. I tore into them and told them that I was not coming for the shoot. They profusely apologized; and finally I relented and reached Haridwar. The arrangements for my stay were also not very good. I was displeased with the whole affair. I started the work in a real bad mood. But once I got into it, I forgot about everything else. Later, Pravesh and Sanjay explained that I had to face all the inconveniences only because nobody had told them anything about my travel requirements.

It was a three-day shoot. By the end of the shoot, the three of us became close friends. We even had a tearful farewell. It was a remarkable change of mood from the bad note that we had started off on.

A couple of months passed. I was on the shoot of Sanjay Leela Bhansali's *Saawariya*. A call came.

'Resul bhai, would you do the sound for a Danny Boyle film?'

I told him: 'Pravesh bhai, if it's with you, I'll definitely do it. But I'll call you back in two minutes; I'm in the middle of a shoot right now.'

I quickly logged on and read up on Danny Boyle on the Internet. I wanted to check whether the Danny Boyle I knew of and this Danny Boyle was the same guy. When I checked the IMDB (Internet Movie Data Base) website, there was only one Danny Boyle—the same Danny Boyle who had directed movies like *Trainspotting* and *The Beach*. Ah! I remembered the time I was completely stunned by *The Beach*.

I called back immediately!

'Is it the same Danny Boyle who did *Trainspotting* and all?'

'Yes, the same man.'

I said, 'I am on.' I didn't have any second thoughts.

What came to mind was my hostel room at the Institute—D22—which had a poster of *Trainspotting*. It was a cult film of that time. Later, when I was in London to mix for the film, *Snip*, the director Sunil and I were drinking beer. There was another guy across the road, also sipping beer. Sunil pointed him out to me and said that this Scottish guy across the road had acted in *Trainspotting*!

All those details lying in the backyard of my memory suddenly came alive; like a dream coming true.

I remembered watching *The Beach*. That was the time when Leonardo DiCaprio was at his peak, right after *Titanic*. Satheesh and I had gone to see the film together. We both loved the film. The travel element in it had appealed to us, especially because both of us were avid trekkers. The film itself had the mind of a traveller. Even though the climax had its problems, the rest of the film was fantastic. I was sure about working with this amazing director.

Danny Boyle was in Mumbai. Pravesh asked me whether I could go and meet him.

'Oh, yes.'

Thrice the meeting didn't take place. Either he or I wasn't free. Finally, we met after a week. It was a breakfast meeting at nine. Danny entered with a wide grin, the same grin he still has on his face. From there on, we worked together for months. Yes, we did have our share of problems too. But he still maintains his characteristic grin, that's what's special about him. He is a magnificent man—a great human being with love, compassion and respect for the lives of others. This is not an opinion that I alone hold. For anybody who knows him closely, what makes him such a great guy is not the greatness of his cinema—that may be the case with people who don't know him personally—but his great sense of humanity. When you speak to him, you might end up thinking that you yourself are Danny Boyle, while the real Boyle is like you, some insignificant guy. This is what I see as the special quality in a person. Danny Boyle is a greater film-maker than all the film-makers I have worked with so far; and he is also the most ideal human being of them all.

So we started talking about things. He had a rolled-up paper in his hand. I was dying to ask him a lot of things and finally settled on a question: whether he had seen any Hindi films. The films he said he liked had nothing to do with the kind of work I did. He loved *Black Friday*. He really liked the sound in that film: 'The dialogues were very good and audible.' He also believed it's very tough to do live sound in India. I told him that the film was completely dubbed in a studio: 'It might be a novelty for you. But we consider that as rubbish. It sounds like that. You like it probably because you haven't worked with ADR (Automatic Dialogue Replacement also known as dubbing) before. Here we are sick of it. Also, dubbed sound is a tasteless thing. I see ADR as something that doesn't communicate the environment of the actor to the audience. So it seems, in the matter of ADR and live sound, we belong to two completely different schools of thought.' Then he opened the roll of paper and asked me which films he should watch from this list. I looked at the paper. It was a list he had downloaded of all the films I had done! He had done enough research on me already! I shrank to the size of a tiny worm. He knew everything about me. He was asking me to recommend my films for him to see. I was a bit taken aback. As far as I was concerned, I was dying to work with him. And I thought, which one should I suggest?

Finally I told him to take his pick and whichever film he chose, I was wholly there in that.

He said, 'Okay, do one thing, you read this script. Then we meet again next week.' He gave me a copy of the bound script of *Slumdog Millionaire* that day.

I thought, okay, Bollywood also gives you bound scripts; most of them blatantly cooked up after watching other DVDs. Even so, to get a copy of such a script, you needed to sign a non-disclosure agreement first!

And here was one of the most acclaimed film-makers of the world, handing over his script just like that and telling me to read it first before we discuss it next week!

That is the difference.

A month before this, a famous woman had called me. She told me I should do the sound for her film. It was a big project and her directorial venture. I agreed. Her secretary then called me and gave me a date and time for the meeting. Just the day before the scheduled meeting, I got a call from the secretary again. This time she wanted my address. I gave her my address and asked her what it was for. It was for the confidentiality agreement.

'But why am I signing a confidentiality agreement?'

'That is because you are going to have a meeting tomorrow. You can't disclose the contents of that meeting anywhere. This is the agreement for that.'

I said, 'Hold on, hold on. It is my decision to work on your film or not. This person I am going to meet tomorrow, how many films has she done? I have done sound for thirty-five films. On what basis of quality should I meet this person?

That's one thing. The other is, what this confidentiality agreement means is that you don't trust anyone, right? If I have to sign something like this just to meet someone, I am not even interested in meeting that person. This is an insecurity you have that comes from your own lack of confidence in the material that you have. I am not at all interested in working with someone so scared. You call me back only if these conditions are agreeable to you. And please convey this message to her.'

She was stunned. She called me back after half an hour to tell me that she had rescheduled my appointment and would call me back later. That somewhat summarizes my experience with the Hindi film industry. I am not saying that everybody in Bollywood is like that. But I know of another celebrated director who behaves exactly like that. I have worked with him. He kept everything so close to himself, never showing anything to anyone. These people are insecure and live in constant fear. I have chosen not to fall into that trap. I don't have that fear in the way I work too. Even my colleagues are the kinds who are reluctant to go and work in another studio. They don't leave their regular studio; they fear that a new studio may figure out their work techniques from the sessions that they play there. I don't worry about such things, so I can work in any studio. If someone gets inspired and follows my working methods, it's a good thing. Let them.

Everybody uses the same software. What makes me different is my knowledge about the software and how I use it. My knowledge about the sound art and how I use it in my work is what makes me and my cinema unique. Nobody can copy that from me. Even if someone copies my sessions and makes a mix, it won't have that same quality unless I personally work on it. Even my sound editors who work with me have the fear of our work leaking out. I would say, 'So what? Let it leak out.' When I was working in Satheesh's studio, I have seen similar concerns among the people there too.

As far as I am concerned, none of these materials that we use is our exclusive private property. If ten guys want to work with this material, let them! Sometimes I feel that it is its fear psychosis that drives the Hindi film industry.

Then came Danny Boyle. He lived here for eight months. He understood Mumbai in and out, better than anyone from Mumbai itself. He internalized Mumbai and let his film take form in this place. This is something that goes even beyond art—a special quality that's above the art and craft of cinema. His greatness lies in the fact that he didn't want to change Mumbai for his film. He elevated his art to a level where human beings were recognized at deeper planes. That's what made *Slumdog, Slumdog*. If you feel joy, hurt or sadness seeing that film, it's because one man had experienced all that in this city. The film is a product of that range of experiences; a range shared by everyone who worked on that film.

I met Danny again after a week. The script, written by Simon Beaufoy, was fantastic. I must tell you something about Simon Beaufoy. When I had just come to Mumbai, it was not very simple to watch Hollywood films. There were no multiplexes. All of them were single-screen theatres. There's a theatre called Sterling, the first theatre in Mumbai equipped with the Dolby sound system. It screened Hollywood films in its late-night eleven thirty shows during weekends. After leaving the Institute, the frequency of my movie watching had come down drastically. So going to Sterling for a film was a much-awaited full-day event.

Three or four of us guys would make a plan. At around noon, we would leave for Churchgate from Andheri. Then Kerala lunch at Fountain Plaza. After that, we would spend some time hanging around in Fashion Street and then head towards Café Mondegar. That was the only place you got draught beer in those days. They also had a juke box. We would sit around drinking beer, listening to some Pink Floyd in the juke box till about seven. Then we would head back to Fountain Plaza for dinner—Kerala parotta with chicken or mutton curry or dry chicken, and a sweet banana fry to finish off. Like how we working Malayalis were deprived of cinema, the food, too, was the stuff of fantasy. Then we would carry our inflated abdomens on foot to the Sterling Theatre. The film would start at eleven thirty sharp and we attained bliss. Those days, most of the industry people landed up for these shows. It was before the time of DVDs or even VCDs. As for laser discs, only the super rich had them then.

Full Monty was a film I saw like this; a fantastic film. It was written by Simon Beaufoy.

I got very excited at the prospect of meeting the man himself. I couldn't believe that I was holding in my hands and reading something that had been typed by this man! A man whose film I had celebrated as a big event many years ago. I couldn't contain my happiness. Not only that; I found out the film was to be shot by Anthony Dod Mantle. He was even more terrific. He had shot a film called *Dogville,* and more recently, the brilliantly shot *The King of Scotland*. He had also been nominated twice for the European Academy Award.

Actually, I was the most insignificant guy in the project!

I had finished reading the script in one go. I had carried on reading it in full thrill almost till the end; then suddenly, the whole thing became a mess. It turned out to be an out-and-out Bollywood film with a completely uninspiring end. When I met Danny again, I told him that it was a full-fledged Hindi movie and that I didn't like the ending at all. He said, 'That's it! I want a Hindi film. I am making a Hindi film. Song and dance are terrific things. We don't have them in our films.'

I was hit on the head and a bulb flashed inside, 'Oh yes, that's true!'

Then I told him that I felt such and such parts of the script dragged. He said, 'It's exactly those parts we have been discussing. I am planning to go and come back from London with a fresh version of the script, which I definitely will show you. I am glad you, too, pointed out the same areas.'

During that second meeting, we discussed the film in more detail. That's when he started talking about his real ideas. He didn't want a dubbed film. He wanted it recorded live. He also wanted a mobile dubbing booth, because all the locations were going to be extremely noisy. He had no hope of getting live sound from many of these places. In such situations, he said, with a mobile dubbing booth, we could get the actor quickly inside it and record the dub while the scene was still fresh in the actor's mind.

I said, 'Look, Danny, I don't think these things are going to happen, considering the dynamics of how a shoot happens here. I am not saying I won't do it. I'll try hundred per cent. But I can't guarantee the success of it. And the shoot is going to be in summer and it will be extremely hot. Still I am going to try. Finally, you see, dubbing is a post-production decision; also, we can't know which performance we are going to choose in the final edit. It won't be possible for us to dub all the takes of a shot either. We would be dubbing what we decide as the best take, but that can change at the editing table, right? So we will take the wild track anyway. Let's see what the dynamics of the shoot is going to be. We'll decide after that.'

In essence, I had rejected all his ideas; at the same time, I hadn't completely ruled them out either. I am sure he must have felt a bit uncomfortable at that point. But he said he was okay with it.

While these discussions were going on, one concern I had was about how to shoot the *Kaun Banega Crorepati* show.

Danny told me the producers of his film were the same guys who had conceptualized the *Who Wants to be a Millionaire?*— the British original of the *Kaun Banega Crorepati* show in India. The producers were very clear that in the film, the format of the show should be the same as it was in TV, because of the show's immense popularity all over the world.

I said I wouldn't be able to do the recording for a film keeping the show in the same format. 'That's possible only in TV.'

The recording of the show became a road block for me. I had no problems with the rest of the entire film. The film was going to be done in 'surround sound' and then appear in Dolby Digital later. So the recording had to be in the surround-sound format which is a rather tedious process. If the shooting style of the show wasn't changed, it was going to be almost impossible for me to record that part.

I told Danny that if they wanted to retain the show's TV format, we should understand that in TV, it's a live show. So when it came to the show's questions and answers, right or wrong answers, there would be specific music pieces, all lined up on a computer and played by two recordists according to the cues. That, I told Danny, would work in live TV because it was being edited online according to a pre-determined plan. But cinema is not a live show; it is shot, edited and recreated completely. Cinema is recreated reality. The TV show in *Slumdog Millionaire* bothered me a lot.

At that second meeting itself, I had told Danny that I needed to open the computer screens used in the show and fix two mikes each inside. I had also asked for all the tech specs of the process, including information about the makers of the monitors. The producers had promised all that, but nothing seemed to be happening about it before the shooting began.

*

Amitabh Bachchan has a story that he often narrates. The moral of the story is that his many years of experience have taught him never to trust the production team. This was in my mind. So I did my own research and discovered a special mike. It was a surface mike. I got two of them and started walking around everywhere with that in my pocket. Now I was ready for anything!

The shooting date was drawing near. They fixed a date for the first shoot and another date a week prior to that for a pre-shoot. My dates were not available for the pre-shoot and anyway, I wondered what the hell was this pre-shoot. It was the first time I was hearing about anything like that. They said it was just a trial shoot, mainly to check the equipment like camera and lights and also to check the visual quality of the location. There wouldn't be any sound recording or anything.

I said, 'Okay, fine. But please note I'll be there only from the date of the actual shooting; not for this so-called pre-shoot.'

A couple of days into the pre-shoot, I started getting phone calls every night, asking for the sound to be ready the next day. After two days in a row dealing with the same thing, I lost my cool. I told them I had no idea what was going on in the name of a pre-shoot. 'First you said you didn't need sound; now, in the middle of the night, you tell me you need sound for the next morning. What do I look like to you guys, someone sitting on the footpath and selling sound by the kilo? Didn't I tell you guys I won't be there for this? How the hell am I supposed to know what you guys want and why you are calling the sound unit?'

I was waiting for some special equipment that I had ordered to arrive. It was coming in a week's time. I was also all prepared to go to London in the next few days. Finally, things got very messy. The producer started calling me, the editor started calling me—everybody started calling me. The producer then told me that Danny had been taking all of us for a ride—it was not a pre-shoot; what was going on was the real shoot!

I blew my lid. I asked him whether they were making a documentary instead of shooting a feature film. Finally, I told him I would send them a sound crew. 'Whether you want to use it or not, my crew will record whatever you shoot!' I sent two of my assistants. They promptly came back and reported to me, 'There is no way you can do sound there. It's a set-up of five or six cameras. Nobody knows what's being shot. Nobody tells us anything. There are some new cameras and a laptop kind of a thing. We can't figure out anything.'

I said, 'Okay, so be it!'

I made my entry on the date I had agreed upon. The shoot was at the gate of the old Centaur Hotel in Juhu. The generator was whirring close by. A vanity van was also right there. A huge crowd had milled around and it was quite a festive atmosphere altogether.

There were no visible traces of any discipline on the sets. Nobody had any idea what was going on. Like it's mentioned in the film itself, all of this was 'bizarrely plausible'.

I yelled at the camera assistant during the first shot on the very first day for not giving the clap properly. I deployed ten guys for 'sound policing', and went on to control everyone. I told the cameraman that it was I who would tell him when to roll. The scene came under some sort of control then. Simon Beaufoy was standing there, staring in absolute disbelief at the whole thing. The cameraman came and told me, 'You're the man! Now we can see that there's a sound man out here. Great going, stay firm, we want to hear your voice!'

That's when they figured out that if you need to do sound in the Indian context, you need to increase your own sound levels. They are all very polite people. They wouldn't shout and tell someone standing across the road to move over; instead, they would cross the road—first looking at the right, then the left—and approach the guy and ask him whether it would be really inconvenient for him to move over and come to our side.

This approach just doesn't work here. If you need to get the guy moving from there, you really need to shout: '*Arrey!* Come here!' That's what we are all about—completely opposite to the etiquette they are used to.

So that's how I began with *Slumdog*. The next thing to tackle was communication. I started asking everyone—what is it that they were doing, why and how . . . Slowly, I grew into the responsibility of the shoot. I started seeing what was going on.

Then the seriousness of the whole thing dawned on me. It wasn't a small film as I had thought. It was technically a very elaborate film. At any given moment, there were three cameras rolling. In the case of Hindi cinema, we use a maximum of three cameras for only very expensive and elaborate action scenes. It's a tough thing. Traditionally, we have always shot with a single camera. That means we only deal with one magnification at any given point. The mike is also used accordingly.

If three cameras are running simultaneously, then we have

three different spaces. When these three cameras cover one close-up from three different angles, it will give you three different dimensions. And if it's a wide angle, you can't get your boom mike in. That means you'll have to do the sound for a multidimensional space at one go. This is not the conventional method of one shot after another—first the long shot, then go in close. They were doing the shooting spontaneously. There were kids in the shot. If something didn't go right, they went for another take with a completely different set-up—a new take with completely changed dynamics!

For me, this meant relentlessly keeping track of at least two camera angles at any given time. It came to a stage where I needed to keep Danny next to me all the time, so as to understand the interactions and communication between him and the cameraman. Also, I needed to make him hear what I was recording. Then I figured out that for me to do anything, I really needed to know exactly what was happening. The only way to achieve that was to do a technical rehearsal of what was going to happen in the scene, and closely follow every detail of it.

By this time, one thing became very clear to me: for me to work properly in this film, I needed to keep aside everything that I had learned so far! It became the biggest unlearning process in my life. So far, as a professional, what I had been doing was to record at the given location precisely. The performance takes place in a certain space, according to the script; I used to cover that space by recording the sound according to the camera angles. That had been my way of doing sound recording for cinema. Here, I figured out, that was not going to work. So I said to myself that I had to go beyond recording the cinema, and instead, first know how a space functions in a particular scene and understand how the cinematic elements are going to perform in that space. For that, I needed to have a good understanding of what was going on. So the only way available to me was to record a space where an event unfolds, with a wide understanding of the overall happening.

For years, I have been working as a technician in cinema. This has honed my technical skills considerably. I can go into any messy space and record the film in the middle of it. But I realized here that I had to use all my skills to understand the space in which an event unfolds, more than just recording the sounds.

By the third day, I was completely convinced that I was not shooting a cinema, but covering an event that happens in a particular space. Today I am fully aware of the fact that, in many places in that film, I haven't done a professionally balanced recording job. Many areas of the film completely lack technical finesse. You can hear all those technical imperfections. At the same time, it does work beautifully in the film.

I think the Academy has given me the Oscar, not for the sophistication, but for this idea in my work. I know, as a professional, this was not the most satisfying recording job I have ever done. I knew I was taking a big risk by taking this path—it might work (good if it does) or might turn out to be a big flop.

But I did take the risk as I felt it was important. I think it's important for any artist to take this kind of a stand.

So I started a detailed recording of the film as an event. At all points, I would ask Danny whether this was what he wanted to be heard. And he would tell me what he wanted to hear in that particular shot. For example, when the boy goes inside the water, he told me he wanted a certain sound, and when the boy comes up, he wanted the sound that would be made when someone emerges from water. 'I need to hear the drops of water falling through the ear,' he said. I would always find ways to achieve what he wanted. The riot scene, he explained to me in great detail. By the time we finished it, we got a very beautiful sound. Glenn Freemantle deserves praise for how the sounds of that part were cut and used. Though I had done an extremely detailed recording of that part, Glenn deserves superlative compliments for the way he used those sounds. It was unfortunate that he lost his Oscar to another film, *The Dark Knight*.

Now let's take the moment in the film when the last question of the quiz show is asked. For the answer, Jamal calls his brother. But the brother's phone is with Latika; moreover, she leaves it behind in the car. No one picks up the phone. Anil Kapoor's character, the gameshow host, scornfully asks, 'You have the kind of brother who goes to take a leak exactly the moment when the question that's worth two million comes?' Latika watches this on TV and runs back to the car, picks up the phone and says, 'Hello . . .' It's an emotionally tense scene. During its recording, Danny came up behind me and put his mouth close to my ear and intoned a 'hello'—that was how Latika's 'hello' should sound; the audience in the theatre should feel that *hello* behind their ears as a magical word.

For shooting that sequence, we brought Latika to the studio. I arranged a mike and speaker system separately for this. We sat Latika behind a curtain, without the characters of Anil Kapoor and Dev Patel knowing. While shooting them waiting for someone to pick up the phone at the other end, I played Latika's 'hello' in her own voice exactly as Danny wanted. That came as a surprise. When her voice was heard like that in the studio, it created a natural feeling of surprise and excitement among the artistes. That was a first-rate sound event. Danny used to repeatedly ask for things like this.

When the director gives me an idea, I carry it in my mind for months, thinking about the ways to record it, until I find a way to do it. Even when small details of many sections in *Slumdog* had to be recorded in the studio, I could decide precisely upon the miking I needed because the original ideas were still in my mind.

I had made Danny listen to every recorded detail. Mainly because I wasn't going to London with Danny after the location recording, even though he had wanted me to be with the film till its final mixing stage. He was interested in the Indian convention of one man working through the entire process of location recording, sound editing, sound designing and mixing. Still, even for minor dialogue recording, Danny used to come to India and get it done by me. But after the shooting and some preliminary editing, he dropped a bombshell.

Danny came to India with the eighth version of the edit and showed it to us. I felt this film was something special. It had the texture and feel of something like *The City of God*. I liked it very much. Then came the shock. Danny told me that he had decided to dub the entire film. I was on the verge of tears. What did he mean? All my work was useless? How? Why? I just couldn't believe it.

The same night I called up Glenn Freemantle, without Danny knowing, and told him what Danny had said. I asked him what we should do.

Glenn told me he also had heard about it, and if it was true, it was a serious issue and spelt trouble.

I asked him to immediately check all the tracks I had recorded. I was very sure there was no need to dub. I had recorded many tracks for every performance. There would be enough good recordings out of that many, for sure.

Only when I met Danny again the next day did I figure out what he had in mind. His idea was that much the same way that Bollywood dubs films, if we too dub, in effect, we would be getting one more performance. So there would be one more set of material in our hands; and then we could select the best out of the whole lot.

Even I got excited. The point was, I knew I would not get this opportunity with any Bollywood films. Now one more performance was going to evolve when we dubbed. I told Danny that we were going to dub like how we had shot the scene, not just by getting someone to the studio in front of a mike. 'We will get them to perform like they did during the shooting and record it, except we'll be doing it for just the sound this time.' Danny agreed. Then I encountered a version of one of Murphy's Laws: if everything was going right, it only meant that something would go wrong. In this case, it was the producers. They secretly intervened. For them, this was unnecessary extra expenditure. Danny then returned to London the next day. After that, there was no news of any dubbing.

After a week, Danny called and said, 'We've mixed the film. We took all the rough tracks you had recorded. Everything is great. We need to dub only some small sequences in some sections; especially some of Irrfan's dialogues.'

Irrfan Khan's dubbing is quite a story. After dubbing each part, Danny would look at me and I would look at him; and sometimes Danny would tell me, 'Resul, I know what you're going to tell me.'

I had told Danny during the time of the shoot itself that Irfan's diction was not correct. 'Irrfan has mistaken mumbling for acting. We would need to dub him.'

Irrfan and I are great friends and on first-name terms with each other. He had also acted in my diploma film in the early part of his career. He was also there with me at the Film Institute in the beginning. (When I got the Oscar, he sent me a message: 'What good news. Now nobody in the Hindi cinema industry is going to call you for work. They will be so scared of you. You're finished! Ha ha ha!')

The issue with Irrfan was that, like a lot of Indian actors, he seemed to get intimidated by a language he didn't know too well. Now suppose we are not very sure of the pronunciation of a word like *magnificent*—whether it's *magnifishient* or *magnifisent.* This doubt makes us swallow a part of that word. Then for the audience, the word becomes inaccessible. Fear of a language is the basic reason why sometimes people mumble. I know this very well because I too have experienced this fear. I may not be correct in saying this with confidence,you never know what goes on in an actor's mind while shooting.I recently experienced this when I did a guest appearance in a Malayalam movie.I have great respect for actors after this experience

While dubbing, I told him that if he had walked while performing in a scene during the shoot, he would have to walk while dubbing too.

'What about the mike?' he asked.

'I will sort out the miking.'

I had modified the dubbing room; I also got the boom man to swing the mike accordingly while dubbing. Apart from the studio mike, I had taped mikes on his body as well. I was making him act the way he had during the shoot.

He was not very amused about all this. He stepped out of the dubbing room and shouted at me and the producers. He wanted to know why we were repeating all this when the shoot had taken place in sync sound and when everything had been recorded on location already. He said he didn't have time for all this. Pravesh came and asked me, 'Resul bhai, are we dubbing the whole thing?'

I asked him, 'Why, did Irrfan say something?'

'No, no . . . nothing like that.'

I told him to tell Irrfan that if he had any issues regarding this, he would have to take up the matter with either me or

Danny. 'These are not actor's decisions. Tell him to do his work. How many dubbing dates have you got from him?'

'Five days.'

'How many days have we dubbed?'

'One.'

I said everyone should just relax then. And I went ahead and dubbed for about ten days with the various artistes. We did some crowd sounds too. The dialogue editor from London, Gillian Dodders, had come to supervise everything.

I have no count of the number of mikes I used for this film. In many instances, there were more mikes than I could handle. When a shot would change, I would shift to another mike. I had bought many special microphones for this purpose. In fact, I designed many things for this film.

But there was a point during the film-making when I threatened to walk out of the entire thing after an argument with Danny. That was a very emotional moment.

You see, I had been called to do sound for this film because of my professional capability. That entitled me to have my own professional opinion and judgement. But when this opinion and judgement were not given adequate attention, it didn't go down well with me.

As I said earlier, in this film I was working with some big names of world cinema. Compared to them, I was insignificant. I didn't have much to show in terms of an international portfolio. That had made me slightly worried— in the sense that it would be really bad if there were to be any errors of judgement on my part. The editing for the film was going to take place in London, and I didn't want the people out there to point to my errors. During the entire shooting process, I was conscious of such a thing. That's why, under any circumstances, if I couldn't do something the way I wanted to, I used to bring it up very strongly.

The camera used for filming this movie had a 'gyro' system. Most of the time, the filming was done with the camera held in the hands. A hand-held camera will always be shaky. It was to avoid this shake that the gyro system had been developed for this film—it's like the ones used in the binoculars of a ship. Ship binoculars need to be steadied with a gyro system in order to counter the bobbing movements of the ship. A similar principle was at work with the camera in this film. It was essentially a hydraulic system with a vertical and a horizontal motor. This always countered the slant of the camera by moving in the opposite direction. And we would get a steady shot. The whole thing looked like a big ball, with a camera attached on top of it. The recording was taking place on a computer through data cables. All these were specially developed for this film—and indeed praiseworthy. But the motor of the gyro system would always make a whirring sound. This sound would get completely submerged in the exterior noise of Mumbai—even in many night scenes like the one where the orphanage kids are blinded, I could mask this sound because there were gas lights used in the shot which themselves made a hissing sound. But there were many occasions when I couldn't mask this sound with anything. It used to happen while shooting indoors—like during the police station scene or the brothel scene where the character Maman gets killed. In such instances, there was no other sound that I could use to mask the sound of the gyro motors.

Typically, during the indoor shooting for the film, the sound would get naturally amplified in the confined space. If that was not enough, the crew would be walking all over inside the room and shooting. It was not a pre-planned shooting process. They were shooting by going around, at a full 360-degree angle. That made it impossible for me to place a boom mike anywhere. I couldn't even take a video feed from the camera. And mixing live sound without seeing what is being shot is next to impossible. At least, if I could see the scene that's being enacted, I would be able to do something. The 360-degree camera movement didn't allow me to be inside that room either. I sat on a ventilator that opened to the roof. I was recording even as I was looking on at the scene. At some point, during the camera movement, the cameraman spotted me and the ventilator in his viewfinder. He immediately closed the ventilator.

I told them it would be impossible for me to record if they closed the ventilator. The cameraman insisted that he had to close it.

I said, 'We are shooting a film; it would have some limitations of its own. We have to realize that a certain kind of shot-taking is just not possible inside this room. In cinema, we have to work within a certain context. It's not as if we are trying to capture a once-in-a-lifetime event. This is cinema that we are doing.'

But they didn't listen to my arguments.

Then I brought up the issue of the noise of the camera. They didn't care about it either.

At that point I said, 'Okay, then I am not recording any more. I'm off after lunch. You better look for someone else from tomorrow onwards.'

Danny called for a lunch break when he realized that things were getting out of hand. I had become all emotional. I am like that. I cry when I feel like crying; I quarrel when I'm angry; I laugh when I'm happy. I don't hide my emotions. And it is a big problem for me if I have to compromise on the quality of my work because of someone else's sloppy workmanship. Those characters instantly become my enemies. Sometimes, people would place noisy lights at the sets. There are lights that make no noise. But because these lights were at a slight distance away and because they were too lazy to get them, they would plug in these noisy ones. Then, there would be times when the generator would not be parked at a distance. These are all trouble for me. I am not asking for people to do anything extra; all that I am asking for is for people to do their duties sincerely and precisely, and if they did so, the world would transform into such a beautiful place. That's what the liberal Basheer's worldview was. So, I was reacting at the sets to such contexts.

At lunch break, I told Danny that my problem was that nobody was listening to what I had to say. 'You do one thing,' I told him. 'Send all these tracks to Glenn. Let him hear them and take a decision. In my opinion, if you are planning to shoot the whole thing this way, then you will have to dub the entire scene.' I was on the verge of tears.

By that time, all the producers had landed up. Christian Colson came; the producer from London came. The latter said that they couldn't afford to dub the scene; that it was not in their plan. I told him that if this was the camera that would be used, everything would have to be dubbed. 'Leave alone this scene,' I told him, 'there's the police station scene coming, which would be about forty per cent of the rest of the film. All full of dialogues. So if this is the camera that's going to be used, it's going to be a problem.'

The producer said, 'You must not leave. That would be a pity. If you leave now after doing all the tough parts of the film, someone else will do the rest and will get the credit for the work.'

I said, 'Don't try to emotionally blackmail me. Credit is not the issue. That's all up to you. What I am saying is that the work is not going on properly. You are artists and good people, but you are not accommodating my problems. I also feel that you're refusing to accommodate my problems because it's me. Maybe I am wrong about that. But this is a very sensitive issue.'

When I returned after lunch, Danny had sorted out everything. He had understood my problems completely. The shooting had been re-organized for me to record! As a craftsman, you could start a project based on a completely worked-out and concretized set of ideas. But if that comes in the way of someone else's process of work, something is not quite right then. In the event of such not-so-right situations, Danny has the mind to stand up for the right thing, above the compromises that have to be made for cinema. That is the reason why for me, he is first an ideal man, then a film-maker.

So Danny asked the cameraman to change his approach. Later, when the scene was shot, it turned out to be a very energetic and powerful one. Now I have to mention some pleasantly surprising incidents without which the narration of this whole episode won't be complete.

That day, we hadn't changed the camera when we shot. So the whirring sound was there on the track, slightly irritating. Thus we had to dub that whole scene. This irritating sound was mainly on one character's track. In London, during the mixing when this track was replaced with the dubbed one, it was generally felt that the tension present in the original had been lost. This was something that Danny told me about later. In the so-called clean track, the tension was no longer there. The whining noise of the motors in the original had given the scene a tension. Finally, they replaced only a couple of dialogue parts where the noise was too much. Then they added the motor noise to this part, like in the rest of the recording. In fact, that scene in the film turned out to be one that created a good bit of tension. See how something which we had initially considered to be a disturbance, later turned out to be something that complemented the drama of the scene. There I realized that no pre-conceived judgements are quite valid in the making of cinema. Many unintended accidents in the angles or story structure can actually work towards making a film better.

Though the stand I took that day on location was largely an emotional one, it was professionally correct. I was deeply

touched by the greatness of Danny's humaneness on that day.
I also learned a lesson about cinema and the role of chance.

*

In a way, *Slumdog*'s recording process was very tough. Initially,
I had thought that recording the TV show part would be the
toughest. But in three days, I was doing that like it was the
easiest thing in the world. I would come in the morning,
memorize the whole script, and then all I had to do was to just
move my hand on the console controls. It became that easy.

Memorizing the script was very important—for me and the
boom man. It was after studying the script that we planned
on how and when to swing the boom mikes. We were using a
lot of microphones. We had to react to each dialogue. And if
we kept all the mikes open all the time, we wouldn't be able to
control the noise levels. So, we had to turn off one character's
mike as soon as he finished his dialogue and switch on the
next character's who was about to speak.

Shooting at the VT railway station was particularly
difficult. But it was an enjoyable difficulty. It was Danny's
vision that made it an enjoyable process. Danny believed that
we had no right to disturb someone else's life only because we
were making a movie. At the same time, he wanted to bring
into the film, the same spirit with which the city of Mumbai
functioned. And he was successful in accomplishing both.
Usually, film guys think of how to alter a place to make it
convenient for filming. Here it was just the opposite.

What we got from VT station was an awesome scene; but not by setting up anything for the shoot. You can see how music and sound combine beautifully in that part. Nothing was staged. The VT station was shot as it was. There were two trains when we started the shoot. We had to shoot before the trains left. Only minutes were left. The character was coming towards us, running through the space between platforms one and two. There were cameras on both these platforms. We were taking close-ups and long shots simultaneously. I had no time to go from one side to the other and place mikes. I did the scene by 'multi-microphoning'—dividing the space into zones and placing multiple wireless microphones. I placed the boom man inside the train. Within minutes I had to control and execute the whole thing. I could see only one camera; the rest was speculation.

Cinema shooting has its ethics. Shooting ethically is as important as making films. It has to do with a value system. Danny making *Slumdog* and creating history is one thing, but more valuable was how he conducted himself, conforming to this value system. I could see that process very closely and it will always remain with me as a valuable lesson.

Some time during the making of the film, I told Danny about the *Trainspotting* poster that I had in my hostel room. He refused to hear anything about it! He might have encountered such things countless times. He prefers living a simple life without ever accepting the star status that people pin on him. Danny's *Trainspotting* was about drugs and 'tripping'. As an artist, he likes to explore the extremes. Extremes like the kid jumping into the pit of shit in *Slumdog*. Many might think that that shit scene was not strictly necessary in the film. But Danny tends to push certain points for a reason. *Trainspotting* is a film of such an extreme. Danny's personality is all about simplicity, while his films are about extremes. Between these two facets, he has an artist's honesty about his art and a sense of values. Dynamically balancing all these, Danny has influenced me more as a great man than as a director.

2

THREE PRESTIGIOUS NOMINATIONS

I have never ever received a National Award for any of my works. I got one very recently after I wrote this book. I have done enough good work to deserve such an award. But in this country, like someone said, you need to believe in astrology to get awards. Anyway, never mind—I can say 'never mind' because the awards I've got are all highly reputed international ones; that too, all in the span of one month. Among all of them, I feel the most proud about the Cinema Audio Society's award.

In December 2008 Kabir Mohanty and I had planned to be in Italy for a sound art project. But that didn't materialize; same was the situation a second time around. It was only after the release of *Ghajini* and the completion of the Indian version of *Slumdog Millionaire*, could I make it to Italy—that is, some time in January 2009. When we finally reached Italy, as I had been working day and night, the first two days I just slept.

We were staying in a village about forty kilometres outside Rome. It was very cold and the atmosphere kind of gloomy.

The whole day I would shut myself in the hotel room and work. I would step out only to eat something once in the evening. The only connection with the outside world was through email.

One morning I opened my email and saw that I had been nominated for the CAS (Cinema Audio Society) award. A CAS winner had sent me the mail, congratulating me. Kabir was there with me at that time. I shouted, 'Kabir, I've been nominated for the CAS award!' Kabir had no idea what the hell was CAS. He asked, 'What is this CAS?' Cinema Audio Society, I told him.

There is a background story to it. It has to do with the time I was in Los Angeles, doing work on *Gandhi, My Father*. There, I happened to chance upon CAS's quarterly magazine, and I went through it—primarily to find out how I could become a CAS member. For that, one needs to possess a minimum of eight years' experience in the film industry, which I had. One also needs to be recommended by two or three people—but there was no one I knew who could recommend me. I badly wanted to be a CAS member. It's a very prestigious title for a sound recordist. CAS has only about 500 members all over the world. It's 'dedicated to the advancement of sound'. Every year, it presents an award for Outstanding Achievement in Sound Mixing. It's like a life-time achievement award.

I was stunned when I heard I had a nomination for the award. It's high recognition, the biggest a sound man can get. Like a cameraman getting an ASC (American Society of Cinematographers) award. It's a guild award. My mind started wandering: where will it go from here; what if an Oscar nomination comes by; I will have to give an Oscar speech and all! I couldn't sleep that night. I tossed and turned all night seeing visions of the Oscar.

I wanted to make sure that I had indeed bagged the CAS nomination. The next day when I had a bit of time, I checked the CAS website. Ha! My name was indeed there. Apart from my movie, the other nominations were for *Quantum of Solace*, *Iron Man*, *Wall-E* and *The Dark Knight*! I froze seeing all these titles. I can't really describe the state of my mind at that point.

Usually, I'm not candid in front of guys like Kabir. He is a very serious man. But that day, I just couldn't rein in my excitement. I called up Vikram Jogelaker. He was staying in Italy. I had met him when I landed in Rome. My name had already gone for Oscar nomination at that time. He had been very happy to hear that and had given me a big bear hug. When he now heard of my CAS nomination, he got even more excited.

Soon, the official announcement of the nomination came from CAS. In its forty-five-year history, I was the first Asian to be nominated. I wanted tell everybody about this. I sent an SMS to friends and asked them to forward it to everyone. A lot of friends replied, saying that it was a huge achievement.

In the meantime, I was struck by a severe bout of viral fever. I was bed-ridden. Yet, I was following all that was happening around my nomination. A number of people contacted me from Europe and America. Many of them had already seen the film. Meanwhile, several social websites of sound recordists started discussions on my nomination. I also found an article in an international magazine about my work in *Slumdog* and sent its link to many. I wanted guys to know what kind of work I had done in the film. And since this was a guild award, I emailed this article to some friends in America and asked them to forward it to all the CAS members who they knew. The members should know about my work, I thought.

My fever was intense. I could only do such things for half an hour at a stretch; after that, I would fall back on the bed. Like those white men who come to India get bitten by mosquitoes and then fall prey to malaria, I was down for a week.

Then next week came the BAFTA (British Academy of Film and Television Arts) nomination for me. Apparently, I had become the first Asian to be nominated! I was all restless with excitement. I messaged everyone.

'It's not a joke, nor a small affair,' said Vikram. 'It's only going to get bigger. You have to throw a party right now.' So we went to Vikram's favourite place called Braciano. There we went to a little restaurant with a view of some ancient ruins of the Roman Empire. An amazing place. I luxuriously opened a 100-year-old bottle of wine for Vikram, to wash down some excellent rabbit meat, and then we came back.

Now I was dying to get back to India. I didn't care about the work I had in Italy; all I wanted was to return. Somehow, I finished the work and got back here. The first thing that everybody told me was that TV and the rest of the media were buzzing with the news of *Slumdog*; anyone and everyone who was remotely connected with the film were getting interviewed; 'except you'! They told me that the guys who were mere assistants and the guys who had painted the sets and such were all there in the newspapers every day, and only I, who had done important work for the film and got nominated for international awards, was missing.

I said, 'Never mind, I wasn't around, that's why. Now I'll let everyone know.' I called up many of the Chalachitra Academy guys and gave them all the details. I also informed A.R. Rahman about everything through emails. He was very happy and kept sending messages, saying '*Alhamdulillah*' (God be praised).

All my friends were telling me that it was a major thing to be the first-ever Asian to be nominated for CAS; then there was the BAFTA nomination. They exhorted me to make a big splash in the media with the whole thing. The Chalachitra Academy guys asked me to come up with a press note giving them all the details and then send it as an attachment; they would make it into an official press release. I did all that. I also forwarded the same to all the news guys I knew in Delhi, Mumbai, Calcutta and all. But nothing happened.

One day, I told my manager Kalluvila, 'This is it, my friend! Maybe I need an Oscar nomination to create any ripples, no?' His reaction was immediate: 'If that happens, I'll do a forty days' fast and go to Shabarimala!' That was quite a remark for someone who had vowed never to enter a temple!

We just looked at each other.

*

Around that time, Danny Boyle came to India. He told me that the CAS nomination and such happened only to the biggest of big films. But even that statement from Danny couldn't give me much idea as to where my life would be heading henceforth. Danny had come for the Indian premiere of *Slumdog Millionaire*. Before that, there was a premiere to be held for the cast and crew. I was thinking of skipping it. I was feeling a bit let down—after such major nominations and all, nobody was giving a damn to me. I was thinking this was the lot of technicians—so what's the point of toiling day and night; does anyone realize the value of our work?

This line of thinking took me to the lowest possible point of depression and when there was no further to descend, my spirit started looking up. I thought it might look bad if I didn't go. I told myself that after all, it was my film too, and that there was no point in stepping out of the whole show at the last moment. So I went and reached the venue five minutes before the show.

There were a lot of people. Danny was very happy to see me. He said, 'Oh, you are coming from work, are you?'

It was true. There was some urgent work I had to finish on a film. I was coming from the middle of it. He continued, 'I just can't understand you and Rahman. You guys are working all the time!' I told him that we had no other option, that's how we were and that's how things happened here.

He said, 'It's the premiere of your film. You have received some of the biggest nominations in the world. Celebrate is what you have to do!'

I agreed.

At the premiere, they had brought the four Golden Globe awards which *Slumdog Millionaire* had won recently. Winning the Golden Globe was a powerful indicator of the position of the film. Now we had reasonable hopes about the Oscar; we might get a couple of nominations; Rahman would definitely get one for the two songs that had been submitted; then there was the possibility that *Slumdog* would win a nomination in the best-picture category. That's how our calculations went.

The kids from the slums who had acted in the film were also there at the show. They were happily moving around the crowd holding the Golden Globe trophies. I stood away from the crowd. You see, I was a crew member who had been nominated for both BAFTA and CAS, and yet no one was paying me much attention. No, I was not really feeling bad about it. Yet I stood away from the crowd.

The film started and I had the shock of my life! The sound was completely wrong. What I was hearing wasn't the sound I had done. That was the last straw. I felt very weak. After the screening was over, the chief of Fox India asked me, 'You must be feeling really proud, aren't you?'

But I said 'no' and he wanted to know why. I said there was something seriously wrong with the sound of the film. That was not the sound I had prepared for the Indian version. Something had gone wrong. I told him that it was a film that had won a CAS nomination and if this was how it was going to be played, I would be the one getting a bad name. I called up Danny and told him that there was something terribly wrong with the sound of the film. 'You need to intervene and stop dispatching the prints,' I said. He immediately demanded that all the prints be cross-checked.

I didn't hang around there after that. I was very tense. I went back to my studio and listened to the track. That was not the track I had heard at the premiere. At two in the night, I called up the mixing studio and reached there in the morning. Actually, there was only a minor difference, but I was sure the track that I had heard at the premiere was not the one I had done—even if nobody had noticed it.

My investigations finally took me to the place where the HD had been printed. I went to their mastering unit and checked the track. It was the same thing that I had heard last night at the premiere. Then I figured out that a mix-up had happened when the sound was sent for HD printing. By then, sixty to seventy prints had already been dispatched. It was six in the evening. I stopped further printing, and overnight I brought the correct files and re-punched them.

The next day I went with the Dolby guys to line up the premiere theatre. We needed to make the necessary corrections in each theatre's speaker system. We reached the theatre at two in the night. *Ghajini* was running there then. The track wasn't sounding bad. Still, I lined up four theatres that night. By that time, the new print had come re-punched.

From the day of the premiere for the cast and crew till the big premiere day, I had been awake three whole nights, working. I left the premiere venue at eight on the morning of the big premiere day. I was driving through Dharavi. A few moments ago, I had been watching and checking the riot scenes in the film; those had been shot in Dharavi. I showed the spots to the Dolby guys who were with me in the car. I said, without thinking much, almost as if it was a joke, 'It'd be great if we get an Oscar nomination, no?'

I reached home at nine. I couldn't sleep. After lunch, I managed to catch an hour and a half's sleep. The premiere was at seven in the evening. I should reach there by six latest. While driving, I called up the Chalachitra Academy people once more to find out whether they had sent my stuff to the press people or not. I hadn't seen anything in the media yet. They said they'd do something soon.

I was depressed again (my readers might be getting irritated with my constantly recurring state of depression! What to do Sir, sometimes my life is like that only!). I wondered why people were refusing to see the importance of the whole thing. There was nobody to even support me. Was this a fight that I had to wage all alone? Perhaps people were thinking that my nominations were no big deal.

When I lost all peace of mind, I sent an SMS to Rahman: 'Nobody recognizes the importance or gravity of the nominations I have got. At least, if you could mention it in any of your interviews, people might take notice.'

Rahman's reply came as I reached the premiere: '*Inshallah*.' If Allah wills so.

And within the next forty-five minutes, my fate changed incredibly! The Oscar nomination list was out. I had been nominated for the Oscar! What followed was a media frenzy that I had never before experienced.

The nominations were declared at seven thirty in the evening, Indian time. When we heard about *Slumdog*

Millionaire getting a nomination in the best-picture category, we screamed in ecstatic excitement. Dev Patel, Frieda Pinto and I were all hugging each other and rolling on the floor. The best-picture nomination—for a film that I had worked on! For the life of me, I had never expected such a thing would happen! It was chaos all around. Everybody was there, including Danny and Anil Kapoor. We then heard that our movie had won two more nominations. Then we started counting—till eight. Eight nominations! Sound, sound—yes, for sound editing and sound mixing too! Two nominations for sound!

Oh! Oh my . . .! I . . .! What do I do . . .? I thought I was going to collapse right there! I jumped on Danny's back and hugged him. All of this was being captured on camera. But I didn't care. I was naked. Emotionally completely nude in front of everyone! I had never behaved like this before. I was screaming and shrieking.

I didn't know what exactly to do. There was wine and champagne flowing. I called Baiju. His phone was busy! Somehow I got through. I shouted at the top of my voice I had been nominated for the Oscar. He had already heard about it and had been trying my number! This was pure joy. My phone went mad ringing. I saw messages piling up; when I received message number 252, the phone crashed, because of the overflow! Then I went about trying to fix my phone like a mad monkey.

When I turned around with the phone, there was no one around. Everybody was on the stage. Someone then dragged me and sat me on the stage. Then I lost complete control. I went on to perform all sorts of Kerala folk art. I remember talking to a couple of Malayalis too. After that, I don't remember much. I can't even remember how much I danced that night. All I remember is going for an interview with NDTV the next morning—on crutches! I was limping as my knee had swelled up. It must have been some dance performance! Then began the endless press conferences. I was not even in a position to respond to my name when it was called out. I was in a total daze.

That was an unforgettable night. I didn't sleep the whole night. Around five thirty in the morning, I reached home. At seven, NDTV's car came to pick me up, or was it a kidnap? The press meets continued non-stop for weeks on end. Those days, sometimes I would be on phone for almost fourteen hours at a stretch. But at that grand moment, when I received the greatest piece of news ever in my life, my wife and kids were not around!

I kept telling Shadia that she had no idea what was going on here. 'You come with the kids right now.' She said, 'But my ticket is for the 20th . . .' 'Cancel that ticket and come tomorrow!' When I had gone to Europe, she had gone to Dubai to her sister's place as she didn't want to be alone with the kids. She rushed back. I was very happy.

But then I heard about my eldest brother suffering a cardiac arrest. An angiography had to be done immediately. I was crestfallen. He was not that old. He had no health problems either. Those were very tense days. I called up my cousin, a cardiologist, and asked him to do a thorough check-up of my brother. I organized the money for the surgery and went home. The surgery went off well. In Kerala too, I was bang in the middle of a media frenzy. The people of Vilakkupara gave me a grand reception.

I haven't had a moment of rest since that Oscar nomination. I have been constantly on the run. And in a constant state of intoxication. Within just one week, I even went to America twice. Five days in a plane. That was the only rest I got those days. The rest of the time it was all about celebration and the media. But I was not feeling tired yet. In between, the BBC guys came; they wanted to talk to me, and also cover me going for the BAFTA ceremony. Ah!

3

ON THE AWARDS TRAIL: FROM BAFTA TO CAS

Before the Oscars, I had to go for the BAFTA function. But what should I wear? I have a designer friend who had worked with me on a couple of films. She was also the one who designed my outfits for my wedding. So I called her up, for the first time after my wedding. I told her, 'Three major functions are coming up. I have no time for anything. I need to go to Kerala also in between.' That was her brief for the design. I didn't even see the material that she had selected. At the Oscars, one designer, one of the big names in the fashion world, said my outfit was one of the best of the evening. He said I looked elegant. The whole credit for that goes to Isha and Darshan.

I had never even dreamt that any of this would happen to me. For me, the nomination itself was like getting the award. February came. I reached London on the 6 February for BAFTA. On the 7th, when the award functions began, I started getting very tense. That morning itself I had been under stress. I had felt as if I was feverish. The whole day I had been busy with the Indian media. With the BBC too; its crew had been panning its camera on me the whole time. They had wanted to cover all my movements while going for the BAFTA ceremony. All of this must have stressed me out.

London is a city I have visited on work many times. I have walked a great deal through its streets. During one trip, I had lived on a ten-pound daily allowance. Today, I was in this city with a BAFTA nomination. There were red carpets for me. How fast life changes. Half a second is all that it takes; and life becomes wonderful ever after! Like they say in the film world, a Friday can change your life.

The BAFTA proved to be tough competition. I didn't expect us to win against films like *The Dark Knight*. During my London visit, I visited all the unit members of *Slumdog Millionaire*. It was a London production. Danny is also from London. Most of the people who had worked on the film are from London. Danny had huge support in the city and *Slumdog Millionaire* had the backing of the entire media there. They asked me, 'So you're going to get a BAFTA, aren't you?'

I said, 'At the moment, I'm not interested in thinking about whether I will get or I want to get a BAFTA. So please don't ask me that question. It stresses me out.'

I went inside the hall and met Rahman. We sat in the same row. The first award of the evening was declared, for music. The award went to *Slumdog Millionaire*. The first Indian to get a BAFTA—A.R. Rahman!

I shrieked in excitement. The white men sitting in the front row turned around to take a look at me. The British, you see, are very structured people. There is a precision in their movements and manners. Now they were seeing one guy in a gentlemanly tuxedo making very primordial sounds, like a joker gone nuts. The BBC was telecasting everything live and people were in their best behaviour, except me! I was shrieking and shouting in full thrill the way I used to in my college days in Kerala, long ago. Anil Kapoor got inspired by my performance and started on a similar sound effect. By then, everybody had marked us out for special attention.

After twenty minutes came the awards for sound. Those, too, went to *Slumdog Millionaire*.

I walked through the aisle, screaming and laughing. On the way I met Danny and gave him a hug and a kiss.

Five of us had won the award. Glenn Freemantle and Tom Sayers were the sound designers, while Ian Tapp, Richard Pryke and I were the sound mixers. BAFTA gives only one award for sound—for both design and mixing.

One great thing about the BAFTA award ceremony is that, unlike the Oscars, there is no time limit for the winner's speech, unlike at the Oscars. If there are five people, all five could speak. They have serious respect for anybody who contributes to cinema.

So I received the award and started speaking. I don't remember exactly what I had said. But I had said things like, what I held in my raised hand here was not a film award, but history. I thanked everyone. Thanked a billion people. Then the anchor said in wonder, 'Did you mention one billion prayers! What a magnificent statement! How beautiful!'

How could I say anything else? I knew everyone was praying.

On the stage, all five of us had to share the single BAFTA mask that was given to us. I thought, oh, so I was not going to get one for myself! But they assured me that I needn't worry—everyone was going to get one to take home. I felt a sense of relief. They also told me that there would be a photo session afterwards.

Then I sent everyone messages, saying that I had won the BAFTA. Congratulations started flowing. I heard Shadia screaming in excitement over the phone. At the function itself, a grand dinner and a big press meet followed. By the time the show finally wound up, it was two in the morning. In the wee hours when I was returning to my hotel, a lot of Londoners stopped their cars, seeing the BAFTA mask in my hand, and posed for photographs with me. Look how things had transformed—here I was, at an odd hour, signing autographs for white people, standing in the same streets where I had once wandered like a destitute! What a satisfying experience! It was such an amazing feeling. I felt my life's purpose had been fulfilled. At that moment, I felt there was nothing left to achieve in life!

I was returning home the next day. At the London airport, the security staff saw the trophy in my bag. They asked me, 'Which film?'

'*Slumdog Millionaire*!'

The immigration officers and checking officers at the airport got very excited hearing this. They sang me the 'Ringa Ringa' song from the film and stopped me at three places to pose for photos with them.

I landed in Mumbai airport during the day-time. Baiju

had sent me an SMS saying that I was to come out only after he gave the signal. He had run around and organized a bunch of news guys. But they were waiting at the wrong terminal. Baiju was in a state of panic to get the guys to the right spot. I was dying to get out. I was coming home with my first international award and wanted to see my wife and kids before anything else. I got sick of repeatedly asking Baiju whether it was time for me to come out. I was beginning to get angry too. I knew he was up to something and not telling me anything about it. I thought: why should he be running around and gathering the news guys when the news guys should have been coming to us on their own.

Finally, I lost patience and came out. There were a few Malayalam journalists and some others waiting, and they came running to me. Then there were some guys from my studio, my studio partner Akhilesh Acharya, Baiju, Shadia and the kids. I took out the BAFTA mask and posed for photos. But all this was nothing compared to the kind of news coverage I had received in London.

Here I must point out one difference that I felt. When Rahman brought home the Golden Globe and the BAFTA awards, the entire media fraternity in India celebrated it. Rahman's achievements are huge; and his personality, sublime. My achievements are in a technical category—a category in which the general tendency is to belittle Indians and their work. The general notion is that we don't know anything, say, about sound. The value of my achievement needs to be seen in the context of this undervaluing of the kind of work that the technical people have been carrying out. Unfortunately, most of our media people are only bothered about stars. Often, it's only stardom that creates news. In many ways, such a trend has come about because of the laziness of our media folks.

That said, even the larger society's attitude in this regard is pretty pathetic. I will tell you of one experience that Baiju had while waiting for me at the airport. He was running around getting the news guys to one place. Then I entered into the field vision. A cop in plain clothes came and did secret investigations. He found out from Baiju who I was. Then he wrote down the relevant details on a piece of paper and passed on the findings to the cops in uniform. Then a lady cop asked, 'Is this guy a south Indian?' Maybe, this was a stray incident. But this is the general pattern in which our society's curiosity works. I couldn't help comparing this with my experience with the officers at the London airport.

The lady's question infuriated Baiju. He told me, ' . . . As if you brought the BAFTA for south India! Only when you bring an Oscar will this attitude change!'

After a week, I had to return to America for the CAS awards. And following that: Oscar night!

*

I went to Hollywood for the first time, in 2003, to mix for the film *Amu*. I was staying at director Shonali Bose's house. The mixing was taking at Burbank in West Hollywood. Daily, we would drive to work. We would drive around the Kodak Theater, take a left, cross Hollywood Ball, cross the Barham freeway and then pass famous studios like Universal, Warner

Brothers and NBC. Every time we passed Kodak, my mind would flicker and I would tell myself, I'm passing in front of the Kodak Theater!

Life went on like this and one day, there was no mixing. Holiday! I went to see the Kodak Theater with a friend. We couldn't get in. We walked around and checked it out in detail from the outside. It's actually a big shopping complex. There's a Chinese theatre on the front façade and right at the entry of Kodak, there's a shopping mall. There, you'll find listed the names of all-time great Hollywood movies. The aisle leading to the inside is called the Walk of Fame. On either side, you have the names of superstars engraved in star-studded brass plaques. You can also see the foot impressions of Charlie Chaplin and Donald Duck. The whole mall is a big treat for any film buff. In the evenings, the place will be full of regular people dressed up as celebrities—there you can find John Lennon, Ingrid Bergman and Michael Jackson, even Batman would be there. You can pose with them for photographs for what was then one dollar. The Kodak Theater and its surroundings become a teeming tourist attraction every evening.

This is one of the most active spots in Los Angeles. You get to see lots of people and lots of memorabilia. There's also a big book stall, then there's the Virgin store with its huge collection of music and books. Bang opposite is the Capitol Theater which houses the world's biggest dome theatre. At many places in this Kodak complex, you can get to read the wise words of people who came to Hollywood as nothing and then went on to become superstars. You get very inspired reading such lines. The entire place is such that any cinema

lover would want to spend the rest of his life there. The
memories and the sense of belonging this place gives are
beyond words. During this first visit there, I made a mental
note: I'm going to enter this place once.

Hollywood Ball is a big open-air theatre. I have a beautiful
memory of attending a John Williams concert there. It was
also a function commemorating all the American Olympic
winners of all time. On the occasion, Williams played out
the Olympic theme song as well as the theme songs of several
films. Before each theme was played, we would speculate
about which one it would be, like, 'this one would be Harry
Potter'. We also made him play some themes again and again
by applauding non-stop. It was hugely exciting.

That first visit to Hollywood brims with cinematic memories.

The next time I was in Hollywood was while working for
the film *Gandhi, My Father*. I was staying at the Oakwood
Apartments in Barham. In the evenings, after work, I would
go straight to the Kodak Theater. There I would do some
shopping, hang around in the book shops, or check out
some memorabilia. Then, too, I thought: I am going to sit
inside this theatre one day.

For the Foley recording of *Ghajini*, I once again went to
Hollywood. It was there that I recorded all the bone-crunching
blows and punches that are very much part of that film.
During this time, on the last day of October, I was walking
into the studio where I worked, carrying a big pumpkin on
my head, a big watermelon and a parcel of raw mutton in
my hands. All the people were staring at me. But they were
not really people! They were all ghosts and demons in orange

and black. I got a little worried. Later I found out that it was Halloween's Day. I hadn't known what it was. Then it was explained to me—that Halloween's is the day when the spirits of the dead return; it's celebrated as a big holiday. People get into bizarre costumes that day. So when people were staring at me when I was carrying all those exotic things, they were actually wondering what kind of a fancy costume would I come up with! But I was heading for work. Who remembers public holidays and all while working on sound! Anyway, it was an entertaining situation. I did *Ghajini*'s Foley recordings with the same guys who had worked on *Rambo* and *The Bourne Ultimatum*. And the pumpkin, the watermelon and the raw meat were all meant to create the sound effects for all those blows and punches in the movie.

After many visits, the Kodak Theater and its surroundings became my most familiar place in LA.

Recently when I went to Rome, I saw the street where Federico Fellini had shot *La Dolce Vita*. It invoked a special feeling inside me. I felt I was treading the grounds where cinematic history had once been sculpted. The street looked the same as in the movie. Something stirred inside me, a deep impression formed, and I went through that déjà vu feeling of proud excitement that I had experienced while watching that film.

But Hollywood cinema had never created any such impression on me. At the same time, I knew that the ultimate recognition for someone like me—who was involved with the technical facet of cinema—was the Oscar. So Hollywood's acknowledgement was what I had always kept in mind as a touchstone. Hollywood had also touched me a great deal with its vibrancy and love.

In Hollywood, there is an annual evening event where the Motion Pictures Sound Editors' Association makes a presentation on the sound aspect of the most outstanding film of the year. I was in town doing *Ghajini*'s sound effects when that year's presentation was to take place and I was invited. The film presented was *The Dark Knight*. Its sound designer Richard King, along with its music director and music editor, made a detailed presentation about the sound features of the film. A lot of people were asking them questions and clarifying doubts. I sat in a corner of the full house listening to everything carefully. I was astounded when I heard of the varied details that had been gone into while doing sound for that film. It had taken them over two and a half years of hard work to create such a sound!

I went for this presentation with a friend of mine, Kunal. On our way back, as we were coming out through the Kodak Theater, I told Kunal, 'One day, I am going to come here, my friend!' He blushed and smiled. But I never thought it would take me only a few more months to be inside there—and in competition with *The Dark Knight*!

*

I landed in LA for the CAS awards function which was to be held on 15 February 2009. The ceremony was to take place at the Millennium Biltmore Hotel in downtown LA. It was the season of cinema and television's technical awards—around the Kodak Theater, such awards were taking place one by one, while Kodak itself had been closed down in preparation for the Oscars.

Biltmore is a very famous and old hotel. The function was in the crystal ball room. When I arrived there, as a CAS nominee, many people came to me and said, 'You must be Resul.' It wouldn't have been very difficult to spot me. I was the only Indian around. The president of CAS, Edward Moskowits, came up to me and introduced himself. Many more such introductions followed. They were all very happy to meet me. I posed for photographs with a lot of people.

When I had confirmed my arrival for the function, they had told me that they would like me to present one of the awards. As a part of its aim to promote sound mixers from around the world, CAS had wanted me to present the award for television mixers, and I had agreed. So my very first ascent to a Hollywood stage was to present this award. A big-time television anchor was introducing the people who were on the stage. He announced to the audience: 'With an Oscar nomination to his credit, Mr Pookutty has become a superstar in Bollywood.' A thunderous applause followed. I presented the award. I had an incredible feeling of community and belonging when I stood there! It was like a big family gathering. The hall was full. About two thousand people from various fields of sound were present—sound mixers, renowned equipment makers, sound researchers, studio heads etc. They sat behind tables arranged in a big circle. It was both an award function and a dinner ceremony. Mellow music flowed; the awards were being declared . . .

The last award of the night was declared. For *Slumdog Millionaire*! I sat with my head in my hand, looking down. I just couldn't believe it! I was sharing a table with a television mixer and his wife; along with Richard Pryke, Ian Tapp and John Coffey, who owned the renowned sound equipment maker Coffey Sounds while also being a member of the CAS board of directors. I don't know how I got to the podium—but there I was, addressing everyone, saying that this was something way beyond anything I could believe. I continued: 'My friends in America, I have to say two things. In many ways, there was no production sound in India thirteen years ago. In 1995 when I started on my profession, I remember collecting equipment from my friends, putting them in bags, hailing a cab and going for shoots like a porter, carrying those bags. Now I am standing here! In the biggest if not the only platform for sound and sound mixers, receiving an award like CAS! This is the success story of thirteen years of hard work by my colleagues and me. We worked hard to bring a change in the sounds heard in Hindi cinema. This is the reward for our hard work in an industry where dubbing has grown massively and bloomed into an art form. Also, this is a recognition for our industry's openness to changes. As for me, just being able to share a platform with a stalwart like Ben Burt itself is an honour and gives me immense joy!'

Then I looked at Burt and told him, 'Sir, you might not know me, but we have always looked up to you. Whenever we thought of good sounds, we thought of you and got inspired by those thoughts. I feel like I am standing in front of my guru. I have been honoured just by that!'

That was the day the famous sound recordist Dennis Maitland was presented with a lifetime achievement award. He was the one to introduce wireless microphones in production sound recording. I greeted him and told him, 'Dennis sir, I'm a stranger to you and you may not even have a reason to know me, but I know you since my film school days—since the day I saw the film *Pawn Broker* there! For someone like me who comes from another continent, someone who knows the work you have done over the years, it's a great privilege and honour to share this platform with you or even just to stand in front of you; I thank the Cinema Audio Society from the bottom of my heart. I would like to express my gratitude in the name of my industry for this privilege and honour. It certainly is like giving history into my hands. Thank you!'

I got a standing ovation which went on and on! I stood there, teary-eyed. You won't believe this: As many as fourteen Academy members came and hugged me—I counted! They told me in my ear that they had voted for me! They said, 'We're rooting for you!' Their gesture, their kindness and appreciation, shook my very being. I kept thinking about it: why did a society and its people behave like that with no trace of selfishness? I thought, maybe it had to do with the cinema that we had made and the ordinary lives of Mumbai shown in it—yes, I had touched their hearts with the very same ordinary Indian life! It was as if someone had softly strummed at the depth of another's heart! I think that was the source of the overwhelming flood of love and kindness. I haven't had a more fulfilling moment as far as my soul is concerned.

Ben Burt hugged and congratulated me. Dennis Maitland came to me and said, 'It's great! People like you from another continent come to give us insights into that civilization. So amazing! We feel privileged and we feel special that you have come to tell us what is happening with your lives and your films—it's amazing!'

When I was stepping down from the stage, I felt that now it really didn't matter even if I didn't get an Oscar. That was how satisfied I was.

My wife and children were at home. I really wanted to see them. Also, I had to pick up Shadia for the Oscar function, which was to take place the same week. So immediately after the CAS function, I returned to India.

4

OSCAR GLORY

I reached Mumbai on a Wednesday. I briefly met some close friends who were waiting at the airport and headed straight home. Shadia's mother and sister Shindi were there. The idea was to leave the kids with them when Shadia and I went for the Oscars. They had come a little early so that they could spend some time with the kids and become friends. I told my son Monu that we would be away for a couple of days. I spent most of my time with Monu and Mia to make up for the days I was going to miss them. Actually, I lied to Monu. I told him that I had to take his mom to the doctor because she was not feeling well. For him, the doctor was someone who gave injections, and he was sure he didn't want to go anywhere near one. With the added promise of ice cream from my mother-in-law, he was ready to stay without us. I felt a bit sad about playing with a little kid's trust. Meanwhile, I tried out my Oscar outfits and Shadia decided upon what she would be wearing.

The night of our departure, I prayed to my parents and

left home, thinking that they were always with me, sitting on my shoulder.

The child actors were also travelling with us and there was a huge media presence at the airport. Nobody paid me much attention. I checked in. There were a few Malayalis in the flight. Some of them got down at Frankfurt. I also met a few people who worked in Barack Obama's office. Many people came up to me and told me that they were praying for me. All in all, I felt good and humble. At the same time, I was beginning to get slightly tense.

But there was a nightmare waiting for me at the Los Angeles airport. The computer had picked up my name for random checking. Of late, I had been travelling to America quite frequently. I also carried a name that can make American computers suspicious: Resul Pookutty.

I had heard of enough horror stories of this so-called random checking. You might have heard of the actor Kamal Hassan's experience. My friend Feroz Abbas Khan too had faced a similarly tough situation. I was a bit upset when they asked me to step aside. It was Shadia's first trip to America. She wasn't aware of what this random check could lead to. That was my biggest worry. I asked her to stay calm as this might turn ugly.

The officer who had chosen me for special attention was an African-American, hugely built, imposing and quite a tough guy. He asked me rudely, 'Okay, why are you here?'

I said I was an Oscar nominee.

'So, which movie?'

'*Slumdog Millionaire.*'

His attitude changed instantly, as if those were some magic words.

'Wow! *Slumdog Millionaire*! What did you do in the film?'

'I am one of the sound mixers.'

Now this creature turned into a human being. He looked at me for a moment, then went to his senior and came back with two other officers. He said, 'Sir, please come with me.'

They took me to the immigration counter. As three officers were escorting me, the immigration officer might have even taken me for a VIP.

My immigration card had been already marked in violet. The immigration officer said that once it was marked in violet, they couldn't stamp the card and that a separate procedure had to be initiated. Now they were taking me to a corner. I knew these guys knew that I knew the shape of things to come. I was shaking inside. I knew what was waiting for me: X-ray scans, all kinds of body frisking, a complete examination of every item in my luggage . . . and after all that, there could be a humiliating interrogation too.

They patiently waited till my luggage arrived. Then they walked Shadia and me to a desolate corner. I started getting scared. I asked where they were taking me. Politely, but without a change of expression, they said that if we were interrogated there, people would notice and we might find it uncomfortable. This matter-of-fact answer only deepened our sense of horror. Suddenly, Shadia started coughing.

'Madam, would you like some water?' they asked politely. But even that politeness was intimidating.

When we reached the corner, they started with the questions. Into a few questions, all our apprehensions dissolved away. I am quite sure that nobody who had been picked up for a random check would ever have come out of it like us, feeling so good. They were checking each paper and asking questions very kindly. They kept saying, 'Don't worry, we had to do this to you only because the computer picked your name randomly. Once we feed our findings back into the database, you would never have to face this again, we assure you. So please co-operate with us for half an hour.'

After the examination, the officer said, 'I haven't seen the whole film. Saw it only in parts. Still I wish you all the very best. I'm going to watch that film today only because I met you. Certainly I'll be there in front of my TV watching the Oscars' evening tomorrow and I'll be cheering for you.'

Tears welled up in my eyes—isn't it all because of one film? In one way or the other, *Slumdog Millionaire* has touched the hearts of people. This officer accompanied us all the way to the exit to the waiting limo, shook my hand and said, 'Thank you. Best of luck! And I am going to cheer for you!'

I told him if I get to meet him on my way after winning an Oscar, I was going to give him one big hug. Between us, it was like two complete strangers discovering the same idea at the same time. Cinema can trigger love between two individuals; or even introduce a common language between two civilizations!

*

That evening there was an award night of the Motion Pictures Sound Editors' Association. I had been invited to introduce Danny Boyle at that function. I considered that invitation as an honour for the industry I represented.

It was a stupendous function. Ben Burt was getting a lifetime achievement award; there were guys like Richard King, George Lucas and Steven Spielberg, and top guns of big production houses like Sony Pictures, Fox and other studio heads. Around 2500 people! *Slumdog Millionaire* was in the foreign film award category because it was not a Hollywood production. And it won the award. I went up to the stage. I had not prepared any speech. I saw some really major guys who had done major work in front of me. I didn't know how to deal with the situation. I said, 'Ladies and gentlemen . . . This indeed is an intimidating crowd!'

Everybody burst out laughing and gave me a big hand. I had got them. I talked about Indian cinema. Then I said, 'One man's vision is the reason why I stand here now. The unique distinction of that vision has transformed the ordinary lives of Mumbai into a work of art. Today that man has become a household name in my country. That man is Danny Boyle!' I also went on to talk about how I once kept a poster of his film in my hostel room in the Institute.

When I finished, there was unending applause! Danny Boyle came to the stage. He said some kind words about me and performed the award distribution that he was supposed to.

A lot of my friends were present at this function. Everyone came to congratulate me. Even guys whom I had never met before hugged me and wished me all the best.

As the next day was the much-awaited Oscar night, I returned to my room early. Meanwhile, there was a rumour floating around of the Oscar winners' list being leaked. There were a lot of Oscar predictions as well. I didn't feel like paying attention to any of this. But I couldn't sleep much. I must have slept about two hours that night. You can imagine the strain of something as big as the Oscar.

When I had returned to India with the CAS award, there had been a request from the Oscar committee. They had wanted to know, since we had been nominated as a group for the sound mixing award, which one of us was going to give the Oscar speech. Fortunately, I was the one who had been selected. I shall be eternally thankful to Ian Tapp and Richard Pryke for that. I had thought many times about what I should be saying if I went in to win the Oscar. I had called Feroz Abbas Khan regarding this matter. He is a very close friend, someone who knows me and my work. I also share a very good rapport with him as an artist and as a colleague. He is like an elder brother to me. I had asked him, 'Feroz, what shall I say?' He had said he would think about it and let me know.

When I was leaving for Los Angeles, I had called him again. He had then read out a few sentences to me. In that, there was some mention about the sound of *Aum*, and it had touched me deeply. But I didn't have the time to write it down. I had asked him to email me everything.

The night before the Oscars, I came back to the room and read Feroz's email many times; wrote down all the names of the people I wanted to thank—from teachers to Christian Colson and Danny Boyle who had given Rahman and me the opportunity to work on this film.

My dear friend Shonali Bose came early to our hotel room the next day. She helped Shadia with her outfits. I wore my clothes. Shonali took some pictures of us. She asked me about the speech. I read out what I had. She suggested some changes. My problem was, I could never read out a speech; it had to come from within me. And what I had written was a long speech. I had already started forgetting the sentences one by one.

We drove to the Kodak Theater. The place had been completely transformed. Lot of arrangements, lots of security, and a crowd that happily cheered for every Indian that passed by. *Slumdog Millionaire* had huge ground support there. I couldn't take pictures of these moments because cameras were not allowed inside.

After the preliminary introductions, we walked on the red carpet and entered the venue. I met Ben Burt and his wife there. Mrs Burt wished me success and told me not to forget to mention my mother if I won the Oscar. Those words touched my heart. Then Rahman and his wife came, followed by the entire *Slumdog Millionaire* team. We all hung around there for some time.

I was in a hurry to actually experience the Oscar show first-hand. I had always wanted to see how this whole show functioned; so without wasting much time, I went and sat in my seat and watched. They had earlier sent me a video and a book explaining the etiquette of the Oscar night. They had also got me to sign an agreement in connection with this. All these formalities had made me a bit anxious.

The Oscar night is also a timed TV show. Every second of the evening is part of a thoroughly pre-planned programme. When it is a commercial break for you watching the show on TV, it's a break for us too. We have nothing to do in those three minutes. We can go get ourselves tea or champagne; or go to the bathroom to release the tension!

The opening performance started at five thirt-eight p.m. At five forty-five, the first award was announced—for the best supporting actress. The sound mixing award was the sixteenth in the order. One official came and told me that my award was going to be at seven twenty-six and that I should be back in my seat by six forty-five no matter what.

The first award went to Penelope Cruz. She was sitting right behind me. I was watching everything. For the Oscar winner on stage, there was a big display showing a countdown from sixty seconds to one second. After fifty seconds, the count down would start flashing in red. Towards the last seconds, an official would promptly gesture you to move out. If you still hung around on the stage after that, the remotely controlled mike would be slowly muted. Then you would be lead out of the stage. Being on the Oscar stage had these additional tensions as well.

I started getting tense sharp at six forty-five. I tried reading the paper where I had written the speech, but couldn't concentrate. I saw just some alphabets on a paper. Shadia and I were holding hands. Shadia could feel my tension from the tips of my fingers. She was telling me, 'Relax, relax . . .' I tried to tell myself that everything would be okay even if I didn't win and that at least I had reached till this point. I told myself to just sit back and enjoy the whole show.

By that time, they started announcing the awards for the post-production category. My tension meter was going into red. Until then that night, *Slumdog Millionaire* had bagged all the awards it had been nominated for. Then came sound editing. The Oscar went to *The Dark Knight*. Our sound editor Glenn Freemantle was sitting next to me. Our hopes fell.

The next announcement was for the award in sound mixing. Names of the nominees were read out, and snippets were shown from the nominated films—*The Dark Knight*; *Wall-E*; *Wanted*; *Quantum of Solace*; *Slumdog Millionaire*. I felt that our film clip had a pathetic sound—it was a mess with no trace of sophistication. I was certain we were not going to make it.

Then Will Smith announced: 'And the Oscar . . .'

I had always wanted to receive this award from Will Smith. I like him very much as an actor. We had made an acquaintance and chatted earlier on.

'And the Oscar goes to . . .'

In my mind, I was chanting *Slumdog Millionaire, Slumdog Millionaire, Slumdog Millionaire* . . .

' . . . goes to . . . *Slumdog Millionaire!*'

For a moment I sat inert as if I was coming back to life after death. Then I screamed at the top of my voice but no sound came out. The next thing I remember was getting the Oscar statuette in my hand. Later, even from the video I couldn't recollect how I had reached the stage. I couldn't even find the paper with the speech. I looked at the crowd. On either side of me, I saw Ian Tap and Richard Pryke as some sort of a mirage. The countdown timer had already ticked quite a bit. There were only a few seconds left for me to say whatever I had to say. Words came out in panic from my parched throat:

'This is unbelievable. We can't believe this . . . Hhoo . . . Ladies and gentlemen . . . Sorry . . .' Ian and Richard tapped on my shoulder saying 'You are rushed son!', I pulled myself up and continued ' . . . I share this stage with two magicians, you know, who created the ordinary sounds of Mumbai, the cacophony of Mumbai, into a soul-stirring, artful resonance called *Slumdog Millionaire* . . .'My throat went dry and I started to slur, but continued ' . . . I come from a country and a civilization that has given the universe a word (I wanted to say 'Sound', but mixed up. Read 'word' with 'sound'). That word is preceded by silence, followed by more silence. That word is *Aum.*So I dedicate this award to my country. Thank you Academy, this is not just a sound award, this is history being handed over to me. My . . . sincere and deepest . . . gratitude to my teachers, Danny Boyle, Christian Colson, Paul Ritchie, Pravesh . . . and everybody who has contributed to this film, Glenn Freemantle and all the sound mixers. I dedicate this to you guys. Thank you, Academy. Thank you very much . . .'

Richard Pryke and Ian Tapp, too, expressed their thanks. I felt as if all that I had wanted to say had flowed away from me at that time. I forgot my crew and I forgot to mention my Umma. Whatever Feroz and I had discussed came out of my mind in a different language.

After receiving the award, you can go to the back stage and talk as much as you want to the Oscar camera. But by that time, my throat had completely dried up. I was looking for water. I kept asking for water in Malayalam. Finally someone gave me a bottle. Ian Tap and Richard Pryke spoke while I stood sipping water. I remember thanking my crew; I don't remember anything I said after that.

The next event of the night was the customary Winners' Walk. We were reverently led through a corridor lined with portraits of past Oscar winners and then champagne was popped for the new winners. While walking through the corridor, Rahman's agent came running to convey Rahman's congratulations. I was told he was back stage and going to sing next. Then I met the international press. They asked me why I had said history was being handed over in my hands. I said, in the eighty years of history of the Academy, it was the first time that an Indian technician had got an award. After that, when I was standing for the photo session, I heard the good news of Rahman getting two Oscars. From backstage, we then watched Danny Boyle receiving the award. Spielberg was standing there. He walked up to me and shook my hand. Wow! I had never thought that Spielberg would ever shake my hand. His palm was soft, like cotton.

Except for the category of sound editing, *Slumdog Millionaire* had won all the rest of the awards. Backstage, I met the sound designer of *The Dark Knight*, Richard King. I told him that just four months back, I was there among the audience, listening to his presentation on the sound features of *Dark Knight;* I told him that I had never thought that I would be able to meet him like this that night. He spoke to me with love and kindness. He praised our work and told me not to forget to meet him whenever I came to Hollywood.

Messages were gushing into my phone. Four hundred of them in the first few minutes. Moreover, people were calling me from all over the world.

Then I went for the official Oscar dinner, the Governor's Ball. I was not hungry at all. I just drank water. Then I moved to the next party by Fox Searchlight, then *Vanity Fair*. Our film's entire crew was there. We were all sad about Glenn Freemantle not getting the award. As a sound editor, his contribution to the movie's sound had been huge.

It was a night of celebration.

*

I finally stumbled back to my room only at four in the morning. Feroz Abbas Khan called and congratulated me. He said the speech was fantastic and that people were deeply touched by my words—indeed, a lot of discussions were happening about my speech.

The same morning was the photo session by James Goodings.Later on he created a beautiful limited edition book called *Nineteen Hours and Fourteen Minutes* with the photographs of the Oscar winners and gifted it to all of us as record of that historic day. Relieved after days of anxiety, everybody looked happy and glowing. There was pure joy and excitement; and a table full of wine, champagne and the Oscars we'd won. So as to avoid confusion later, everybody had stuck the first letter of their names on the Oscar statuettes. But I had to stick 'RP' as Rahman and my names start with the same letter. I met every single one of the crew and posed for photos. I was bursting with happiness and also feeling impatient to get back home.

That morning at around eight, I got a call from the reception. Someone had come to see me. I went down and saw an Indian man waiting for me, to congratulate me. He had been in America for the last twenty-five years. He had brought with him a big basketful of clothes for Mia. He said, 'I know you have a little daughter and you'll be reaching India on her birthday. This is a present from me for your baby.'

'But how . . .?!' I was a bit taken aback.

Then he said, 'I bet on your name and made fourteen thousand dollars! This is a little present!'

When I boarded the plane, I was carrying that present.

During the journey back home, I slept most of the time. The first leg of the trip was from Los Angeles to Frankfurt. A couple of people recognized and congratulated me. Otherwise, it was an uneventful flight.

I must tell you a story at this point. When I was working on *Gandhi, My Father*, I used to have a lot of free time in the evenings. The work was only till six. So I picked up and watched a lot of old films. One of the films was *Dances with Wolves*, directed by Kevin Costner. That film had won seven Oscars in 1990. After the film, I watched the making of the film. There was an interview with the cameraman, Dean Semler, an Australian. The interviewer asks him about his best memory of the Oscar. He starts by saying that he was not expecting any Oscar. Then he goes on to narrate an incident that happened while he was on the flight back home, carrying the Oscar statuette with him. While he was dozing off, he was woken up by an announcement: 'The cinematographer of *Dances with Wolves* and Oscar winner Mr Dean Semler is travelling with us in this flight. He is carrying the Oscar statuette. It's an honour for all of us to fly with him. So dear Mr Semler, please stand up, so that we can all see you!' He stood up to the applause of his fellow flyers. He showed the Oscar statuette to all. They approached him one by one and congratulated him. They took photos with him. That was his best memory of winning the Oscar.

This story was lying dormant somewhere in my mind. My flight took off from Frankfurt. I dozed off after dinner. I woke up when somebody touched me. It was the German air hostess. She asked me, 'Sir, are you Resul Pookutty?'

'Yes!'

'Wow! That means we are flying with an Oscar?'

'Yes!'

'Where is it?'

I pointed to the overhead luggage hold. She said, 'You have a fax message from the cockpit,' and gave me a fax print-out.

It was from a certain Janardhanan; not someone I knew. He had tried meeting me in Los Angeles, but couldn't. Then he had found out my flight number and sent a message to the flight. I don't know how he had managed to send that fax to the plane. It was a congratulatory message for me. Everybody in the flight now recognized me. The passengers and the crew came up to me to congratulate me. When the plane landed in

Mumbai, the captain personally came, took me to the flight deck and congratulated me.

At the customs clearance, Shadia and I gave our passports. A lady was in charge of the counter. She looked at the passport and stood up.

'Resul Pookutty . . .!' she shouted. 'Where is the Oscar? We all want to see!'

On hearing my name, everyone stopped working and surrounded me. I said, 'First, give my passport back.'

They said, 'You have become the man of the country. Now nobody will stop you. We want to take pictures with you.'

I took out the Oscar statuette to show to the huge crowd that had gathered around me. They started shouting: 'Oscar! Oscar!' My eyes welled up. When I bent down to pick up my bag, everybody said, 'No, you needn't!' Someone carried my bag and there was a long applause. While the cheering continued behind me, I came out of the airport.

There was an incredibly big crowd outside. I saw Monu and ran and took him in my arms. I stood there with the Oscar in one hand and Monu on the other. Within minutes, the crowd grew out of control. Somebody carried Monu away. I didn't know what was happening. The police escorted Shadia and me into a van. I sat in the police van clutching my Oscar. The van was surrounded by TV and other media people. It then started moving, blaring its siren. It was like the scene in *Slumdog Millionaire*, when Jamal heads for the show towards the end of the film.

I had no idea where my kids were. The police brought us to the closest police station, Sahar. We spent almost an hour there. For once, the cops and the criminals behind the lock-up bars seemed to be united—they all congratulated me! They were all shouting, 'Hello, hello'. In the meantime, the police was trying hard to figure out about the security arrangements that needed to be made to take us home. By that time, Akhilesh came with Monu and Mia to the police station. I managed to leave by about three in the morning. Still, a lot of bikes and cars accompanied me to my house. When I reached the Saibaba Complex, I heard someone shouting my name, it came from the road level. Shantanu, my senior from FTII, was standing across the road to welcome me and congratulate me, all the windows lights came on one by one and people were looking at me.

Mia's birthday, too, fell on that day. I had brought her the greatest possible birthday present I could bring. I felt very happy about it. While looking at the crowd at the airport, I had decided there itself that I would go to Kerala only after the public excitement had settled down a bit. I stayed in Mumbai for a few days before I headed to Kerala. The moment I landed in Kerala I became an honourable guest of the government; they provided me with a state car and police escort. Now I was really impatient to reach my village, Vilakkupara.

*

When I embarked on the journey to my village, there was a huge crowd waiting for me on either side of the road at a place called Aayur, some nineteen kilometres away from

Vilakkupara. They had been waiting there for hours. When I reached there, the crowd got me out of the state car and put me in an open jeep for the rest of the distance. But as we got close to Vilakkupara, the size of the crowd had grown so big that we couldn't drive any further. And the police and others couldn't control them. When the pushing and shoving became too much, I started running. The function was arranged at the village's open field near its temple. I arrived at the venue running! It was twilight. A crowd of more than ten thousand people sat there listening to what I had to say. What I said I remember very well. My words were prompted by my memories of the place.

During the Vilakkupara temple festival, the local Muslims would perform one of their traditional art forms, inside the temple itself. And someone would always light the lamp at the turn in front of the temple. Nobody ever bothered to check whether this guy was a Hindu, a Christian or a Muslim. All that mattered was that someone had to light the lamp. That has been the tradition of this temple right from its inception. Even today, for the ten-day-long temple festival, all the announcements to the public are made by none other than John Achayan. No one else gets to do that work.

The temple of Vilakkupara was built by the people of the village. The mosque and the church too were built by the same people. I used to go to the temple festival with the same gusto with which I attended the Eid procession holding a green flag and chanting '*bolo taqbeer*'. On Christmas day, we would all assemble at the church and eat cake. For us, a festival did not belong exclusively to a particular religious section. We viewed all this as being part of our lives.

I reminded my audience of the trust and love we all shared; I told them of my childhood and of Vilakkupara's collective mind—consisting of the likes of Thothyachchayan, Kochchannan Mesri and Azhathi Kovalan, and the rest of the whole village community. I said, 'It's just that I happened to have an opportunity to narrate at the Kodak Theater some of the things I had absorbed from you and here. The world listened to that. But the true reason why I was able to say those words is us and our lives here. It's precious and we must not trade that for anything at any cost. That's our identity. Vilakkupara is not just a village; it's an entire land and culture with its own unique character. I want to you to give me your word that you are going to maintain this and sustain this!'

The crowd gave me their word while their tears streamed down their faces. I was one of them and of their culture. Tears flooded my eyes too.

EPILOGUE: SOME FINAL THOUGHTS

I feel major changes between the circumstances of my growing-up years and what I see now when I return to Kerala after fifteen years.

There was a range of coconut trees around our home with clearly distinct personalities. The ones that gave long coconuts, the ones with round coconuts and the ones that bore tender coconuts from which we could drink. There was another one called *chentengu* or red coconut tree, laden with orange-red coconuts. Then there was a stud of a coconut tree specially kept for seeds with an alpha-male personality. There was a variety of tapiocas too; and yam; and beans; and peppercorn; as well as a range of exotic chillies. I recall how frequently Umma would dig up sweet potatoes to mash into a quick meal for us after a long day; or how often Kochumon and I would climb trees to pluck pepper from the vines that curled around those trees—or else collapse into a fistfight over who deserved more rest from the chore.

When I finished my time at the Institute and returned home, all these things had disappeared. There was no yam in the front garden; no purple yam, no elephant yam, no beans—nothing. Nobody was growing vegetables in between the cash crops any more. Nothing was being grown. There were still people to work in the farms. But the coconut trees didn't have the same yield. The time before I left for the Institute, we always had enough coconuts to sell. But when I returned, I saw that we were buying coconuts from the market. There was no firewood either. Everything had completely changed.

It was a big transformation—in all aspects. There were no cashews any more! And to think that there was a time when I used to get sick of picking up the cashews. Saif would be the one shaking the tree from the top, while Kochumon and I would pick up the fallen cashews. Umma would be sitting in one place plucking the cashew seed from the fruits and counting them as it piled up in a heap. In those days, when we felt like eating candies from the neighbourhood shop, we would run towards the cashew tree and throw stones at it, get some nuts, and trade them for the candies. But that's not what kids do these days. They ask their parents for money. If it's refused, they pinch some money! There has been a total cultural change in a relatively short duration—ten or twelve years! It has fundamentally affected the experience of living in Kerala. I won't be surprised that this is happening elsewhere as well. We have become a totally consumerist society.

Now we believe only what we see in the newspaper! This medicine is good or this man fries the *pappadom* like this—if we see such things in print, we believe it, without ever pausing to think that it's merely an advertisement for the medicine or that pappadom roasted in the fire is far better. All this is a side-effect that the Malayali is suffering from due to literacy. We have been converted to consumerism through education.

This is a major paradigm shift. And dangerous at that. Without any basis whatsoever, people are involved in making as much money as possible in order to improve life's conveniences. This is also what capitalism is about. It keeps people in a never-ending circle, constantly chasing after objects. Just your salary is not enough to stay in this chase. So you need bribes. What you get is not enough; because everything needs to be bought—there is nothing growing in the kitchen garden, nor are there chicken to lay eggs at home.

Earlier, whenever guests would visit, we would catch and cut up the rooster hanging around in the kitchen, and make a dish out of it. That's why, when our rooster would make a mess of the dishes in the kitchen, Umma used to tell it: 'You're getting too arrogant and fearless, no? If you don't watch out, I'll cut you up and make a curry!' The rooster would immediately sense the dire consequences of its actions. There was a communication of sorts between them.

As for bribes, people have now become completely shameless in demanding them. To move a file in an office, you need to push a hundred rupees to the man sitting on it. If you want to file a petition at the police station, you need another hundred there. Cops coming for passport verification expect a minimum of three hundred rupees. Now things move only if we bribe; and the giver is mentally prepared to give, while the taker takes it as his right. This is an appalling change that has taken place in Kerala.

In my growing-up years, sometimes we wouldn't even have proper food. But when my son was born, what a variety of packaged food I brought from America, paying hundreds of dollars—there was so much to choose from. I had neither seen these things before nor tasted them. Yet, I couldn't comprehend the lifestyle that made all these a necessity; I would say useless necessities. When I carried these things from America, the cinematographer Ravi K. Chandran teased me, 'Look at you, you grew up eating cashew fruits under the trees; but when you have a son, you bring his food from America! Amazing! This is the real Malayali!'

Ravi really teased me about it, to the extent that I had to think about it; then I realized the magnitude of my own change. Our cultural changes are drastic. And we have dangerously named it progress, in some strange language.

A lot of the changes that we see today around us are not geared towards progress. Earlier, behind the changes that led to progress had been a thought or a conscious desire for improvements. But I just can't see that driving force behind the changes I see today.

You see, the circumstances I grew up in, gave me both the awareness and the ability to face new situations. Here's a simple example.

When I was recording for the film, *Split Wide Open*, a crow landed on the set. It was making a lot of noise, making life impossible. Each dialogue I was trying to record was being spoilt by a 'caw, caw'. What to do, I thought. I had seen people drying chillies in the sun, back home. The chillies would be spread on a bamboo mat and a small mirror would be kept on one edge of the mat. The crow would never land on the mat seeing the reflected sunlight. Another technique was to hang one chilli on a stick so that the crow would peck at just that single one. I asked the production guys to get me ten mirrors. And I gave these mirrors to the assistants, asking them to flash it on the crow's eyes when it came again. The technique was a super hit.

Director Dev Benegal had a joke ready the next day: 'If Resul is doing sound, the crows would land up wearing sunglasses to deal with his new weapon!'

Jokes apart, my question is: would our new generation have any practically useful childhood experiences? That's what makes me anxious about the changes around me. Among the new generation, if a kid gets slapped by someone on his way, he might immediately search the net on his cell phone to find out what to do!

My point is, there is a danger in thoughtlessly copying— you shouldn't be tackling the situation you find yourself in by imitating what you have read of how somebody else had tackled a situation.

As a sound man, my strengths are rooted in the village life of my childhood and the careless abundance of my college days. This energy is still there in our Indian villages. It's important for our government institutes to know how to tap this raw energy. I have travelled to many such places as part of my work. When you enter villages with camera and gear, a crowd will always gather around you, especially when you are travelling in Bihar or Uttar Pradesh. What you see in those places are the ailments of a whole nation.

Once I worked with the BBC anchor Mark Tully and a London cameraman, for a documentary on power plants. The film grabbed worldwide attention. International bodies like the World Bank and IMF were in support of these power plants. Our documentary was trying to look into the First World's view on this and why the Third World was eager to push this hazardous technology. We visited the areas around the Singrauli Power Plant. What we saw was an ecology that had completely collapsed. Water surfaces were covered with ash; with no fish left in the water. The greenery of the region was charred in the drizzle of ash. And the authorities were still acquiring more land for dumping the waste.

The power plant has come up in a land that had been used for agriculture for generations. Their farmland had been acquired and they were settled elsewhere. Their huts had been demolished; concrete and asbestos housing colonies built in that place. A peacefully living self-sufficient community had overnight been forced to live in a slum. The farmers had not wanted to give up their farmland. They told us that theirs had been a completely self-sufficient community—the eggs had come from the chickens roaming around home, the vegetables from the backyard, and rice from their own paddy fields. Now they had to buy all these from the shops.

Our investigation was to find out at whose expense the so-called development had taken place. I thought in those days: what is it that I can do? The maximum I could do was to do the sound for this documentary as properly as possible. The only hope was that the film would melt the heart of a bureaucrat or a minister and inspire him or her to do something about it. But what kind of a hope was that? Then it dawned on me that I was living a life where it was impossible for me to do anything worthwhile for my own people who were suffering. I felt that there was no point in having a great education or feeling proud that I was an ace professional in my field. Such thoughts filled me with extreme helpessness; I also developed a sense of helplessness where my profession was concerned.

This is not progress. We don't need progress of this kind.

Our middle class is now smart enough to go and study anywhere in the world. I am a guy from an underdeveloped village called Vilakkupara. There are many such underdeveloped villages in other parts of India. If guys from such places get to study in our national institutes, they would be able to make a much more valuable impact because of the kind of images that they have seen, the kind of sounds that they have heard and the kind of ideas that they wish to communicate.

It's high time our institutes had reservations for this section of the populace. But the government agencies and the ministers who are expected to do such things are busy running around garlanding me! All that they are interested in is to be seen alongside this guy who has won an award from America, and who they think is sophisticated and popular. Before I became famous, no leader of the working class here had ever recognized my work. That's another danger of our times: you can become a leader without doing anything in particular—just focus on public relations and image building, and you can become a leader.

I need to mention one more change that I came to hear about, recently. It has to do with the Film Institute.

It seems the students these days don't sit in the main theatre to watch films. So, no discussions on movies take place in this theatre any more.

'So, what do they do, instead?' I asked the person who told me this.

It seems now they see films on their computers, sitting in their rooms. Mostly pirated stuff. They have all seen *Slumdog Millionaire*—or, more exactly, its pirated version. During my days at the Institute, I had never seen any pirated cinema from there. Those were the days of landlines—when the hostel phone at the Institute rang, everybody would come out running to find out who the call was for. Today, almost everyone has a cellphone. Technology is changing human behaviour. And it is creating more human cocoons. The Institute is losing its distinct collectiveness.

I remember sitting under the Wisdom Tree or at the front of the hostel, discussing endlessly a film, say, *Rashomon*, that we had just seen. Then we could discover the reactions of people from different cultures—the opinions of an Oriya, a Bengali, a Malayali . . . We would relate to a film despite having extremely different opinions about it. While we studied a film, the study would not be just about the film, it would become a study of ourselves, of the similarities and the differences amongst the cultures that we each individually represented. But now it seems such discussions have reduced drastically. But this trend is not something we should be fighting against; we shouldn't be telling the present-day students of the Institute that they are doing things the wrong way. The change can happen only through awareness. But I have felt helpless wondering what would bring this awareness. You see, these kids don't live in an isolated island like we did in our times. They have special, *live* relationships with the world outside. But these relationships—and the technology that makes possible these relationships—are the kind that can dilute their convictions about cinema. It will only help them to make more of those middle-of-the-road films. In my opinion, we must make either extremely serious cinema or completely accessible cinema. I see lesser chances of such films being made by this generation of Institute students.

During my days at the Institute, whenever I would watch a movie there, I desperately wished I could get a copy of that film. In fact, I had copied a lot of those films on VHS. But that's like your love for books. When you see books in the library, you feel like stealing them. But if you steal and have that book in your possession, then you will never read it! That's what would happen with the present-day Institute students because of their taste for pirated cinema. These students need to realize the fact that screening films and discussing them together in a collective forum are part of the curriculum.

As I try to understand these changes, let me ask a couple of questions. Are the selection processes of our national institutes subconsciously designed for the middle class and the upper middle class? From which class should our cinema come from?

Cinema is a powerful medium. It can be strategically deployed to usher in a variety of changes. But considering how things are not necessarily changing for the better, I still hope that the future does bring some welcome changes.

ACKNOWLEDGEMENTS

2̲8 November 2009. I was sitting one evening in a serene and lovely guest house in Bangalore, absorbed in a very special activity. Suddenly the mobile phone rang in a special ringtone. That tone was set to announce the call of a very special person in my life—my dear and eldest sister Kunhumolitha, someone who became famous in family circles and local folklore as the 'Umma who kissed Danny Boyle'. Being preoccupied with my work, I had postponed attending this phone call many times.

The next day, Kutnhumolitha called again. I had just reached Mumbai. I picked up the phone immediately. She asked, 'You have any idea what day is this?'

I said, 'Yes, Eid!'

'Oho! So you know! Then why were you not picking up the phone when I was calling?'

'Oh, Itha, you know . . . I was busy with my book and . . .'

'Listen, I want to tell you something. That thing you

have, no? That thing like the gizmo that Mandrake has? That damn Oscar you got? Will you do me a favour and return that thing to whoever gave it to you? Imagine! You can't now be contacted even on phone! Even on the day of Eid!'

This came from the person who ran and kissed the TV screen when she saw me getting the Oscar! By the time she had reached and kissed the screen, the image had changed, and instead of my face, it was Danny Boyle's that appeared on the screen! That split-second slip had earned her the title of 'the Umma who kissed Danny Boyle'. She truly takes after my Umma—she's her true heir. Now, as I am concluding this book, I thank my Bappa and Umma and their legacy.

No matter what my Itha says, returning my Oscar is completely out of the question. In this matter, I hope I have the strong backing of Shadia's parents who are also now my parents, Dr Mohammad Basheer and Advocate Laila M. Basheer; I express my gratitude to them. I am also hoping that Shadia, Monu, Mia and Kalluvila are all with me in this regard.

I also want to thank my friend K.K. Muralidharan who encouraged me immensely on reading the very first chapter of this book. That was when I had just begun penning my memoir. He then enthusiastically went on to translate it into English and also design the cover for the Malayalam edition of this book. A big thanks to Baiju N. Natarajan aka N. Baiju who helped me to discover the narrator in me, and also to Dileep Raj, the resident editor of *Malayala Manorama*–Penguin, for conceiving this book and for discovering Baiju. However, I would like to clarify that neither Dileep, Baiju nor

I will take responsibility for any perceived, felt or real faults in this book; but at the same time, we will have no issues whatsoever if the responsibility for the same is assumed by the great phenomenon called Time!

I thank the publishers—Manorama and Penguin Books India—for bringing out the Malayalam, and now the English, edition of this book.

I express immense gratitude to Udayan Mitra for commissioning the English edition of this book, and I especially thank Ambar Sahil Chatterjee for his marathon task of editing the tome to half its length.

Meena Murali deserves special mention for giving me her house in Mumbai to work on this book.

I'm grateful to Amrit Pritam, Vijay Kumar, Arunav Dutta and Reena Kumari at Canaries for giving me my time as allowances to finish this book.

I thank Shadia for finding precious moments despite her hectic schedule, to read many chapters of this book and give many creative instructions. I also humbly thank Monu and Mia who displayed the largeness of heart to give Shadia that much time to look into this book.

My love-laden salute to all the good souls who buy and read this book.

As if compelled by Allah, let countless people come and buy this book!

Alhamdulillah!

FILMOGRAPHY

Sound Department

1997 – Private Detective: Two Plus Two Plus One
1999 – Split Wide Open
2000 – Snip!
2001 – Bombay Eunuch
2001 – Everybody Says I'm Fine!
2002 – Agni Varsha: The Fire and the Rain
2002 – Boom
2003 – Raghu Romeo
2003 – Matrubhoomi: A Nation Without Women
2004 – Kyun . . . ! Ho Gaya Na
2004 – Musafir
2005 – Amu
2005 – Black
2005 – Bluffmaster!
2006 – Zinda
2006 – Mixed Doubles
2006 – Bombay Skies

2007 – Traffic Signal

2007 – Gandhi, My Father

2007 – Chaurahen

2007 – Saawariya

2007 – Mithya

2007 – Dus Kahaniyaan

2008 – Woodstock Villa

2008 – I'm 24

2008 – Slumdog Millionaire

2008 – Ghajini

2009 – Kerala Varma Pazhassi Raja

2009 – Blue

2009 – Fatso!

2009 – Raat Gayi, Baat Gayi?

2010 – Prince

2010 – Endhiran: The Robot

2010 – Walkaway

2010 – 10ml LOVE

2011 – Pappu Can't Dance Saala

2011 – Ra.One

2011 – The Best Exotic Marigold Hotel

2012 – Nanban

2012 – 3

2012 – Liv and Ingmar (Sweden)

2012 – The Good Road

2012 – Sans Voyage Retour (French)

2012 – Chittagong (Sound Design & Executive Producer)

2012 – Gandhi of the Month

2012 – English Vinglish

2012 – ID (Producer & Sound Designer)

(Slated for 2012) – Gaur Hari Dastan: Freedom File

(Slated for 2012) – Shootout at Wadala

(Slated for 2012) – Warning

(Slated for 2012) – Aankhon Dekhi

(Slated for 2012) – Blemished Light

(Slated for 2013) – Scarlet Poppy